Poetic Argument

Poetic Argument

Studies in Modern Poetry

JONATHAN KERTZER

McGill-Queen's University Press
Kingston, London, Montreal

ISBN 0-7735-0679-9

Legal deposit fourth quarter 1989
Bibliothèque nationale du Québec

Printed in Canada on acid-free paper

This book has been published with the help of a grant from the Canadian Federation for the Humanities, using funds provided by the Social Sciences and Humanities Research Council of Canada.

Canadian Cataloguing in Publication Data

Kertzer, Jonathan, 1946-
Poetic argument
Includes index.
Bibliography: p.
ISBN 0-7735-0679-9
1. Poetry, Modern - 20th century - History and criticism. 2. Reason in literature. I. Title.
PR604.K47 1989 809.1'04 C89-090107-4

Portions of some chapters originally appeared in, and are republished with the kind permission of, the following journals:
Wascana Review 13 (Fall 1978): 19–39.
Contemporary Literature 20 (Summer 1979): 292–315.
Modern Language Quarterly 45 (December 1984): 373–94.
Mosaic 18 (Winter 1985): 27–43.

For my parents

Contents

Poetic Argument

CHAPTER ONE

Poetic Argument

the duty and office of rhetoric is to apply reason to imagination for the better moving of the will ... The end of rhetoric is to fill the imagination to second reason, and not to oppress it.

Francis Bacon, *The Advancement of Learning*[1]

THE ARGUMENT OF ARGUMENT

This book is a defence of reason in poetry. It does not follow the "moralistic" and "absolutist" principles proposed by Yvor Winters in *In Defense of Reason*; it is closer to the cautionary critique of avant-garde "unreality" offered more recently by Gerald Graff in *Literature Against Itself*. My main purpose is to trace the fate of reason as it engages in and is challenged by the arguments of modernist poetry. Such poetry argues with itself, within itself, with its resources, with its author, and with its readers. As I intend to show, it grows argumentative by making paradoxical demands of itself, setting tasks that can be accomplished only through a strenuous logical, verbal, and dramatic dispute. The dispute is so contentious and aggressive because modern poets insist that their work is defiantly problematic in its means and ends. According to extreme versions of the dilemma, poetic thinking demands an intricate display of reason, which must call forth and submit to its mysterious double, known variously as unreason, the irrational, visionary, intuitive, or transcendent. Meanwhile poetic language must also engage its opposite, known as the unspoken, ineffable, or nonsensical. Together, thought and speech produce an argument sustained by what T.S. Eliot calls the nondiscursive logic of the imagination, a lyrical logic through which poetry argues its case with the help of the famous ladder extended at the end of Ludwig Wittgenstein's *Tractatus* as a necessary but disposable prop to understanding. Poetry uses reason and language as aids to mount above their limiting conditions. It renounces the vehicles by which it argues, but only by employing those same vehicles. I hope to prove, on the contrary, that in the course of arguing, reason is actually reinstated, sometimes explicitly, often surreptitiously, because it operates with unexpected deviousness within the rhetorical and dramatic means by which it is renounced. The problematic nature of thought and speech can be explored only within the resources that they provide. There are no alternative forms. Poetic theory and practice are therefore at odds, with argument – the discursive power of reason – sustaining the oddity.

At issue here are a series of interrelated problems, many of which are familiar but have not, I believe, been studied sufficiently from the controlling vantage-point of argument. These problems include the complex relations between argument and ideas, words and things; between poetic thinking, seeing, and knowing; between the immediacy of experience, the detour of discourse, the progress of argument, and the mystery of understanding; between the poetic self that argues or is constituted by its argument, and the conclusions that it seeks. To give a full account of so immense a field would require a book much longer than this one. I intend more modestly to survey the subject in the first chapter and then to study selected poets who illustrate some of the issues. My discussion will be guided by three recurring questions: how does modern poetry claim to argue, how does it in fact argue, and what does it argue about?

Let me begin with the argument of argument, that is, with the network of ideas suggested by the word as it applies to poetry. An argument is an inferential pattern, a train of ideas that are logically connected and lead to a conclusion entailed by the premises originally accepted and unifying the preceding discourse into a meaningful, satisfying whole. All the terms in this definition are useful, especially the notions of power and form, which traditionally have served to explain the energy and shape of poetic language. Modernist theories of argument and of its display in poetry – my main interest – focus on the power of logic, which is the principle of dynamic connection, and on the form of discourse, which is the pattern of continuity. As we shall see in this chapter, these accounts usually question how mental faculties operate (reason, intuition, imagination, the subconscious), and how poetic language functions (via symbol, image, metaphor). In short, they investigate the locus and the trajectory of argument: where it is located and how it proceeds. Later accounts by postmodern and deconstructive critics – a secondary but nagging concern – are still concerned with logic, but they shift attention to the axioms, conclusions, and unity, that is, to the beginnings and ends of argument. Hence their criticism of the self, the scene of writing, origins, closure and enigma – all ways of launching and concluding, or failing to conclude, an argument.

Because my subject is so broad, there is danger in being too vague. In the following pages, I may sometimes seem to use "argument" to mean the structure of a poem; and so I do, if I can discern the way that structure articulates, asserts and proves itself. Even more generally, I may seem to mean discourse; and again this is true, if I can stress the way discourse is aggressive, purposeful and refractory. For instance, in "After the Funeral" Dylan Thomas finds he can lament the death of his Aunt, Ann Jones, only by disputing his own powers and duties as a poet. He concludes:

> These cloud-sopped, marble hands, this monumental
> Argument of the hewn voice, gesture and psalm,
> Storm me forever over her grave until
> The stuffed lung of the fox twitch and cry Love
> And the strutting fern lay seeds on the black sill.[2]

Thomas discovers that he must prove his worthiness to himself and to the reader, if he is to be "Ann's bard." He must question his art and his competence in it, if he is to make sense of his confused thoughts and feelings about her. He discovers - and works his discovery into the poem - that, despite his overwhelming grief, he cannot mourn for her, he cannot animate his elegy and build it toward a final, inspired vision, until he has deliberated through a finely-chiselled "Argument of the hewn voice." His poetic vision requires a poetic argument. "What I like to do," he wrote, "is to treat words as a craftsman does his wood or stone or what-have-you, to hew, carve, mould, coil, polish and plane them into patterns, sequences, sculptures, fugues of sound expressing some lyrical impulse, some spiritual doubt or conviction, some dimly-realised truth I must try to reach and realise."[3] The truth must be won through all the craft he possesses. Calculation permits illumination. In the same way Marianne Moore delights in the "lion's leap," the sudden, thrilling conviction that only poetry can give; but she too emphasizes the precise, disciplined effort of thought and attention that makes possible this final spontaneity.[4]

The notion of argument in poetry is an old one. Edmund Spenser, Shakespeare, John Milton, and William Wordsworth all speak of the argument or heroic argument of their poems, meaning subject, theme, and demonstration. Quintilian describes argument as the topics of orations, the subjects of plays or of any writing, as well as the process of reasoning which involves "proof, indication, credibility, aggression," and rhetorical persuasion.[5] The *aggressio* (attempt, effort, force of argument) is traditionally considered the motive power of poetic argument. It recalls the "energy" which Aristotle praised in vividly visualized metaphor, but which was subsequently interpreted as poetry's essential force of thought and expression.[6] Through energetic imagery - or what in the Longinian tradition is called "the language of the passions" - poetry enforces its meaning in a way that is more compelling than logical assertion.[7] Modern poetry extends the tradition by insisting, with Dylan Thomas, that it must storm, and strut; it must be impulsive, even when its aims are elegaic or peaceful. Everything in it is at issue because nothing can be taken for granted. It must encourage, according to an energetic critic like Harold Bloom, "the aggression of reading and the transgression of writing."[8]

Poetry argues in several related senses - logical, rhetorical, dramatic - and these will be the operative terms in this study. Poetic logic involves the way poetry asserts, entertains, organizes, and displays ideas. Through its own inner necessity, a poem argues its case and, according to Thomas, proves itself. It is both hypothesis and solution. Following the example of Giambattista Vico or an ideal of primitive language, some poets and critics recommend a mythical thinking that is distinct from discursive thought and conducts itself by means of image, symbol, metaphor, and metonymy. Its argument is figurative. In this view, rhetoric is a means of knowledge as well as the traditional art of persuasion. It enables the reader to think in a new (or very old) way, by mystifying him before earning his assent. Therefore an argument is conducted within the poem, in opposition to or collusion with the reader, but also within the poet. As drama, poetic argument is a performance displaying the poet's quarrel with words and ideas, with his own experience, which resists his effort to turn it into poetry, and with his competence as a writer. For Matthew Arnold, "the dialogue of the mind with itself" was the mark of modern culture;[9] for W.B. Yeats, dialogue becomes dispute: "We make out of the quarrel with others, rhetoric, but of the quarrel with ourselves, poetry."[10]

Paradoxically, all this effort is designed to arouse an effortless vision, affirmation, or epiphany: the monumental argument culminates in a cry of love. Consequently, poetic argument must contrive to subdue or even efface itself, although self-effacement is an effect of, not an escape from, argument. Accounts of lyric poetry especially stress the instantaneous appeal of what Northrop Frye calls "the lyric of mental focus," a focus achieved through the rhetorical compression of metaphor, image or symbol.[11] Such accounts are impatient with the leisurely discursiveness of narrative and argument, which seems to interfere with the urgency of direct experience. But, as I intend to show at some length, vision in poetry is the reward of argument. Wallace Stevens describes their interplay as "A horror of thoughts that suddenly are real. / We must endure our thoughts all night, until / The bright obvious stands motionless in cold."[12] Aggressive poetic thought ends in revelation because, according to formalist theories, poetry is an autonomous activity whose arguments are different in kind from those of prose. Their conclusions have a special resonance that persuades, proves, and approves in a unique and powerful manner. In more enthusiastic versions of this theory, poetry not only conducts, but liberates thought and invigorates language. Octavio Paz, the Mexican poet, critic, and surrealist, claims that poetry "says the unsayable,"[13] because it "violates the laws of thought" (86), such as the principle of contradiction, in favour of a logic of its own: "As if they were obeying a mysterious law of gravity, words return to poetry spontaneously. At the heart of all prose, more or less attenuated by the demands of discourse, circulates the invisible current. And thought, insofar as it is language, suffers the same fascination. To set thought free, to wander, is to return to rhythm; reasons are transformed into correspondences, syllogisms into analogies, and the intellectual march into a flow of images" (56–7).

Paz's desire to think the unthinkable by saying the unsayable carries poetic aggression and autonomy to an extreme that raises basic questions about how poetry can be argumentative and how arguments can be poetic. After all, rhythm, correspondences, analogies, and the flow of images, all of which he cites as the subversive principles of poetic reasoning, are not themselves illogical. On the contrary, they are systematic, rational, and discursive. The very forms he seeks to escape have quietly reasserted themselves within his system of denial. Nevertheless, the modern mistrust of reason and language has prompted poets to propose an independent domain of "poetic unreason," where only the arguments of poetry are valid. Throughout this study I shall use the awkward term "unreason" in order to discuss the locus and the course of poetic arguments, both as they are perceived to operate and as they actually operate. I like the word, both because it has been widely used to suggest how poetry opposes or cooperates with reason, and also because it preserves in its awkwardness a hint to be developed in this chapter, that the notion of unreason is an elaborate poetic fiction created by the contradictory demands made of poetic argument.

How does poetry claim to set thought free? By musical enchantment, according to Stéphane Mallarmé's famous account of the powers and duties of the poet: "Je dis: une fleur! et, hors de l'oubli où ma voix relègue aucun contour, en tant que quelque chose d'autre que les calices sus, musicalement se lève, idée même et suave, l'absente de tous bouquets." [I say: a flower! and, out of the oblivion to which my voice consigns any contour, in as much as it is something other than known calyxes, musically arises the fragrant idea itself, the one absent from all bouquets.][14] This passage has served as a point of departure for histories of modern poetry, because it evokes so succinctly the symbolist legacy. By stressing revelation, Mallarmé seems to suggest that the poet has no need to argue. He is perfectly composed and merely utters a sonorous word. But again, lyrical ease is the flower of intellectual effort, and Mallarmé challenges his successors to cope with the twin paradoxes of poetry in which reason defies the rational and language defies the verbal. The poet must build his arguments from recalcitrant materials. In the first place, the fragrant ideas of poetry blossom only when reason has been subverted, when clear and distinct ideas grow hazy, when memory yields to forgetfulness, so that a natural fact can be transformed into "sa presque disparition vibratoire,"[15] its own musical illusion. Poetry is a means of seizing the unseizable, a shadow or mirror image of reality which is prized for its elusiveness. The very effort to grasp the poetic flower puts it beyond reach; its remoteness confers its value. Paul Valéry agrees that in the "lyric universe," " 'ideas' .... do not play the same part, are not at all *currency of the same kind*, as the ideas in prose."[16] Poetic thought is "musicalized." Nevertheless, the mind is not passive, and Valéry, even more than Mallarmé, stresses the calculated discipline of poetry. Although "the most beautiful thoughts are shadows," they can only be captured by "the most precise faculties of the intelligence" (4): "the more restless and fugitive the prey one covets, the more presence of mind and power of will one needs to make it eternally present in its eternally fleeting aspect" (11–12). Consequently, the poet's intelligence is devoted to evoking what will defy the reader's intelligence to grasp.

In the second place, the poet is for Mallarmé a craftsman in words that he must use to express the ineffable. Words are essential yet flawed, and his task is to purify them, to invest them with a meaning that they resist. Poetry is a verbal art that arises from a defect in language. If there were a supreme language perfectly able to express reality, then poetry would be unnecessary because all words would be poetic; but because words become debased, we require verse philosophically to reward the failure of language as a superior complement to ordinary speech ("philosophiquement remunère le défaut des langues, complément supérieur"). The poet's word is "total, neuf, étranger à la langue"[17]; it is foreign to its native language. Valéry agrees that the poet can draw a "pure, ideal Voice"[18] from soiled, everyday words only by suppressing their natural tendency. He can only sing by refusing to speak: "The poet's use of words is quite different from that of custom or need. The words are without doubt the same, but their values are not at all the same. It is indeed nonusage – the *not saying* 'it is raining' – which is his business; and everything which shows that he is not speaking prose serves his turn (98) .... Here language is no longer a transitive act, an expedient. On the contrary, it has its own value which must remain intact *in spite of the operations of the intellect on the given propositions*. Poetic language must preserve itself, through itself, and remain the same, *not to be altered by the act of the intelligence that finds or gives it meaning*" (171). In the symbolist ideal, therefore, language eloquently defies the intelligence it serves. The poet neither thinks nor talks in the customary sense, yet mind and verbal music combine in "lively, rhythmic, or spontaneous movements of thought" (176). Elsewhere Valéry called this ideal "a poetry of the marvels and emotions of the intellect."[19]

In the discussion that follows, I intend to examine the symbolist legacy as received by the Anglo-American imagists and to criticize its intransitive, autonomous model of poetic argument by studying its formative paradoxes. Delight in paradox and in artistic subversion as a means of achieving mysterious power is a mark of the avant-garde; it recurs in a less mystical tone in poststructuralist criticism. The history of poetic theory from romantics to modernists to deconstructionists reveals repeated attempts to contest this model, usually by reassessing and reassembling its components. Nevetheless their reformulations retain the model's combative structure – which, I shall argue, for all its pathos is basically a festive and ironic structure – even in the case of deconstruction, which questions the very notion of structure. My purpose is not so much to provide a countersystem as to expose the disparity between theory and practice; to show how proposing the model has served as an argumentative strategy or generative fiction; and to find a practical way of assessing the arguments of the poets whose work I study in later chapters. The disparity between theory and practice actually works its way into poetic arguments and reinforces their recourse to fractious, self-validating, and self-defeating proofs. Ultimately, it testifies to their deep ambivalence concerning the powers of human thought and speech.

I have divided the discussion into three sections, in keeping with my analysis of the logical, rhetorical, and dramatic modes of poetic argument. Each section follows a roughly parallel course, the first dealing with reason, the second with language, and the third with the dramatic interplay of the two. In each case I examine how, in concert with and opposition to romantic precepts, modern theories challenge these terms and force them to dispute themselves by conspiring with their opposites – unreason, silence, and vision. I then show how the powers of reason and discourse are not truly surmounted, but subtly reinstated with an unruly energy that renders them problematic. In this way we shall see how modern poetry insists on arguing about itself and its career in the world.

LOGIC: REASON, UNREASON, AND VISION

Logic in poetry need not display strict deductive or inductive patterns; it need not even respect logical categories and relations. But it must employ these patterns, categories, and relations in the course of its disrespect. Nevertheless, symbolist theory contends that poetry can resist (Mallarmé), musicalize (Valéry), or violate (Paz) the rules of thought in the service of vision, unreason, unified sensibility, mythical thinking, orphic divination, and so on. In this section I shall concentrate on unreason and vision, especially as they appear in imagism, in order to show how the modern mistrust of reason has made poetry more, rather than less argumentative. The revolt against reason is, of course, a commonplace of modern cultural criticism. It is so common that we overlook how readily we assign reason a comic role by linking it rhetorically with icy abstraction, linear thinking, and impersonal science, and then treating it as a convenient adversary, a Malvolio to be ridiculed and humanized. Imagination in turn becomes the hero or clown that makes reason undergo a lively festival. In the process, however, reason exacts its own mischievous revenge. Logic is the dynamic and sanction of argument, yet modern poets and critics have repeatedly made the self-defeating claim that poetry argues by subverting logic systematically, that is, logically. The tricky circularity of this puzzle should alert us to the fact that reason need not be cold and linear.

Viewed historically, Mallarmé's first paradox of poetry as engaging but defying the intellect is the modern flowering of an old dispute. It continues the long contest between philosophy and literature, which goes back at least to Plato's *Ion* where the poet must be inspired out of his senses before he can sing. When modern poets joined the debate, however, the issue had been redefined in romantic terms. The major premise, as described by Friedrich Schlegel, was a separation of mental faculties, a disjunction which then made possible the ideal of reuniting them: "It is the beginning of all poetry to abolish the law and method of the rationally proceeding reason and to plunge us once more into the ravishing confusion of fantasy, the original chaos of human nature."[20] Friedrich Schiller agreed that poetry must not be crucified "upon the cross of grammar and logic," because "it absolutely cannot flourish in the realm of concepts or in the world of understanding."[21] The hypothesis that there are two independent modes of thought, one governed by reason, the other by imagination, has proven powerful and seductive, if misleading. It provides the first axiom for P.B. Shelley in *A Defence of Poetry* and for his literary heirs like A.E. Housman, who declares: "Meaning is of the intellect, poetry is not."[22] For the young Yeats, poetic truth lies in the twilight world of unreason: "When all is said and done, how do we not know but that our own unreason may be better than another's truth? for it has been warmed on our hearths and in our souls, and is ready for the wild bees of truth to hive in it, and make their sweet honey."[23] Unreason has a rationality of its own that sweetens poetic thought.

Three interwoven problems bequeathed by this romantic legacy have a special bearing on the arguments of modern poetry: poetic unreason, vision, and unity. First is the division of mental faculties whereby poetry employs an aggressive form of reasoning that is parallel to, but distinct from, conceptual logic. Benedetto Croce calls aesthetic logic the "science of intuitive or expressive knowledge" and treats it as an independent, intuitive system that is "the true analogue of Logic."[24] This expressive science continues to haunt and to inspire, but stubbornly to elude modern poetics in its pursuit of a rarefied vision that, like Mallarmé's visionary flower, endows the freshness of worldly sensation with other-worldly significance. Poetic unreason is supposed to reconcile the competing qualities of immediacy and mystery and so to fuse sight with insight, being with meaning. The antagonistic co-operation of these terms is preserved in the connotations of the word "intuition," by which Croce means not mystical knowledge or Schlegel's "ravishing confusion," but the formative power of the mind as it experiences objects, events, and feelings. Thus aesthetic logic (argument) generates poetic perception (vision), which in turn permits a unified consciousness. Accounts of poetic argument usually follow the pattern of Thomas's "After the Funeral," by raising a stormy dispute in order to proclaim peace. They endorse the ideal of unity as a dominant value in the triple sense of the fullness of perception, which is instantaneous rather than discursive (Ezra Pound's image as intellectual and emotional complex); the union of human faculties (Yeats's unity of being, T.S. Eliot's unified sensibility, D.H. Lawrence's integrated consciousness); and, since mind and poem reflect each other, the corresponding unity of a work of art. This threefold unity can be envisaged, however, only when we discover that it has been lost and must be regained. We treasure it all the more because it is absent and ideal and because we lack the means of realizing it. Because it presupposes a state of alienation to be overcome, it imposes an argumentative form on the work of the poet, who now is obliged to write himself out of his dilemma. Given this legacy, poetry inevitably becomes a project in understanding and redemption; it is the redeeming of thought by thought. This is the aim of poetic argument.

But what kind of argument can enable thought to outwit itself in order to transform logical discourse into a unified poetic vision? To answer this question, we must clarify what is at issue in asking it, and what demands are being made of poetic thought and language. Few modern poets are as confident as Schiller is about the total separation of reason and imagination, and most try to accommodate reason in the imaginative process, but in a way that will not threaten the autonomy of poetry. For example, after collecting the honey of unreason in *The Celtic Twilight*, Yeats feared that rejecting logic would disqualify the intelligence and put at risk the relationship between the poet and the world. It would make him too escapist ("l'on tourne l'épaule à la vie," wrote Mallarmé in "Les Fenêtres"[25]), and it would free him only by trivializing his work. Rejecting logic would mean endorsing the philosophical impotence of poetry proclaimed by logical positivism, that permits literature only the pretence of making pseudo-statements in pseudo-arguments. Reason was, Yeats discovered, a virtue of John Donne's writing, where "the more precise and learned the thought the greater the beauty, the passion; the intricacies and subtleties of his imagination are the length and depth of the furrow made by his passion."[26] The intricate furrow of the imagination traces an argument whose validity demands a reconciliation of logic and passion, reason and unreason. The problem is to discover the relationship between the opposing terms and to find a suitable way of expressing the extraordinary twist in thought by which reason manages to outwit itself. Yeats's visionary system of gyres is one image of the spiralling interweaving of mental faculties, but there is another that is less mystical and more useful for our purposes.

English romanticism had always been wary of the German example and had treated poetic reasoning as a passionate but thoughtful apprehension of reality. As Michael G. Cooke puts it: "Even while being rejected in its standard, prescriptive-analytical sense, reason is deftly reordered and redeemed for a romanticism that is anti- rather than irrationalist. Wordsworth calls imagination 'reason in her most exalted moods.' "[27] Samuel Coleridge praises the poet for combining imagination with "depth and energy of thought," or aggression in Quintilian's sense.[28] By the end of the nineteenth century even the antirational was suspect. H. Stuart Hughes contrasts social theorists of the 1880s and 1920s and observes that the former, in their revolt against positivism, sometimes adopted an openly anti-intellectual stance. They were interested in unconscious, intuitive, and subjective experience; they sought a "new definition of man as something more (or less) than a logically calculating animal." After the First World War, however, they were more cautious, especially on the question of rationality: "In defining their attitude toward reason, the social thinkers of the early twentieth century were obliged to walk the edge of a razor. On the one side lay the past errors of the eighteenth century and of the positivist tradition. On the other side lay the future errors of unreason and emotional thinking. In between there remained only the narrow path of faith in reason despite and even because of the drastic limitations with which psychological and historical discovery had hedged it: however much 'intuition,' free association, and the other unorthodox techniques of investigation might have broadened the criteria of evidence in social thought, reason alone remained the final control and arbiter."[29]

In their desire to reconcile passion, logic, and unreason, poets walked the same razor's edge, accompanied by their critics, and in *The Tightrope Walkers* Giorgio Melchiori again uses the image of precarious balance to portray their position. They, even more than social theorists, feel the vertigo of the irrational. However, the waking dream is a more useful figure of speech to explain the role of reason and to chart its resurgence. By combining the contrary states of sleep and wakefulness, it illustrates how vision and logic, sight and insight co-operate for poetic ends, even as it enforces their essential opposition. It supplies a locus or domain for poetic argument. Most important but most misleading, the waking dream appears to free poetry from the labour of consecutive reasoning while permitting it the cogency of an argument.

At first the preference was for sleep. John Keats longs for a life of sensations and visions rather than of "consequitive reasoning," and he compares the imagination to Adam's dream: "he awoke and found it truth."[30] But in "The Fall of Hyperion," Moneta introduces the dilemma that later bothers Yeats, when she warns that illusion may be indulged at the expense of sensation. The poet must not turn his back on life:

> "Art thou not of the dreamer tribe?
> The poet and the dreamer are distinct,
> Diverse, sheer opposite, antipodes.
> The one pours out a balm upon the world
> The other vexes it." (l.198ff.)

Charles Lamb also recommends vigilance and advises: "the true poet dreams being awake. He is not possessed by his subject, but has dominion over it. In the groves of Eden he walks familiar as in his native paths. He ascends the empyrean heaven, and is not intoxicated."[31] In this assessment the poet exercises the powers of sober craft within a world of dreams. His true home is Eden or heaven, and to this wonderful realm he devotes his thoughtful attention. For Lamb, reason operates within the domain of the imagination, and therefore it is more accurate to say that the the poet calculates being asleep and that he remains alert within a dream that he seeks to dominate; or, in Henry David Thoreau's words, that "Our truest life is when we are in dreams awake."[32]

The figure of the waking dream remains popular, but the emphasis gradually shifts to suggest a different balance of reason and imagination. The poet begins to awaken. For Mallarmé, visionary power must be earned by a crafty poet, who does not so much walk in a world of dreams as create the intricate illusion of such a world and convince the reader of its validity: "Here, the supreme act consists in showing, through a faultless possession of all faculties, that one is in ecstasy, but without showing how one rose to the summits."[33] Valéry stresses the poet's calculation even further, calling him "a cool scientist, almost an algebraist, in the service of a subtle dreamer." A further shift in perspective occurs when Valéry reverses his terms and makes the dreamer serve the scientist. Now the state of wakefulness is primary, and the true home of the poet is reality: "The true condition of a true poet is as distinct as possible from the state of dreaming. I see in it only willed inquiry, suppleness of thought.... My image of the poet is of a mind full of resources and cunning, feigning sleep at the imaginary centre of his yet uncreated work, the better to await that instant of his own power which is his prey."[34]

The poet's mind requires supple thought, cunning, and resourcefulness – all features of a good argument – and his sleep is now an elaborate pretence that permits him to seize his own imaginative power. Vision is the reward of calculation. He does not so much awaken within a dream as convey the power of dreams into the state of wakefulness: imagination invades the domain of reason. The emphasis is no longer on gazing into heaven with sober eyes, but on confronting reality with poetic insight.

The waking dream has retained its fascination, appearing in the work of Yeats, Robert Graves, Stevens, Edwin Muir, W.H. Auden, and others. In the course of its history, however, as emphasis shifts from vigilant dreaming to dreaming vigilance, the question changes from the romantic, "How can unreason be reasonable?" to the modern "How can reason be unreasonable?" Posed in this way, the questions indicate that the figure of the waking dream expresses a problem rather than a solution and that, as it shifts in emphasis, it redefines the problem. Although the change might seem minor, I think it has major implications because of the way it reconstitutes the domain of poetry so as both to encourage and to complicate its appetite for argument. The elements of the image are realigned to acknowledge the importance of logic in poetry, but, in so doing, the figure renders reason problematic. Far from being comically inept, cold, and impersonal, reason now assumes a disturbing waywardness. It behaves unreasonably. It may even appear grotesque, as we discover in "Poetry," where Marianne Moore allows Lamb's "groves of Eden" to be invaded by an ungainly creature. Following Yeats, she describes true poets as " 'literalists of the imagination' " who "present / for inspection, 'imaginary gardens with real toads in them.' "[35] It is characteristic of modern literature, and of Moore in particular, that the lion's leap of poetry can be executed just as well by a toad. As Bonnie Costello shows in her detailed commentary on the image,[36] the toad sets off a chain of associations, linking reality, imagination, fable, superstition, transformation, the uncanny; but I prefer to treat the toad as the voice of reason, precisely because of the associations that remind us that reason has a darker side. It can speak equivocally in arguments that must allow for *logical* contradiction, ambiguity, transformation, circularity, and regressiveness – all created by the regular exercise, not by the flouting, of logic. The oxymoron "waking dream" poses a problem by maintaining a split in the consciousness that it seeks to unify. In the case of "dreaming vigilance," however, the rivalry is not between two independent faculties (reason and imagination) and not within a secluded domain of poetry (reverie, the groves of Eden), but within reason itself.

How can reason be unreasonable? This question recalls, but differs in its assumptions from our earlier one: how can thought outwit itself in order to transform rational discourse into poetic vision? I must postpone investigation of the problematic of reason until I have prepared the ground further. Meanwhile, I can return to the first question in order to see how modern poets claim to answer it through the ambidexterous skills of dreaming vigilance. It permits them to solve the threefold romantic puzzle of unreason, vision, and unity, by using the second category to justify the other two. Because vision suggests both clear-sighted vigilance and visionary dreaming, it serves the contrary aims of defending the cogency of poetic thought while offering an alternative to logic. It appears to use vision in order to triumph over argument, when in fact it is the product of argument. Since imagism is the theory that most clearly promotes the visual qualities of poetry, I shall use it to illustrate the disparity between theory and practice, whereby reason is rejected on behalf of vision, only to insinuate itself unnoticed within the means of rejection.

It is convenient to contrast vision and thought in poetry as if they were utterly distinct, but their relation is far more complicated. As noted above, Croce tries to justify the contrast in his aesthetic by proposing a distinct science of intuitive knowledge; unfortunately he does not elaborate its principles. Susanne Langer explains that he cannot succeed, because any attempt to explore those principles and their expression will reveal their prevailing rationality and will break down the mistaken opposition between logic and intuition as two fundamentally different "methods of knowing": "But there is, in truth, no such opposition - if only because intuition is not a 'method' at all, but an event. It is, moreover, the beginning and the end of logic; all discursive reasoning would be frustrated without it. The simple concatenation of propositions known as "syllogism" is only a device to lead a person from one intuition to another - [The] emergence of meaning is always a logical intuition or insight. All discourse aims at building up, cumulatively, more and more complex logical intuitions."[37] Langer touches here on what I have called the darker side of reason, and when I trace the trajectory of argument in Eliot and Stevens, I shall examine two attempts to reach "the beginning and the end of logic." All arguments, including poetic ones, depend on the interplay of experience and understanding, intuition and logic. "All cognition of form is intuitive" but all form is rational.[38] Behind all logical recognition of relation, correspondence, resemblance, and difference lurks a prelogical activity (strictly speaking, it is *logically* prior); but all such activity must be articulated logically. As Langer shows, modernist aesthetics tends to ignore this dialectic when it sets vision against thought and thereby necessitates an alternative to thought - unreason. This divisive strategy is shared by theories that are philosophically quite different, for example, those of Croce and the imagists. The latter propose a prelogical, unified experience both in poetry and of poetry, but their faith in the visual power of the image encourages them to ignore its rationality and to devise their own form of unreason. In order to follow the twist in the fate of reason from Croce's "intuition," which retains a romantic aura, to the imagists' "immediate experience," which attempts to shed that aura, I must first turn to Langer's mentor, Ernst Cassirer.

Like Croce, Cassirer regards art as a special mode of understanding based on an intuition of the form of things, but, unlike Croce, he proceeds to analyse the rationality of the waking dream. He too claims that art provides real knowledge not through scientific abstraction, but through an "intensification of reality" achieved by "a continuous process of concretion."[39] In *An Essay on Man*, however, he criticizes the purely spiritual character of Croce's philosophy and what he considers its romantic preoccupation with the infinite. He brings art down to earth: "the symbolism of art must be understood in an immanent, not in a transcendent sense. Beauty is 'The Infinite finitely presented' according to Schelling. The real subject of art is not, however, the metaphysical Infinite of Schelling, nor is it the Absolute of Hegel. It is to be sought in certain fundamental structural elements of our sense experience itself - in lines, design, in architectural, musical forms. These elements are, so to speak, omnipresent. Free of all mystery, they are patent and unconcealed; they are visible, audible, tangible" (157). This passage can be read as another attempt to reconcile the vigilance of reason with the dreaming of art. On the one hand, Cassirer defends the rationality of art as a discovery of tangible reality: he calls it "one of the ways leading to an objective view of things and human life" (145). On the other hand, he defends the autonomy of art that obeys only its own imaginative laws: it is self-contained, an "independent 'universe of discourse' " (152). Art is a world of its own, but does not exist solely for its own sake. His concern with artistic autonomy prompts interest in the raw materials ("lines, design"), techniques, and principles ("fundamental structural elements") of art; that is, in the way the independent universe of discourse defines itself. His concern with immanent forms that are visible, audible, and tangible reflects art's commitment to the objective world. By combining vigilance and dream, Cassirer wishes to maintain both the freshness and the mystery of aesthetic experience. He insists on its intensity and richness. He seems to deny it mystery in the passage above, but its forms are "free of all mystery" only in the sense that they are not avenues to a transcendental ideal. The ordinary world is as remarkable as Mallarmé's flower and as elusive, because imaginative insight is necessary to perceive the world as it really is. Not the fragrant idea, but the object itself is the poet's goal. In this way Cassirer reintroduces the reverence and wonder, and almost the otherworldliness, that he seemed to reject: "When absorbed in the intuition of a great work of art we do not feel a separation between the subjective and objective worlds. We do not live our commonplace reality of physical things, nor do we live wholly within an individual sphere. Beyond these two spheres we detect a new realm, the realm, of plastic, musical, poetical forms ..." (145).

The entrancing realm of art is not illogical and does not employ a special logic of its own. Its forms are rational, because reason is essential to both the organization and operation of art. Like Langer, Cassirer insists that art must follow logical principles, because it is organized and articulated: "Every work of art has an intuitive structure, and that means a character of rationality" (167). Even when it is concerned with the improbable, grotesque, or bizarre, and even when it shares their confusion, art retains "the rationality of form" (167). Modernist experiments with free association, automatic writing, hallucinations, and madness do not mean that art itself adopts irrational principles, since principles as such cannot be irrational. In *The Principles of Symbolic Forms*, Cassirer says that scientific thinking and mythic (or aesthetic) thinking depend on the same categories of thought, but employ them in different ways. Their "modality" is different: "The modes of synthesis which they employ to give the form of unity to the sensuous manifold, to imprint a shape on disparate contents, disclose a thorough-going analogy and correspondence. They are the *same universal forms of intuition and thought* which constitute the unity of consciousness as such and which accordingly constitute the unity of both the mythical consciousness and the consciousness of pure knowledge" (my emphasis). I intend to return to this point when I consider the problematic of reason. At present I wish to stress that for Cassirer there is no independent logic of the imagination. The logic is the same, although it is applied differently in the "configurations" of mythical thought. In the different modalities of thought, however, we can still detect the ghost of unreason. Nevertheless, Cassirer insists that reason is essential to the operation of art in the sense that art is "contemplation." It systematically directs attention at the world so as to encourage appreciation, interpretation, and judgment. It teaches us to see. It directs attention inward into the human world as well. It studies passions and is itself passionate, but it is never blinded by emotion: "We are not at the mercy of these emotions; we look through them; we seem to penetrate into their very nature and essence."[40]

Cassirer's aim in the above discussion is to prove the rationality of art by asking: how does art "think" and what does it "think" about? Translated into the terms of this study, the questions become: how does poetry argue and what does it argue about? In the first case, he claims it is a mistake to divide the faculties (reason and unreason) and then to propose exclusive or overlapping domains for each (the waking dream). Instead, there must be appropriate uses of the same faculty operating in accordance with "universal forms of intuition and thought." In the second case, he claims that the aim of art is to articulate immanent rather than transcendent forms. Art argues about "fundamental structural elements of our sense experience" and of our emotional experience. Art is a process of contemplation that gives rise to an intense, aesthetic assurance; it is an argument that culminates in revelation.

The imagists ask the same questions as Cassirer, but answer them somewhat differently. They, too, examine the forms of sense experience in order to achieve an "intensification of reality." Where symbolists pluck the mystical flower absent from all bouquets, imagists observe the actual flower and insist that a rose is a rose and nothing more. Where the former evoke not the object, but the effect or state of mind that it produces, the latter present "the impact of the naked thing-in-itself, not the unknowable ultimate reality, but the essence of the actual."[41] Vision is now vigilant and sensory rather than visionary. However, immanent essences are as unknowable as ideals, and immediate experience proves surprisingly remote. The visual in poetry is supposed to depend on an immediate perception that precedes reason and is falsified by it. Before analysis, calculation or argument comes the mere impact of reality. F.H. Bradley, one source of the modern enthusiasm for immediate experience, claims that in any individual act of experience,"there is no distinction between my awareness and that of which it is aware. There is an immediate feeling, a knowing and being in one."[42] Such experience is prior to rational analysis because it is a simple unity containing diversity without the fragmenting activity of thought. The knowing that accompanies being is the knowledge sought by the imagists, and, if it truly is immediate, there should be no need for argument. If knowledge is a matter of vision, seeing requires no effort or proof.

Imagism aims at a fusion of seeing, knowing, and being, a complex poetic goal that at first seems to disqualify argument. The direct force of reality precedes reason; its immanent value defies rational investigation. Reason, however, despite its exclusion, re-enters unobserved, as Cassirer and Langer show, in the forms of contemplation and articulation. In actual practice, the argument of poetry, and especially the aggressive power of the image, reconciles poetry's two aims: freshness and mystery. The first suggests the palpable vitality of things - all that is given. The second suggests special knowledge - all that is hidden. Combined, the "essence of the actual" becomes the mystery of modern poetry. Reality is not simply given to us; it must be contemplated, pursued, and won. The poet's victory is his vision and his poem. Robert Langbaum maintains that concern with objectivity as a problem to be solved is the true legacy of romanticism, which wished to escape the confines of subjectivity in order to reconstruct the world.[43] Because ordinary things are strange and seeing them clearly demands effort, poetry must become argumentative even to give the impression of simple insight. I intend to discuss Edward Thomas as a poet in this tradition, one who struggles with the conflicting claims of seeing, knowing, and being. He tries to argue himself into a vision of nature, and when he succeeds, the vision comes effortlessly, prompted by a glorious trifle such as an old grange, the sun, or the song of the Ash Grove. When he fails, reality eludes him and his argument becomes a puzzle that he cannot solve. He expresses the failure of vision as a failure of reason, an inability to make sense of his own feelings or of his relation to natural beauty. Instead he portrays himself "hunched up thinking long exhausted thoughts."[44]

Thomas's arguments, whether successful or not, are conveyed through aggressive imagery. Imagism stresses above all the freshness of poetic seeing, but ignores the role of reason in what is apparently visual. When T.E. Hulme speaks of "meaning (i.e. *vision*)," he indicates that the value of poetry derives from the visual impact of the image, that manages "to make you continuously see a physical thing."[45] But poetic images consist of words, not sensations, and the pictures they present to the mind's eye have not an immediate meaning ("a knowing and being in one"), but a growing significance. They permit an expansion of thought and feeling because images are essentially metaphoric, that is, abstract. Abstraction is their virtue and the source of their power, not their defect. Hulme admits that poetry is at best "a compromise for a language of intuition which would hand over sensations bodily,"[46] but he does not consider the nature of the compromise. Images, analogies, and metaphors - the resources of imagism - are figurative devices which may seem to shock us into an unexpected vision, but which really are matters of conception, not perception. Andrew Welsh devotes much of his book, *Roots of Lyric*, to illustrating the intellectual complexity of Pound's "phanopoeia," which favours the visual component in poetic language, but actually combines seeing, knowing, and naming. The image releases its significance only when the reader discovers a structure of logical relations, usually involving undetected and unfathomable resemblances. Therefore, the poem "like a riddle, is not simply a pictorial description but a discovery, a way of seeing that leads to a new way of knowing."[47] I prefer to reverse his terms and to call imagism a pattern of knowing or argument that gives the impression of sight, but Welsh retains a fondness for unreason, not in the sense of irrationality, but of an alternative form of reasoning. Because phanopoeia cannot fully resolve the contradictions it reveals or limit its emotional suggestiveness, he calls it "a paradoxical way of knowing" that operates "beneath the rational and logical forms of discursive language" (76). Welsh is by no means anti-intellectual, but he feels that the riddling quality of lyric poetry gives it an "uncertainty principle" (42) that conflicts with "the logic and syntax of descriptive statements" (78). However, Welsh's own rigorous analysis of the techniques and effects of imagism shows, on the contrary, that they are all logical, and that their indeterminacy does not compromise their logic, but is a product of it. He discusses logical uncertainties, indeterminacies, and paradoxes, which may be condensed in a few images, but which nevertheless depend on "some fundamental structure of overlapping forms." (73). All structure, to repeat Langer's and Cassirer's admonition, is rational.

My point is not that the imagist naively supposed that poetry literally was, or could be, the same as vision. Although Hulme occasionally gives this impression, Pound is more sophisticated and shows that the real issue is the nature of poetic perception and its relation to poetic thought, "when a thing outward and objective transforms itself, or darts into a thing inward and subjective."[48] The point is that using vision as a model to explain what poetry can or should do emphasizes the "presentational" effect of the image and obscures the importance of logic in producing its desired transformation, which is, as Welsh observes, a metaphorical process. Although he redresses the balance, I believe he still obscures the deceptive rationality of the image. Another study of imagism, *In the Arresting Eye*, advances a step further by stressing the surreptitious role of argument. Like Welsh, John T. Gage shows how the allegedly prerational, intuitive impact of the image, which is supposed to bring nature, emotion, and language into perfect accord, really depends on "a structure of thought rather than a sensual stimulus."[49] Specifically, it operates through analogies that operate with argumentative force. For example, in one technique comparisons provide "inductive evidence for the plausibility of emotions otherwise, perhaps, unbelievable. In this case, analogy can provide the 'proof' of paradox" (98). This conclusion recalls the riddles that Welsh finds at the roots of lyric. The poet's unexpected reactions and strained feelings are illustrated and rendered credible through an interplay of images that operates with "the force of an argument" (99). Later, Gage amplifies this observation to explain imagism in general, which in practice presents arguments, yet in theory claims not to argue. Imagism is "a kind of argumentative theory" (131) or "method of moral reasoning" (156), that arrives at truths that it treats as empirically self-evident and therefore not requiring logical proof. We simply see them and so are not obliged to prove them. In this way imagism hopes to achieve all the benefits of argument - certitude, persuasive power, truth - apparently without the strain of arguing. It feels free to reject logic in favour of intuition, but only because of an optimistic epistemology, which presupposes a harmony of words, thoughts, things, and values (159). Healthy language, clear thought, and "natural moral law" (152) are conveniently in accord.

This epistemology has a bearing on poetic diction, the subject of the next section. Now I wish to conclude by reaffirming that the imagists' "argument by demonstration" remains logical, despite claims to the contrary, and that there is no need to appeal to another form of reasoning to explain its visual and intuitive effects. One last example will confirm this point. Here is Archibald MacLeish's version of the imagists' defiance of reason: "Pound's use of 'explicit rendering,' meaning the presentation of the subject not by a generalizing description but by a specific figure, or name, or quotation, or fragment of quotation, standing *for* the subject has become standard "modern" practice. The theory is ... that the true poetic act consists in the presentation of the reality of experience directly in its own often irrelevant terms leaving the reader to puzzle out the pattern of relationships for himself as he is left to puzzle it out in life, rather than having the particulars strained through a sieve of generalizations and presented to him as a series of progressive steps in a logical argument prepared in advance." MacLeish defends the power of poetry to render immediate experience in all its immediacy, but he actually shows that this effect must be achieved rhetorically ("figure") and symbolically ("standing *for* the subject"), and with symbols whose relation to the subject in question may be explicit ("name") or implicit ("quotation") or fanciful and cryptic ("irrelevant terms"). The reader will "see more *seeingly*," he claims, but only by first being forced to puzzle out the poem's unclear logic. Logic operates covertly within the means of rejecting reason – in the linguistic evocation of vision, sensation or revelation.[50]

The discussion to this point shows that reason has suffered a curious fate. It is first excluded as alien (Schiller), then limited to a special field (Croce) or a special mode (Cassirer), and then grudgingly readmitted into poetry (imagism). It is treated so gingerly because of two competing literary aims, whose competition produces the paradoxical demand that in poetry reason must be both exercised and effaced. Modernist poetics is divided between the desire to renounce or to reclaim reason: to give poetry the rigour and responsibility of intellect, yet to preserve its own distinctive power. First comes the reaction against the romantic disavowal of reason. Reason is reinstated. The poet is praised as a responsible and intelligent thinker whose schemes bring him into intimate contact with reality. "A great poet," declares Owen Barfield, "spells a great intellect, and such an one is fairly sure to have the faculty of delighting in abstract thought.... Really, there is no distinction between Poetry and Science, as kinds of knowing at all."[51] However, a second attitude displays a residual dissatisfaction with reason and its apparent blindness. The imagist wishes to move so close to reality that his poem becomes an explicit rendering of experience, its argument so aggressive that it is more than rational. At this point imagism echoes the romanticism it has scorned and offers a modern reworking of Thomas De Quincey's "literature of power" which, unlike the "literature of knowledge," relies on the compelling grandeur of truth rather than on discursive understanding. It does not teach; it reveals. It does not inform; it expands one's sympathetic wisdom.[52] Even a philosopher like Cassirer, who begins by secularizing, and rationalizing poetry, still seeks ways to retrieve the mysterious power that romanticism had granted the poet.

The figures of dreaming vigilance and of Moore's toad suggest a third possibility in which reason is fully reinstated, but its logic is disclosed as problematic. The *Old English Dictionary* traces the word "problematic" back to the sixteenth century, but it is now used so widely that it seems to have been coined especially for modern perplexities. More than a tendency to be sceptical, it suggests a wider philosophical concern with conceptual models and their limitations, with theories of bewilderment, negation, and mystification. It is a system of difficulties, or the difficulties that beset any system of thought, or the systematic difficulty of thought itself. It is the perversity or unreasonableness (but not irrationality) of reason, which enacts a "passion play of thought" through its "tortured thinking. Thinking that devours itself – and continues intact and even flourishes, in spite (or perhaps because) of these repeated acts of self-cannibalism."[53] This sounds like a colourful description of imaginative reasoning, but Susan Sontag is referring to philosophy, not to poetry, The "passion play of thought" could be a description of poetic argument, but here it defines all discourse, because all are poetic, that is sceptical and problematic. Valéry spoke enthusiastically of the marvels and emotions of the intellect. H. Stuart Hughes spoke cautiously of walking the razor's edge of rationality. Sontag's imagery of torture and cannibalism shows how painfully reason can turn on itself as it entangles itself in the language of its devising. To pursue this third possibility, therefore, we must turn to the discursiveness of discourse and the language of poetic argument.

RHETORIC: LANGUAGE AND SILENCE

I have claimed that poetic attempts to subvert logic in order to attain the fresh immediacy of vision have actually reanimated it and made poetry more argumentative by enforcing a fictitious dispute between reason and unreason, discourse and image. As the examples of symbolism and imagism show, the desired subversion can be made only by appealing to the forms and powers of rhetoric. If logic is the dynamic of argument that deploys reason and provides reasons, then rhetoric is an argument's engaging appeal and linguistic aggression. It involves not just techniques of persuasion, but the entire range of poetic diction or *lexis*. In Mallarmé's second paradox, poetry contests the language in which it is written, and we find a comparable tension and contention between language and silence, between words and ideas and things. On the one hand, the magic of words conjures up a verbal universe, a reign of eloquence in which everything exists "to end in a book"; on the other, his ideal is language purified to silence, the "poème tu."[54] Words turn into things; things turn into words; meanwhile poetry mediates both vocally and silently between the two. For Archibald MacLeish, it is the very inarticulateness of words that permits them to fly like birds, and to rise to an "emotion which words cannot come at directly – which no words as words can describe." Therefore a poem "should be palpable and mute / As a globed fruit" and "wordless / As the flight of birds."[55] Both palpable reality and intangible emotion elude the grasp of words for Robert Graves, too, as he tries to escape the "cool web" of language in order to advance "From the unsaid to the yet unsayable / In silence of love and love's temerity."[56]

The temerity of language is that it dares to say the unsayable by setting linguistic limits which it then ventures to transgress. It proposes the same opposition that we have already encountered between conception (argument, thought, discourse) and perception (vision, feeling, experience) and then seeks a way to mediate between them. It, too, imposes on poetry a project in understanding and redemption that, in this case, is best understood as a matter of verbal reference. How do words gesture toward what they replace? Poetic language, like poetic unreason, must bridge a gap that is sustained by itself in its role as intermediary. According to modernist theory, it must reach across the signifying chain that links words to ideas to things, in order to probe into a nonlinguistic reality usually called "silence." Silence is the thwarted reference of language; it is the mute sign of a failure that can nevertheless serve as a valid poetic technique. Just as reason calls forth its opposite, unreason, and the two are urged to cooperate in poetic arguments, so language summons silence as an adversary and ally in what is considered a nondiscursive discourse. Just as unreason proposes the goal of unified consciousness, but through its own opposition to reason enforces fragmentation – for instance, in the oxymoron of the waking dream – so poetic language aims at, but renders problematic, a vision of unity and a unified vision. Norman Holland neatly illustrates the dilemma as follows: "If I think 'Jane,' I not only bring my mate to mind, I also remind myself of her absence or, even if she were in my study with me, the irreducible difference between Jane and the me who says 'Jane.' All language – all naming, anyway – by substituting the word for the thing, establishes both a presence and an absence. One could say, therefore, that in all naming 'desire speaks,' that is, the naming announces both the desire and the absence of what is desired."[57]

In keeping with his psychoanalytic study of identity, Holland stresses the desire of and in language, but we can shift ground and use rhetorical aggression in the same way to explain the thwarted reference that poetic argument struggles to overcome through silence. It argues in order to reappropriate the world that it has obscured. Gerald Bruns outlines the romantic myth of the Fall that expresses the fate of language, when it has lost its paradisal harmony with being and fallen into disunity. Words were once in perfect accord with the world, but after

Babel they can only substitute for reality. Speech now excludes what it names: "The very act of speech is thus an act of dissociation, whereby the word is split off from the world and isolated in vacant space." Language has been cast adrift and must now argue with itself in order to moor itself to reality. According to Bruns, the myth derives from Friedrich Hegel's view that signification can affirm meaning only by negating existence: "the activity of speech annihilates the world of things in the very process of signification; in speech the world of things is displaced by the world of the spirit."[58] Understanding distinguishes the mind, but only by divorcing it from reality. Through its signifying activity, however, thought promises to reappropriate what has been forfeited. For Hegel at least, paradise can be regained. Later theories are less optimistic and, by proclaiming the endless necessity but futility of arguing, they subtly reinforce yet sabotage the view that poetic language is inherently contentious. The space of language may be "isolated," as Hegel claims, but it is no longer considered "vacant," because it is the scene of a busy, self-justifying activity. It is the structural space of Ferdinand de Saussure's *langue*, the elaborate signifying network of language, in which conceptual and phonic differences, rather than positive references to reality, determine linguistic meanings and values.[59] More recently it has become the scene of "textuality," where books are bookish together. In either case, it is the universe of discourse that language constructs for us, and in which it forever confines us. In this view language can only confirm its solitude and can never truly succeed in reappropriating reality.

This legacy of linguistic loss and gain recalls the romantic fragmentation and reunion of reason and unreason, with which I began the previous section; and in the same way, it forces poetry to dedicate itself to self-validating, self-nullifying arguments. The power of language to exclude or annihilate reality has become one of the darlings of criticism, especially following Jacques Derrida's expansion and explosion of the myth of the Fall into language. He too discloses "a power of death in the heart of living speech," because it "replaces presence by ... the ideality of truth and value"[60] available only in the symbolic world of words. However, when Derrida denies that language can redeem itself because it can never recapture the full presence of reality that it only imagines it has lost, he attempts to dispel the Hegelian myth of language and the metaphysics on which it is based. He marks the end of the modernist argument of reappropriation and the start of the postmodernist argument of "différance." I cite him here, not to endorse his deconstruction, which I shall consider later, but to take advantage of the perspective he offers on modernism. He shows that the goal of reappropriation, which can be accomplished only when words grow so refined that they fall silent, is both generated and frustrated by a problematic view of language. The combative linguistic model is apparent in our comparison of Hegel and Saussure. Both are concerned with the isolating effect of "the activity of speech," but where the former locates it in a competent if alienated "world of spirit," the latter sets it within a diacritical system of linguistic differences. Although the terms of definition change, the model of understanding remains much the same, and it is this form that Derrida contests. Saussure wishes to reject the idealist frame of thought, as Frank Lentricchia notes, by discarding "romantic irrationalism" and the "various epistemologies of intuitionism" that it prompted. But in effect he reinstates the model in his notion of *langue*, which he calls "well-defined," "social," "concrete," and open to investigation, but which ultimately exists as an ideal totality of language apart from any individual speech act, a grand, transcendental structure that we know only partially and indirectly through the speech acts (*parole*) with which we analyse it.[61] This withdrawal of language, not only from reality, but from the reach of our attempts to master it, leaves us in a strange territory indeed, suspended between language and the world, unable to trust either. It imposes on literature a dubious task of recuperation and redemption in which ends and means are equally doubtful.

Whether or not modernist poets accepted the Hegelian legacy of flawed language, they were its troubled beneficiaries. Just as they had to find ways of overcoming the romantic disjunction of mental faculties, so they had to heal the self-inflicted injuries of language. In both cases they inherited a dualistic and alienating epistemology, whereby the mind is separated from reality and endowed with powers that confirm the separation even as they try to overcome it. Hence the modernists' recourse to silence as an argumentative ploy. Through it, they accept their fate, mimic the annihilating power of words and, by displaying it, overcome it. Or at least they express the desire to overcome it and so reassert the ideal of reunion with reality. The triad of unreason, vision, and unity now becomes silence, vision and reunion. The poet says nothing, but failure becomes the measure of success.

When language is silenced, however, it tacitly reasserts itself with devious power. Just as unreason is really a figure of thought that engages thought, so silence is a figure of speech within a rhetorical system. It is a felt absence like a pause in music that has rhythmic value in relation to the sounds around it; it is a lyrical pausing that depends on and works against the language surrounding it. By refusing to name things, the poet claims to renounce the mediation of language and to overcome the indirectness inherent in its symbolic function. He pretends not to argue or convinces himself that argument is unnecessary, in order to achieve a knowledge that is actually the fruit of argument. Because the poetic goal is reached through a kind of linguistic asceticism, it has psychological and moral implications that sometimes overshadow its philosophical intent. The strategy of silence is a self-imposed privation, variously associated with humility, negation, reduction, denial, refusal, outrage, renunciation, impoverishment, transparency, purification, withdrawal, death, and so on. Through this self-discipline the poet manages to step barefoot into reality and to touch the outer world of presence (the essence of the actual, the purity of the object), the inner world of plenitude (immediate experience, the purity of the subject), or the void of absence (existence, mere being, death). In *Against Language?* Rosmarie Waldrop considers how modern writers find words inadequate to treat pure spirit (the holy, void, chaotic), subjectivity (emotion, sensuality, energy, the unconscious), and physical objects. Because mystical experience, the mind, and things-in-themselves are ineffable and are falsified by efforts to express them, poets disrupt language in order to overcome its limitations and, paradoxically, to increase its power. All the disconcerting techniques of modernism, such as syntactic and semantic fragmentation, stream of consciousness, and odd typography, are calculated transgressions of thought and speech. Finding words flawed, writers sometimes seek not to perfect them, but to debase them further, resorting in extreme cases to screams, inarticulate noise, and, finally, silence.[62]

It is as impossible to be silent in poetry as it is to be nonrational. Consequently, as a strategy in poetic arguments, silence takes various rhetorical forms, some of them remarkably loquacious. It may appear as the minimal speech, hesitations, and actual silences in Samuel Beckett's work. The ultimate enthymeme (the suppression of the premises of an argument), this technique leaves more and more unsaid, until there remains mere implication, the irony of the unspoken or unspeakable. As irony, silence evokes a world in which nothing is as stated and which must be approached through indirection, denial or omission. Borrowing Waldrop's three categories, we may define this world in spiritual terms, as in Eliot's "Ash Wednesday" where the divine "silent Word" endures though the human word is "spent," "unheard," and "unspoken." It may be the emotional world of Ezra Pound's "Papyrus," where the ellipses argue more forcefully (Hugh Kenner discusses this fragment as a "witticism"[63]) about the yearning of absent love than do the four words:

Spring . . . .
Too long. . . . .
Gongula . . . . .[64]

Or it may be the physical landscape which Hart Crane interrogates in "North Labrador," only to receive silence as a reply:

> Cold-hushed, there is only the shifting of moments
> That journey toward no Spring –
> No birth, no death, no time nor sun
> In answer.[65]

More often and more conventionally, silence appears in patterns of imagery that point metaphorically to experiences beyond words. George Steiner cites three images – light, music, silence – which are comparable to Waldrop's triad.[66] Silence may also appear dramatically as an anti-epiphany, a failure of vision and imagination expressed as a failure of language. The chief model here is Hugo von Hofmannsthal's *The Letter of Lord Chandos*, in which the narrator describes his shipwreck in a sea of words that "congealed into eyes which stared at me and into which I was forced to stare back – whirlpools which gave me vertigo and, reeling incessantly, led into the void."[67] Following his example, many modern heroes of the imagination have lamented the disintegration of language in the face of an inexpressible reality, for example in theatre of the absurd, in fiction (Joseph Conrad's *Heart of Darkness*, Virginia Woolf's *The Waves*, Jean Paul Sartre's *La Nausée*), and in poetry (Eliot's "Burnt Norton," Graves's "The Yet Unsayable").

I offer this list of rhetorical techniques, in order to stress what should now be clear: that silencing language, like denying reason, is a calculated strategy that operates within an argument made necessary by what are perceived as the shortcomings of language. Although silence seems to entail the end of poetry ("Plus de mots," cried Rimbaud in "Une Saison en Enfer," and later took his own advice), it actually makes poetry all the more lively, even as it mourns its own death. More important for our purposes, through the moral, psychological and thematic effects attributed to them, these techniques raise the larger question of the efficacy of poetic diction. If poetry really can argue through a logic of its own (a point I continue to refute), then it demands a language so refined that it appears to evaporate. It requires the "strange rhetoric" of words, whose "exquisite appositeness ... takes away all their verbality," thus permitting them to achieve feats of reference and suggestion impossible in everyday speech.[68] But what kind of language can outwit itself in order to achieve this philosophical enchantment? Does it differ in kind or in degree, or in any way at all, from ordinary language? And if it is different, what relation does it bear to thought and to reality that makes it function negatively, through silence?

The familiar modernist contrast between two kinds of language, one intuitive, the other analytic, repeats the opposition between unreason and reason, and with the same result. It raises the magical prospect of argument conducted by a nondiscursive discourse. To understand the desire for and the claims made of such a discourse, we must return to the epistemological implications of symbolism and imagism and consider two accounts of the relationship between language and thought. They have given rise to two corresponding theories of poetic diction as a means of arguing through silence.

The first account is mimetic and sees writing as an imitation of thought. Language translates a convoluted mental process into more orderly and accessible terms. Northrop Frye explains that "discursive writing is not thinking, but a direct verbal imitation of thought." As used here, "thinking" refers to the entire life of the mind, not just to reasoning, which is disciplined thinking. "For it is clear that all verbal structures with meaning are verbal imitations of that elusive psychological and physiological process known as thought, a process stumbling through emotional entanglements, sudden irrational convictions, involuntary gleams of insight, rationalized prejudices, and blocks of panic and inertia, finally to reach a completely incommunicable intuition."[69] Thinking is prior to language, which subsequently serves as the vehicle of thought by translating thought into verbal terms. To be adequate to its task, therefore, language must be accurate as both imitation and vehicle. That is, it must provide a just translation and it must be internally consistent. In the first case, however, imagination may outstrip the power of words to follow: its intuitions and irrational convictions may be incommunicable. In the second case the discourse, though theoretically possible, may be clumsy, inept, or inarticulate. In Eliot's terms, the poet will not have constructed an effective objective correlative.

In the second theory that relates language and thought, language is not mimetic or correlative, but constitutive of thought. It is interfused with thought. George Steiner traces the theory back to Gottfried Wilhelm Leibniz and Wilhelm von Humboldt and explains that in this view "language is not the vehicle of thought but its determining medium. Thought is language internalized and we feel and think as our particular language impels and allows us to do." Feeling and thinking – the life of the mind – are intrinsically verbal. This does not mean that we always think in specific words, which we have only to write down, but that our thinking depends on the internalized structures of language. Language does not imitate thought as a secondary process; it is already primary and active in thinking: "language is the only verifiable and a *priori* framework of cognition. Our perceptions result from the imposition of that framework on the total, unorganized flux of sensations."[70] Because thought is always subject to the regulation of language, the failure of one entails the failure of the other. In the first theory, thought may continue when language falls silent. Silence may even set thought free or permit the free play of ideas. But in the second theory there is no freedom from language, only within language. True silence would enforce the cessation of thought, although in so doing silence might permit a return to "the total, unorganized flux of sensations." It may bring us closer to our immediate experience of things.

When applied to poetry, these theories sponsor two views of poetic diction, which we must understand as the way in which poetry uses words in order either to imitate or to constitute thought. The two views apparently move in opposite directions, but as we follow their courses into symbolism and imagism, they later converge in a common concern with argument as conducted and enforced by rhetorical silence.

When, in the Preface to the *Lyrical Ballads*, Wordsworth rejected the gaudiness and inane phraseology of eighteenth-century poetic diction in favour of a selection of the language really used by men, Coleridge objected because he wished to preserve as a purely poetic domain the "excited state of the feelings and faculties" that distinguishes the imagination. The language of poetry must be more supple and forceful than that of prose, because it results from and responds to "the modifying powers with which the genius of the poet [has] unified and inspirited all the objects of his thought."[71] In short, poetic thought requires a special poetic language. Coleridge did not doubt the efficacy of such thought or such language because, unlike modern sceptics, he announced that he had faith in the principles of grammar, logic, and psychology, as well as in good sense and good taste. In his "Appendix" of 1802, Wordsworth made greater allowance for the figurative qualities of poetic language, but it is especially through his own practice as a poet that he, too, contributed to the distinctiveness of poetic diction. According to Donald Davie, in the eighteenth century poetic diction meant "the perfection of a common language," but following Wordsworth's example, it came to mean "a private language, a distinctive vocabulary and turn of phrase."[72] This shift from public eloquence to private expression focuses attention on distinctive styles, expressing peculiar casts of thought. Both thought and language become unique to the individual poet in ways that may, when the tendency is pursued, transgress logic, grammar, and good sense.

Poetic transgression is one of the delights of modernism. Pursued far enough, thought may argue itself into an esoteric world in which feelings and faculties grow so excited and so refined that words can no longer represent them. If writing imitates thought, then it cannot do justice to such inexpressible states of mind. Poetic diction will grow increasingly private and peculiar as it aspires to the condition of "resonant emptiness" or musical silence. The French symbolists again provide the best example of this limiting case. Mallarmé said he wanted to invent a language composed not of words, but of intentions and sensations, one composed of all that words can suggest but not state. In one celebrated case he invented a word at once evocative and meaningless. In his sonnet, "Ses purs ongles," the word "ptyx" is usually interpreted as a shell or conch, thereby allowing the poem to speak in the voice of a seashell:"Sur les crédences, au salon vide: nul ptyx, / Aboli bibelot d'inanité sonore" [On the credenzas, in the empty room: no ptyx, / Abolished curio of resonant emptiness]. The ptyx is carefully refined out of existence: it is called abolished, empty and absent, since the room is empty. The lovely, musical second line hints at a silence all the more suggestive because of the mystery of the key word whose dubious sense, Mallarmé wrote to a friend, is created solely by the poem: "try to send me the real meaning of the word ptyx: I am assured that it does not exist in any language, which I would much prefer in order to give myself the charm of creating it by the magic of the rhyme." The words fade into a haunting sensation ("les paroles s'effacer devant la sensation"),[73] and the only way to find a more magical diction is to turn, with Valéry, to utter silence. He, too, was intrigued by the ineffable, and suggested as an ideal the pure, blank page that sets the mind in motion but offers it no content, a "presence of absence" that mirrors the soul's longing for the miraculous. Poetry purified into silence reveals that "there is nothing so beautiful as that which does not exist."[74] The ultimate poetic argument employs the ultimate poetic diction to express the ultimate poetic thought. It also hints at a nihilistic impulse behind the modern rejection of language.

English poets were not given to such extremes, but they too took up the issue of the power, purity, and limits of poetic language. Especially interesting in this regard is Owen Barfield's *Poetic Diction* (1928), which treats poetic diction as a means of creating a heightened state of awareness from which words are finally excluded. Language imitates thought, which it cannot adequately transmit. For Barfield, any word, no matter how prosaic, can function poetically, depending on how it is used by the poet and received by the reader. Like Coleridge, he is concerned ultimately with consciousness. Poetic diction is the use of words to arouse the "aesthetic imagination," a faculty that apprehends the essential unity of experience that it discovers and communicates through metaphor. Poetry grants access to a new, unified world which is really the primitive world of mythic consciousness forfeited by modern man through his excessive reliance on reason. The language of ancient man reported the direct perception of a vitality that we must now rediscover through metaphor: "But we, in the development of consciousness, have lost the power to see this one as one. Our sophistication, like Odin's, has cost us an eye; and now it is the language of poets, in so far as they create true metaphors, which must *restore* this unity conceptually, after it has been lost from perception.... Reality, once self-evident, and therefore not conceptually experienced, but which can *now* only be reached by an effort of the individual mind – this is what is contained in a true poetic metaphor; and every metaphor is 'true' only in so far as it contains such a reality, or hints at it."[75]

Poetry gives us intuitive knowledge that is already latent in language but that must be rediscovered and restored by poetry. To accomplish this end, however, the poet must argue aggressively in order "to fight *against* language," to resist its tendency to grow prosaic, and to make up the "poetic deficit" (112) at which metaphor can only hint. Language falls short of its goal. The visionary state is evoked through words, but it exceeds their range. This is partly because words are now corrupt, but primarily because the visionary state is not linguistic. Originally it was "not conceptually experienced" (89) at all; now it longs for that lost, direct purity. Therefore words can only provide a ghostly paradigm of what was once an immediate, unmeditated, preverbal perception: "Mythology is the ghost of concrete meaning. Connections between discrete phenomena, connections which are now apprehended as metaphor, were once perceived as immediate realities. As such, the poet strives, by his own efforts, to see them, and to make others see them, again" (92). According to the myth of the Fall, thought and language have fallen from grace and must be redeemed by metaphor, with its special power to discover "connections" in reality. Poetry provides knowledge that is really a way of seeing: it renews our half-blinded vision. But Barfield also confirms that, in modern poetry especially, vision requires argument, because reality is no longer "self-evident" and an "effort of the individual mind" is needed to see it. It must be restored "conceptually, after it has been lost from perception." The more sophisticated our consciousness and the more it usurps language in order to impose its rational view of the world, the greater is our need for poetic language to counter that view. As intuition wanes, the poet must fight to reinvigorate it, by discovering a suitable, metaphoric diction. Modern poetry, the product of a highly developed mind, is highly argumentative, because the task of restoring vision is all the more difficult. This explains why modern poetry often gives "a sense of difficulties overcome – of an obstreperous medium having been masterfully subdued" (96). Poetic diction is the means of argument against, within, and beyond language.

Despite his respect for metaphor, Barfield must eventually move beyond language because he treats the "poetic" as a quality of consciousness, not of language, which merely imitates patterns of consciousness. Poetic diction is any use of language that arouses "the poetic mood." This exalted mood is not indulged in for its own sake, but used as a way of regarding the world and restoring its vital unity. In this epistemology, reality, consciousness, and language are all related but distinct, and they are drawn into accord only by the skilful poet. Although his goal is an immediate perception of reality, Barfield concedes that for modern man perception (vision) must yield to conception (argument), which must be mediated further by metaphor (rhetoric). In this attenuating process concrete things are replaced by ghostly myths.

A second account of poetic diction dispels these phantoms by rejecting the abstraction and alienation of Barfield's theory. Proponents of symbolist or mythological thinking wish to expand consciousness, first by establishing a privileged poetic diction, but ultimately by freeing thought from all linguistic constraint. In contrast, the literary reform associated with imagism seeks to integrate thought and language perfectly. Its goal is a mode of thought and speech that can argue without the labour of arguing, because its language does not imitate, but constitute thought. Then language is (or if it falters, can be made) competent to render all the subtleties of mind. Because words are adequate, the poet does not need a unique diction, only a supple one. Imagists tend to agree with Wordsworth that words are "an incarnation of thought ... a constituent part and power or function in the thought,"[76] and that consequently the language of poetry need not differ essentially from ordinary speech. Like him, they reject the artificial diction of their predecessors and seek an idiom suited to "all the mighty world / Of eye, and ear," that is, to the world of sensation. Unlike the symbolists, they turn from the visionary to the visual, only to discover that in poetry, perception as much as conception is a matter of rhetoric – of images, symbols, and metaphors.

Coleridge too wondered if word and mind might fuse so organically that they become aspects of the same essential human energy. All thought might attain the urgent immediacy of sensation, but only if we overcome the aloofness and arbitrariness of words that stand as symbols between us and experience. Instead of eliminating words from thought, like the symbolists, and dispensing with their intermediate function, Coleridge proposed the opposite approach. He asked, "whether there be reason to hold, that an action bearing all the *semblance* of pre-designing Consciousness may yet be simply organic, & whether a *series* of such actions are possible – and close on the heels of this question would follow the old 'Is Logic the *Essence* of Thinking?' in other words – Is *thinking* impossible without arbitrary signs? & – how far is the word "arbitrary" a misnomer? Are not words, etc., parts and germinations of the Plant? And what is the Law of their Growth? – In something of this order I would endeavour to destroy the old antithesis of *Words & Things*, elevating, as it were words into Things, & living Things too."[77] Coleridge wants to draw words into the process of cognition where they become constitutive rather than mimetic and secondary. If words, thoughts, and things can correspond perfectly, then knowledge becomes immediate and poetic. Instead of a gap between reality, consciousness, and language, there is a sensuous apprehension of thought – a knowing, being, and saying all in one: "The focal word has acquired a *feeling of reality* – it heats and burns, makes itself to be felt. If we do not grasp it, it seems to grasp us, as with a hand of flesh and blood, and completely counterfeits an immediate presence, an intuitive knowledge."[78]

Coleridge advocates the reaching out of language to reality, and of reality to language, that was so precious to the early modernists. They, too, envisage a poetic embrace whose passionate certitude should make unnecessary what they regard as the attenuated, discursive hypotheses of argument. Accordingly, they call for direct presentation rather than description of an object, and for language designed to make you see a physical thing and to prevent you from gliding through an abstract process. Above all, through a return to the simple virtues of prose, they encourage a close connection between words and things and try to destroy the antithesis between them. In Eliot's diagnosis: "Language in a healthy state presents the object, is so close to the object that the two are identified." By way of contrast Eliot cites Algernon Charles Swinburne's poetry where "the object has ceased to exist, because the meaning is merely the hallucination of meaning, because language, uprooted, has adapted itself to an independent life of atmospheric nourishment." To a symbolist this would be a great compliment. To Eliot, such idealism is outmoded. Poetry must confront reality and aid the strenuous modern effort to consume and digest it: "But the language which is more important to us is that which is struggling to digest and express new objects, new groups of objects, new feelings, new aspects ..."[79]

Whereas Barfield begins by distrusting ordinary language and designates a compensating poetic diction, imagism presupposes the competence of language not just to represent but to present reality. However, in theory and practice it, too, finds words debased and tries to purify them in ways that grow increasingly figurative. Pound's faith in image, vortex, and ideogram is based on the conviction that "the natural object is always the *adequate* symbol" and that therefore the verbal symbols are themselves adequate, provided "that their symbolic function does not obtrude."[80] Language must be made silent and transparent. Its mediating role must vanish until, as Coleridge speculated, words become the things they signify. To this end, the poet must ensure that his words are precise, concrete, free of "rhetoric," and, above all, accurate: "For when words cease to cling close to things, kingdoms fall, empires wane and diminish. Rome went because it was no longer the fashion to hit the nail on the head." Language is most corrupt and corrupting when most abstract. But Pound trusts things more than words, and he trusts words only when they are most like things. Consequently, he mistrusts ordinary speech, which is often inaccurate, and proposes in image and ideogram a special poetic diction of his own. If words are elevated into things, they become objects that are encountered directly. Pound insists that the effective image is not a symbol or even an idea, but a kind of object: "the author must use his *image* because he sees it or feels it, *not* because he thinks he can use it to back up some creed or some system of ethics or economics. An *image*, in our sense, is real because we know it directly."[81]

Thus Pound's concern for the prose value of verse writing leads him to an increasingly esoteric poetic diction, the virtue of which lies in its special intensity and concreteness. His early confidence in ordinary language leads in his own poetry to a style which, although based on the rhythms of the speaking voice, strays far from the real language of men. It is a style in which words relinquish their verbality, most obviously in the Chinese ideograms used in the *Cantos*. "The point of Imagisme is that it does not use images *as ornaments*. The image is itself the speech. The image is the word beyond formulated language."[82] By "formulated language" Pound seems to mean conventional speech, but he suggests something further. At first he rejects ornamental language, so that he can identify word and thing ("The image is itself the speech"), but then the word is subsumed in its object. It operates like an ideogram, which Pound treats as a thing seen directly, rather than as a sign that represents a sound that recalls an object. Ideally, the image is observed rather than spoken; beyond language and its formulations lies the silence of immediate experience.

The two theories of poetic diction outlined above arise from a common romantic, epistemological concern: they investigate the problem posed by Wordsworth in the Preface to the *Lyrical Ballads*, where he wonders "in what manner language and the human mind act and re-act on each other." Both theories explain how mind and language cooperate to provide knowledge of the world, and both are argumentative in demanding that such knowledge, whether ineffable or direct, must be earned through mental and verbal discipline that transcends language by negating it. They illustrate how modern poetry claims to argue and what it claims to achieve. To understand how it actually argues, we must clarify the relationship between epistemology and the rhetoric of argument.

Symbolists advocate a poetry of abstraction that pursues but "never reaches the conception of the Idea in itself"; imagists advocate a poetry of concretion - "the poem of fact in the language of fact."[83] Following different courses, they nevertheless converge in their desire for a powerful rhetoric with which to compensate for the deficiencies of ordinary speech, a rhetoric based on symbol or image, but ultimately on metaphor. Through metaphor, poetry either exceeds or dissolves the bounds of language and permits a consciousness which, whether it is visionary or visual, they express paradoxically as silence. Both find in metaphoric exchange the aggression that allows poetry to discover, prove, and persuade. The symbolist goal is well served by the significant contrariness of metaphor, but at first glance the imagist ambition to fuse word and thing seems to demand a language as literal as possible. It should indicate rather than prove. It should shun the detachment and displacement of meaning - the abstraction - essential to metaphor. Yet Hulme insists that poetry argues by analogy. The poet's "visual concrete" language attains a "solid vision of realities" only through rhetorical indirection: "Plain speech is essentially inaccurate. It is only by new metaphors, that is, by fancy, that it can be made precise."[84]

Hulme was not troubled by the inconsistency of making poetry concrete by using fanciful abstractions. Ernest Fenellosa, who inspired Pound and the imagists, tried to resolve the paradox through a daring philosophical reversal. He claims that metaphors only appear to be abstract, whereas in fact they are "at once the substance of nature and of language." Reality consists of relations and processes, not of discrete objects. The fusion of word and thing is not of noun and object, but of sentences, directed by transitive verbs and natural activities. The basic natural process is a transfer of power, that is also the form of the metaphor: "This is more than analogy, it is identity of structure." Because metaphors "follow objective lines of relations in nature herself,"[85] they are not arbitrary or even subjective. Viewed correctly, he claims, a poem does not argue by analogy; it makes literal statements. Even more thoroughly than Hulme, Eliot, or Pound, Fenellosa presupposes the happy concurrence of language, thought, and reality, a harmony that Andrew Welsh traces to Emerson's view that language is natural rather than arbitrary, because it "reflects basic structures and processes in nature." The basic forms of all three, if rightly discerned, are identical. The roots of language are metaphorical, but the roots of metaphor are natural.[86] However, in defence of the concrete immediacy of metaphoric perception, Fenellosa is obliged to presume a lost mythic consciousness that can discern the triple identity and appreciate it as a vital unity. The "universe is alive with myth," which unfortunately we can no longer see but must reconstruct in poetry: "Poetry only does consciously what the primitive races did unconsciously." Once again we must struggle to achieve their effortless awareness. Moreover, the calculation needed in "forcing" poetic diction "closer to the concreteness of natural processes" tacitly confirms the very alienation it seeks to overcome. It confirms the abstractness of metaphors. If they really were concrete, they would not have to be argued or forced "painfully back along the thread of our etymologies" to recover their original freshness.[87]

Hulme and Fenellosa are not deceived in believing that metaphor can prove (confirm, approve, attest, convey) the concreteness of things. Metaphor argues equally well on behalf of both abstraction and concretion because, as Paul Ricoeur notes, it combines two "moments" – discursive and intuitive, logical and sensible, a "dynamic of thought" and a "pictorial" power.[88] These two moments recall the dialectic of intuition and logic in Susanne Langer's analysis of aesthetic cognition, because they describe the same process, expressed now in terms of rhetoric. For Ricoeur metaphor is "both a thinking and a seeing" (145). The first is the perception of analogy: recognizing a pattern of resemblance and difference that permits "the transition from literal incongruence to metaphorical congruence between two semantic fields" (145). The second is the "iconic" aspect of metaphor. The interplay of its terms is registered instantaneously and unified under a dominant image. One thing is seen as, or in terms of, another: "If there are two thoughts in one in a metaphor, there is one which is intended; the other is the concrete aspect *under* which the first one is presented" (147). This is the "depicting mode" which gives metaphor its "seemingly essential concreteness" (148). The verbal appears to yield to the visual, and may even seem to transcend language, leaving it in silence. Other effects are also possible. In practice, metaphor presents a varied traffic between abstract and concrete, as well as physical and mental, animate and inanimate terms. It can make us see, or it can tease us out of thought. In either case, it does so by arguing.

Metaphor argues, therefore, whether it is regarded as a model (the mimetic theory) or a mode (the constitutive theory) of thought. In either case, it works logically and has semantic value; it creates or discovers new meanings. As Ricoeur shows, metaphor can argue in this way only if we recognize it as a way of making statements and not just as an unaccustomed substitution of names. It is an act of predication, not denomination, whose locus is the statement, not the individual word: "Thus, we are not dealing any longer with a simple transfer of words, but with a commerce between thoughts, that is, a transaction between contexts. If metaphor is a competence, a talent, then it is a talent of thinking."[89] It is a discursive process of thought. Even though it strikes us instantaneously and seems to overcome the weary discursiveness of discourse by presenting things visibly, it remains a compressed proof the conciseness of which makes it all the more effective. It combines "the sensible moment of figurativity," which is "the power of making things visible, alive, actual," with "the logical moment of proportionality" (34), which is the commerce between thoughts. It attains vision through argument. Ricoeur suggests in effect that every metaphor is a compressed argument, quite apart from the ways in which a poet may incorporate it into larger structures. Moreover, every metaphor is "impertinent" or perverse in its arguing, an impertinence which explains its apparent irrationality. A metaphoric statement is a deliberate "category mistake." It makes deviant or false predication. Because of this "semantic twist," it seems unreasonable or enigmatic, but, far from lapsing into the irrational, it commits a "calculated error," that serves a reasonable purpose (21). By disrupting meaning on one level, the literal, it establishes a new pertinence on another, the figurative. Its "categorical transgression" thus participates in a new "logic of discovery" (22): "metaphorical meaning does not merely consist of a semantic clash but of the *new* predicative meaning which emerges from the collapse of the literal meaning, that is, from the collapse of the meaning which obtains, if we rely only on the common or usual lexical values of our words. The metaphor is not the enigma but the solution of the enigma."[90] If there is a suspension of sense, it is made on behalf of an overriding logic. If there is an apparent challenge to logic, it is made as part of an argument which can reconstrue what at first seems illogical. If there is an affront to our customary use of language, it is not because words have been swallowed up in silence, but because rhetoric allows for their impertinence.

In the previous section I concluded that the subversion of reason on behalf of a superior poetic unreason inevitably testifies to a rambunctious rationality within the very means of subversion and that it forces poetry to argue in devious and self-effacing ways. We see now that language has suffered the same curious fate, making modern literature, in Roland Barthes' phrase, a "problematic of language."[91] Attempts to purify, nullify, or transmute it into a superior lyrical silence have actually invigorated it with a fierce and puzzling vitality. Such attempts have made modern poetry dispute with words, about words, and against words. Wordsworth, too, was aware of the dangerous power of words, but he was confident of his ability to master them. He warned: "Language, if it do not uphold, and feed, and leave in quiet, like the power of gravitation or the air we breathe, is a counter-spirit, unremittingly and noiselessly at work, to subvert, to lay waste, to vitiate, and to dissolve."[92] He cultivated a poetic diction whose precision and tact would avoid such devastation. In contrast, modern poetry impresses us with the element that we inhabit. It sets loose the subversive counterspirit in language and encourages us to entangle ourselves in a perpetually self-confuting, self-affirming argument.

LOGIC, RHETORIC, DRAMA: POETRY AND ARGUMENT

So far, I have shown how the theories and reforms grouped under the heading of modernism both contest and rework the romantic legacy. Following such critics as Graham Hough in *Image and Experience* and Frank Kermode in *Romantic Image*, I have charted the passage from symbolism to imagism, in order to illustrate the modern ambitions, assumptions, and oversights that provide terms - vision, intuition, unreason, silence, metaphor - with which to understand poetic argument. Concern with argument in the enlarged sense that I use it obviously cannot be limited to modern writers, since it enters all accounts of poetic language and thought and all efforts to distinguish their peculiar powers. However, modern poets make extraordinary claims for the aggressive and paradoxical nature of their arguments, and the time has come to examine those claims, to draw together the different threads of my own thesis, and to answer the questions raised earlier about the problematic nature of reason and language. Can reason ever argue irrationally? Can discourse argue nondiscursively? If, as I claim, they cannot, why do they appear to do so?

As in the previous two sections we should begin by noting how the modern fascination with argument shifts the emphasis and recolours the terms of its romantic predecessors. For example, in *The Statesman's Manual* Coleridge neatly unites our three modes of poetic argument, when he defines the imagination as "that reconciling and mediatory power, which incorporating the Reason in Images of the Sense, and organizing (as it were) the flux of the Senses by the permanence and self-circling energies of the Reason, gives birth to a system of symbols, harmonious in themselves and consubstantial with the truths of which they are the conductors." The peaceful reconciliation praised here is really an accomplishment, an effect achieved when poetry succeeds in bringing perception, conception, and language into accord. The harmonious system of symbols (rhetoric) obeys the logic that conducts the mind through its most intelligent and dramatic arguments. It permits the mind, not just to understand, but to seize the truth intimately, as if physically. It manages, not just to represent, but to reappropriate reality, because the "truths and the symbols that represent them move in conjunction...."[93] Despite the reservation of his "as it were," Coleridge indicates that the symbolic argument of poetry is rational; indeed it is reason perfected. As we have seen, however, by the time Mallarmé offers the twin paradoxes that launched our investigation, poetry is said to require a superior "unreason" articulated through poetic "silence," in order to produce an argument following its own nondiscursive "illogic." Its "apparent illogic" Hart Crane explains, "operates so logically in conjunction with its context in the poem as to establish its claim to another logic, quite independent of the original definition of the word or phrase or image thus employed." Following what should now be a familiar pattern, he explains poetic logic by appealing to the rhetorical "dynamics of metaphor":

Twice and twice
(Again the smoking souvenir,
Bleeding eidolon!) and yet again.
Until the bright logic is won
Unwhispering as a mirror
Is believed.

The arguments of poetry must be "won" through "unwhispering" speech, itself vocal, yet claiming the silent authority of reflections that compel belief in a full-blooded yet spectral ("bleeding eidolon") reality. Crane's title, "Legend," suggests that the uncanny logic of metaphor is ancient and venerable. Like Barfield and Fenellosa, he believes that it "antedates our so-called pure logic" and is the "genetic basis of all speech, hence consciousness and thought-extension."[94]

In different degrees, Coleridge, Mallarmé, and Crane contend that poetry enacts a thoughtful, passionate design of its own; that is, its argument is at once logical, rhetorical, and dramatic. It is impossible to talk about one of these categories without involving the other two, but each offers a different avenue into the complex system that they create together. I shall examine their cooperation by considering each in turn, starting with poetry's harmonious or bright logic, which we encountered earlier as the waking dream with its problematic rationality.

The most influential account of nondiscursive poetic logic occurs in Eliot's preface to *Anabase* by St-Jean Perse. Noting the apparent incoherence of the poem, Eliot explains:

any obscurity of the poem, on first readings, is due to the suppression of "links in the chain," of explanatory and connecting matter, and not to incoherence, or the love of the cryptogram. The justification of such abbreviation of method is that the sequence of images coincides and concentrates into one intense impression of barbaric civilization. The reader has to allow the images to fall into his memory successively without questioning the reasonableness of each at the moment; so that, at the end, a total effect is produced.

Such selection of a sequence of images and ideas has nothing chaotic about it. There is a logic of the imagination as well as a logic of concepts.[95]

This passage displays exactly the same inconsistency that we observed in similar explanations by Paz and MacLeish. Eliot claims to distinguish two forms of logic, the nondiscursive form offering "one intense impression" or vision, which triumphs over the apparent disorder that produces it. He at once acknowledges and repudiates the successiveness of the discourse ("to fall into his memory successively"); however, his real interest is in "method" not logic, and the method described - suppression of premises - is a perfectly logical enthymeme. It accounts for both the obscurity of the poem and the way in which obscurity serves to challenge the reader and direct his judgment. Its effect depends not only on an intuition of intense impressions, but also on an orderly contemplation, as Eliot admits: "I was not convinced of Mr. Perse's imaginative order until I had read the poem five or six times."[96] Once he recognizes the rationality of the imaginative system, he sees the "reasonableness" of the poem. Therefore, Eliot has not distinguished between two logics, the one conceptual and the other imaginative, but described a compressed argument that resists and engages the reader's rational powers.

Following Eliot's example, writers like Crane proclaim a unique poetic logic, but they seldom use the term precisely. They use it to suggest that poetry is emotional, intuitive, dreamlike, unreasonable - none of which requires that logic be abandoned. In extreme cases they use it to relish the chaotic incoherence that Eliot disclaims. For example, Alfred Jarry, author of the Ubu plays, celebrates absurdity and madness with his "'Pataphysics," a science of imaginary solutions based on contradiction, hallucination, and monstrosity. It is the ultimate waking nightmare: an unsystematic system of illogical logic.[97] Through its very grotesqueness, however, Jarry's parody confirms the logic that it claims to distort. Through calculated anarchy he follows Rimbaud's advice and seeks vision through confusion, but he implicitly accepts the rationality that he so deliberately defies. In fact Rimbaud had advocated an immense and *reasoned* derangement of the senses ("immense et raisonné *dérèglement* de *tous les sens*") in his "Lettre du Voyant"[98] and so postulated an order ruling his disorder.

More soberly, Wylie Sypher cites Stéphane Lupasco's "logic of antagonism" which, unlike Aristotelian logic, accepts the reality of contradictions, falsities, and illogicalities. It is "a new anti-logic," familiar in literature and now finding its way, with the aid of Kurt Goedel and Werner Heisenberg, into science. Only "by accepting the inconsistencies and contradictions in reality can we get outside the boundaries of our old naïve logic," Sypher concludes, forgetting that only logic permits and creates these same contradictions.[99] Aristotle did not consider contradiction unreal or illogical; on the contrary, it is the prime logical condition of thought, which could not proceed without it. All the conditions of inconsistency, epistemological uncertainty, "complementarity," and recursiveness, which Sypher and other literary critics draw from modern physics, are similarly generated by the workings of logic. Wittgenstein insists on this point in his *Tractatus-Logico Philosophicus*:

> A thought contains the possiblity of the situation of which it is the thought. What is thinkable is possible too. (3.02)
>
> Thought can never be of anything illogical, since, if it were, we should have to think illogically. (3.03)
>
> It used to be said that God could create anything except what would be contrary to the laws of logic. – The truth is that we could not *say* what an "illogical" world would look like. (3.031)
>
> It is as impossible to represent in language anything that "contradicts logic" as it is in geometry to represent by its co-ordinates a figure that contradicts the laws of space, or to give the co-ordinates of a point that does not exist. (3.032)

Since logic is the law of all thought, whether rigorous or wayward, valid or invalid, there can be no escape from it. The very means of escaping would have to be logical. We cannot think illogically, because logic is "transcendental" (6.13). It cannot be chosen or refused at will, because it shapes all choices and all refusals. Therefore we do not contradict logic even when we are illogical. On the contrary, an illogical argument is faulty because it fails in logical terms. That is how we know it is faulty. There are no illogical terms: "What makes logic a priori is the impossibility of illogical thought" (5.4731). If there were an alternative system of thought, then logic would depend on its context for validity, not on its own inner necessity. However, we are not thereby confined in a cold, inhumane prison of logic. Quite the contrary, logical necessity is liberating because it entertains all possibilities, not just what is true, and because it permits us to define and consider what is impossible: "Just as the only necessity that exists is *logical necessity*, so too the only impossiblity that exists is *logical* impossibility."[100]

Finally, then, I can assert my defence of reason. There is no independent logic of the imagination, no poetic unreason, no illogical antilogic. Poetic arguments are not different in kind from any other arguments. The techniques of the imagination are all logical and, as I shall argue in a moment, rhetorical. Logic cannot be antilogical, however unreasonable it seems, however much it surprises or confuses us, however much it entertains improbabilities or impossibilities. As used here, "unreasonable" means unexpected, unconventional, unfamiliar, nonsensical, impossible, incomprehensible, absurd; but in the strict sense explained by Wittgenstein, it does not mean nonlogical. It is the power of negation that reason sustains, as the prefixes in the list of adjectives suggest. It is the problematic that I represented by Marianne Moore's toad, which hops unexpectedly into the enchanted garden of poetry. The problematic has a traditional place in logic: it refers to propositions which are possibly but not necessarily true. To discern possibilities in all their subtle contrariness demands careful thought. When arguments grow ambiguous, contradictory, indeterminate, recursive, or circular, they do not cease to be logical, or propose an alternative form of logic. Instead, they indicate the complications that logic permits us to think, as they encourage and bewilder thought. They are *logically* ambiguous, contradictory, indeterminate, and so on.

What happens now to poetic argument, if it does not enjoy a privileged status of its own? It proves all the more subtle and interesting. Earlier I playfully compared reason to Malvolio, and the problematic of reason might be called Malvolio's revenge. After being ridiculed as stiff, dictatorial, and pompous, reason returns in a puckish form and argues us into amazement. Poetry takes special pleasure in performing what might be called a festival of reason, where the festiveness is rational, not irrational. I use the word festival to suggest the unruly, dramatic character of poetic arguments and to recall festive comedies like *Twelfth Night* and *A Midsummer Night's Dream*, which encourage a spirit of misrule to mock and test a prevailing social order. In a comparable way the problematic of reason forces reason to contest itself by looking into its own dark interior. In the process it may appear to evoke a mysterious double – unreason – with which to dispute. But the ghost of unreason is a dramatic illusion, raised by the conflict between authority and anarchy. Let me illustrate how this festive argument works and how the ghost can be exorcized, by inspecting two versions of it, one modernist, the other postmodernist.

In this way I can bring the history of poetic argument up to date and show how its continuity persists.

In the 1920s Robert Graves worked at Oxford on a thesis which became his book *Poetic Unreason*. Faced with the romantic dilemma of the rational irrationality of poetry, he proposes an independent, poetic logic. The "poet, the mystic, the transcendentalist must be admitted to have a logical system of their own," because they argue through "thought connections discovered in the imagery of dreams." Principles of association, condensation, coincidence, and symbolic suggestion are not rational, he claims, although they still constitute a "method of thought."[101] This is Mr Hyde, the disruptive spirit lurking within poetry and establishing a rule of his own. He represents the outlawed, intuitive element that Graves respects but is not willing to trust. In opposition he also demands craft, commonsense, deliberation, and intelligence - the Dr Jekyll element. The "supra-logical element"[102] alone would tend toward anarchy unless restrained by rationality. Jekyll and Hyde recur in various guises in Graves's later criticism. Mr Hyde courts the White Goddess and insists that poetry is a "non-intellectual" way of thought,[103] a "complete and separate form of energy"[104] generated in each poem. Meanwhile Dr Jekyll demands a stubborn literal-mindedness and refuses to deviate from fact. He reprimands Alexander Pope and Alfred Lord Tennyson for idealizing the asphodel which, despite its delicate literary associations, is really common, tough, and scrubby.[105] He rebukes Matthew Arnold for permitting Sophocles to watch the ebb and flow of tides in the Aegean (in "Dover Beach"), when in fact the Aegean has no tides.[106]

Graves offers a classic example of the antagonistic cooperation of the waking dream. He enforces its antagonism by treating the rival forms of consciousness as separate forms of energy, but he fails to notice that as forms they are the same. That is, the so-called "irrational" principles adduced are actually logical, although they can be mustered in what I have called unreasonable ways. Cassirer has already confirmed this point. He criticizes the cult of irrationalism by insisting that discursive thought and mythical thought depend on the same logical relations (unity, multiplicity, coexistence, contiguity, succession), which they apply in different "modes." These two modes are his attenuated version of Graves's two characters. They indicate a nostalgia for the dualism that Cassirer cannot quite abandon, and that Graves willingly embraces. Graves insists on a categorical difference between "intellectual" and "emotional thought," despite evidence to the contrary, because their conflict generates the lyrical energy that he values so much. Although he speaks of magic, trances, and intuitions rather than of arguments, he grants poetry the aggressive powers of proof and persuasion that I have treated as argumentative. Although he calls poetry a "near-magical art or craft from which the intellect should ... be barred for truth's sake except as an occasional consultant on simple fact,"[107] he shows that reason is more than just a realistic check on Mr Hyde's impulsiveness. According to his own account, Hyde cannot be an independent and valid "method of thought," only a wayward disposition that, in different poems, may or may not be held in check by the authority of everyday experience. Graves implicitly acknowledges the unity of Jekyll and Hyde, since they are aspects of a single man.

This is the modernist version of the festival of reason, haunted by a ghost who has been invoked expressly for the occasion but cannot entirely be trusted. Graves is careful to make reason the final arbiter because he feels trapped by his dualistic model of mind, a model which, I have claimed, is not consistent but has been imposed by the Jekyll/Hyde metaphor. Having granted Mr Hyde the autonomy of a radically different form of energy, Graves is afraid that the energy might prove too anarchic and that poetic unreason might not prove reasonable enough to be serviceable. When we turn to J. Hillis Miller, Paul de Man and the postmodern version of the festival, we find two interesting complications. First, the forum in which it is performed is no longer consciousness (unreason/imagination/waking dream), but language as formulated by Saussure; and secondly, the linguistic spirit of misrule can no longer be successfully restrained . The festival of reason becomes a saturnalia of rhetoric. Miller and de Man endorse Mr Hyde's subversive authority and use him to deconstruct Dr Jekyll's commonsense, but in this case Mr Hyde is "rhetoricity," rather than unreason. He is the constitutive discrepancy in language between assertion and meaning, the nihilistic parasite or "latent ghost encrypted within any expression of a logocentric system" of metaphysics (i.e., the rational discourse of Dr Jekyll). Deconstruction makes poetry relentlessly argumentative, because it treats a text as an abyss or labyrinth of meaning, an "interminable movement of interrogation" that baffles itself into a state of "radical indeterminacy." Thought leads to, creates, and acknowledges its own *aporia*, which is the impasse where logic confounds itself. Fortunately, the *aporia* is not the dead end of unintelligibility, but the ultimate truth of reason and language and of man's fate within them. After his description of the critical abyss, Miller reassures us: "In fact the moment when logic fails in their work is the moment of their deepest penetration into the actual nature of literary language, or of language as such. It is also the place where Socratic procedures [Dr Jekyll again] will ultimately lead, if they are carried far enough."[108]

When de Man and Miller substitute deconstructive "rhetoricity" for modernist "unreason," they shift the emphasis from the logical to the rhetorical mode of poetic argument and recall our second puzzle: the possibility of nondiscursive discourse. The festive structure remains much the same, however, because, according to Miller, rhetorical arguments are "alogical" rather than dialectical. Instead of conducting understanding through an inferential sequence, they disperse it into a "treacherous abyss of doubled and redoubled meanings, around or over which the thought of the poet momentarily swirls or weaves its web."[109] Meaning and certitude are not the reward of a logical conclusion, but a mischievous "tropological effect" that should not be trusted.[110] When he analyses the operations of rhetoric, however, and declares them uncanny, antithetical, and radically indeterminate, Miller actually discloses their rationality, just as Graves did when he cited the "irrational" principles of unreason. For all its waywardness, rhetoric remains governed by logic, and, as Ricoeur showed in the case of metaphor, it is discursive: it argues.

Rhetoricity is our new festive ghost or spirit of misrule, possessing powers like those attributed earlier to poetic silence – the language that triumphs over its verbality in order to tell the truth – in the modernist paradox of nondiscursive discourse. The deconstructive argument is even more spooky, because it tries to show that truth itself is unstable, since it relies on the perverse ambiguity of rhetorical figures. At first glance rhetoric often seems illogical when it opposes figurative to literal meaning. It is impertinent; it contradicts itself and states as true what is clearly or subtly false. Closer inspection reveals, however, that while divergence from the customary practices and expectations of speech may be unreasonable, it is not illogical, because rhetoric acknowledges and directs its own deviance. It makes a *calculated* error or *significant* self-contradiction. It extends meaning by forcing us to discover a new pertinence at the figurative level. Tropes of reversal – irony, oxymoron, paradox – display the twist in meaning most defiantly, but all rhetorical shifts and twists depend on the same procedure. Their deviance nevertheless remains logical in the categories that are substituted one for another: genus/species, part/whole, object/attribute, cause/effect, container/content, instrument/purpose. Rhetoric plays within the regulation of logic; otherwise there would be no sense of playfulness. Even when rhetoric chooses to commit a category mistake, it must respect the categories with which it takes liberties; otherwise there could be no mistake or sense of deviation. It can err only with respect to logical principles of substitution, such as resemblance, analogy, contrast, contradiction, division, predication. Through these operations rhetoric offers a series of hypotheses, or ways of thinking about things.

In practice, then, rhetoricity is directed by the same rational principles as is unreason. The difference is in their aims or conclusions. Modernists treat the literal level as a valid goal that can be attained by poetic thought. It is the limiting, proper, or original meaning. It is the reality to be reappropriated - the bedrock of being, the common asphodel, or, even more basically, what Stevens calls "The the."[111] It is the essential fact which, paradoxically, the modernists can evoke only metaphorically through a poetic diction that aspires to the purity of silence. In contrast, postmodernists treat the literal as a correlative linguistic term, that is, as an accepted norm from which to measure figurative deviation. That norm may itself deviate from an earlier norm, that is perhaps concealed in the word's etymology. Far from being literal, it is a metaphor of a metaphor (metalepsis). This rhetorical shuttling is often used to illustrate the "alogical" perversity of language. Nevertheless, the principles at work remain logical, even if the displacement continues until rhetoric becomes a process of endless deviance. Miller unavoidably reaffirms the logic he is contesting, when he claims that, because every literal meaning conceals a hidden figurative one, the distinction between the two breaks down. In fact his own argument depends on maintaining that distinction. Only as long as there is a perceived difference or distortion can rhetoric wield its subversive power. There must be a sense of impropriety, an affront to meaning, and hence a correlative propriety. Miller welcomes this affront to sense, which he calls "something alogical left over which does not fit any logical scheme of interpretation," and he uses it to reject as an illusory fiction the corresponding proper meaning. Whatever its status, however, the operation of that fiction is logical and necessary. To abolish the literal level, no matter how provisional, is to destroy the measure of falsehood. Even error must be systematic to be erroneous.

Carrying his case a step further, Miller tries to discredit logical and literal sense by appealing to catachresis, a forced metaphor that uses a word figuratively to name something that lacks a proper name of its own (table *leg* and mother *tongue* are his examples). Generalizing on the model, he concludes: "All words are initially catachresis. The distinction between literal and figurative is an alogical deduction or bifurcation from that primal misnaming. The fiction of the literal or proper is therefore the supreme fiction. All poetry and all language are *mise en abyme*, since all language is based on catachresis." The phrase "alogical deduction" is as untrustworthy as "illogical logic," and is subject to Wittgenstein's objection about the impossibility of illogical thought. It indicates that Miller does not want simply to overturn accepted meanings. Like Graves, he wants to establish an overruling poetic unreason in order to carry out the systematic task of deconstruction. Once again, however, the violence of catachresis demands a violation of accepted sense if it is to retain its force, if it is to be aggressive. It defers the measure of propriety another step, but does not abolish it. If "initially" there were a "primal misnaming" (a phrase presupposing a prior naming) rather than a proper meaning, then there could never be a "turning away from the abyss," that is, a rhetorical deviation.[112]

In its own way, therefore, the postmodern critique of modernism reinstates Mallarmé's twin paradoxes of reason and language, making the deconstructive poetic the most argumentative of all. Miller and de Man propose a rhetorical impulse within language that keeps it forever in motion, continually creating and subverting meaning despite a writer's effort to be literal. It is their intensified version of Mr Hyde. For de Man, logic and rhetoric are counterparts in a way not intended by Aristotle. They are at once exclusive and dependent, and in the course of their antagonism: "Rhetoric radically suspends logic and opens up vertiginous possibilities of referential aberration," permitting only the profoundest ambiguity of "suspended uncertainty." When de Man claims that rhetoric and grammar have different epistemologies which inevitably conflict, he repeats the Jekyll/Hyde opposition and refurbishes poetic unreason with the aid of linguistics. He goes beyond Graves, however, when he claims even more problematically that rhetoric "deconstructs its own performance," because "it allows for two incompatible, mutually self-destructive points of view and therefore puts an insurmountable obstacle in the way of any reading or understanding." But even if rhetoric is as delinquent as de Man claims, his own careful analysis shows that its aberrations and "rhetorical seduction" proceed along logical lines in accordance with the familiar principles and categories mentioned above. His own argument depends on the principles that permit him to discern *logical* inconsistencies in both grammatical and rhetorical statements. In effect, he acknowledges the continuing rule of logic when he calls the truth of literature "the recognition of the *systematic* character of a certain kind of error" (my emphasis).[113] Barbara Johnson confirms that deconstruction must rely on systematic inconsistencies even to provide its vision of the abyss. It studies the ways in which a text "differs from itself" through "a certain *rigorous*, contradictory logic," by which it "stages the *modes* of its own misreading" (my emphasis). Even if literature has an "asymmetrical, abyssal structure," its structure and modes of behaviour remain "rigorous." Otherwise they could not be judged asymmetrical.[114]

With deconstruction we reach the furthest point in our survey. It gives the most recent and most uncompromising account of poetic argument by finding it in all texts as the very condition of their textuality. In this view there is no difference between poetic and other arguments, not as I stated above because logic subsumes all arguments no matter how perverse, but because all texts are now treated as poetic. Literary criticism, history, and philosophy are also undercut by Mr Hyde/unreason/rhetoricity, because all exhibit the festive inconclusiveness of arguing, understood now as Derrida's "différance" – the continual postponing and shifting of meaning as it strives for but never achieves completion. They all display the "errant semantics" of a "detour" through language, doomed to waver forever between nonsense and truth.[115] For modernists, argument is the illogical self-effacement of discourse; for deconstructionists, it is the alogical textuality of discourse. But for both, argument is the inevitable fate of the mind and of language. My point is that for all its criticism of romanticism and of modernism, deconstruction has perpetuated their defiance of reason and discourse and has tried to provide alternatives. In providing alternatives, however, it, too, has reinstated reason and discourse within the very means of denial. Despite Geoffrey Hartman's efforts to resuscitate Jarry's "pataphysical heritage," he confirms that the operation of rhetoric is logical and discursive.[116] The difference between modern and postmodern theories lies in how the alternatives are conceived. In modernism they are refined states of consciousness that can reappropriate reality; in deconstruction they are attributes of language that can barely be stated and never mastered. In modernism Mr Hyde can be controlled and used as an agent of truth; in deconstruction, where *mise en abyme* confounds reason and grammatology challenges discourse, he controls and abuses us.

To recapitulate: in order to propose a special poetic argument that transcends the pedestrian restrictions of logic, modern poets have turned to rhetoric, whose operation they deem illogical or supralogical. They thereby confirm Wallace Stevens' dictum: "A poet's natural way of thinking is by way of figures."[117] In particular they favour the presentational property of symbol and metaphor and the power of these to display boldly rather than merely to convey meaning. They believe, for example: "The true symbol flashes the meaning across immediately, and is the most direct method of communication possible to the poet. A symbol is not a compressed logical argument; it is a direct emotional statement."[118] In this view, discursive reasoning must be overcome as a hindrance to true insight, and although argument remains in the symbolic "method," it is no longer attenuated by having to make the detour of logic. Consequently the poet can feel a thought as immediately as the odour of a rose, according to Eliot; or can inhale poetry rather than reason it out at length, according to Lawrence Durrell: "It is a pity that we cannot inhale poems like scents – for crude as their medium is, their message, their content is something which owes little to reason."[119]

Closer study reveals, however, not only that the operations of rhetoric are logical, but that they also display beautifully all the involutions of thought permitted by logic. What poets really admire are their aggressive, entertaining, and bewildering qualities – in short, those powers of argument that are festive or dramatic. The modernist critics invite the reader to participate in the drama by cultivating the same lively state of mind attributed to both the poet and the poem. The deconstructionist critics at first try to be spectators of the festival, as they observe the behaviour of language and calmly note "what is at stake" in a text. They enjoy the dramatic antics of rhetoric. However, they admit that they cannot really be objective or neutral readers, since their own criticism is compromised by the same linguistic behaviour. To be rigorous and systematic, they must accept that they too are writing an "intellectual poem,"[120] since poetic argument informs (or misinforms) all discourse, including their own.

Modernists and deconstructionists also agree that literature provides the most dramatic examples of poetic argument. We must turn, finally, to our third category – drama – to clarify how argument manifests itself as a spectacle. In practice, of course, we have been considering drama all along, but we can now use it to integrate the three functions of poetic argument.

The idea of argument as a dramatic dispute or spectacle recurs in modern theory, where it is often miscast. When Pound speaks of poetry as *logopoeia*, "the dance of the intellect among words,"[121] he indicates that it must obey two rules: that of the intellect and that of the dance. The choreography of meanings is the rhetorical construction of the poem; it is Pound's version of what I have described as a festival of thought and speech. Poetry in which the intellect dances is an elegant argument that persuades us through its elegance. It asks us to admire its artfulness as well as to evaluate the propositions that it offers, both for their own sake and for the sake of the dance. Some modern theory, notably New Criticism, then proceeds to impose a false distinction between the intellect and its dance, because it feels obliged to defend the formal autonomy of poetry by treating it as a drama of thought rather than as a process of thinking. New Criticism regards every poem as a little play which acts out, rather than declares, its ideas and attitudes. Because the poem displays and "tests" rather than asserts propositions, these are more important for their "dramatic propriety" than for their truth. According to Cleanth Brooks, a poem "is to be judged, not by the truth or falsity as such, of the ideas which it incorporates, but rather by its character as drama – by its coherence, sensitivity, depth, richness, and tough-mindedness." While the drama of ideas and the festival of thought are aspects of my account of poetic argument, too, they do not serve here, as they do for Brooks, to defend formalism at the expense of logic. In Brooks's view, intellect is absorbed by the dance of the intellect. Reasoning is assimilated and ultimately disqualified by a semblance of reasoning. He admits that a poem may "accidently possess a logical unity as well as this poetic unity," but he distinguishes sharply between the two. The formal unity of poetry is achieved by "a dramatic process, not a logical" one, because - the argument is now familiar - it depends on irony and paradox. The "essential structure of poetry is not logical" but rhetorical and dramatic. Rhetoric and drama organize the logic of the imagination.[122]

I hope that I have already discredited this assault on logic and the dualistic model that sets it in opposition to poetic thinking. In order to defend the autonomy and power of poetry, New Criticism tries to divorce logic from drama by means of rhetoric (the dramatic display of metaphor, irony, and paradox is called illogical); and it tries to divorce logic from rhetoric by means of drama (ideas are not asserted but rhetorically enacted). Unfortunately, the result of this fragmentation is to put the entire system in doubt by granting it a formal, but impotent, purity. A full view of poetic argument, which I have been building in this chapter, must integrate rather than separate the three functions of logic, rhetoric, and drama; of reason, language, and performance. It must provide a balanced account, if it is to show how argument can be at once cogent, figurative, and aggressive. In Bacon's words, which serve as epigraph to this chapter, poetic argument must use rhetoric in order to apply reason to imagination for the better moving of the will, because "The end of rhetoric is to fill the imagination to second reason, and not to oppress it."[123]

As dramatic displays of thought and speech, the arguments of poetry must "second" reason; they cannot be "accidental" or contrary to logic. Although poetry displays the drama most vividly, all arguments have a dramatic character. They can be elegant, graceful, devious, witty, daring, etc. They can be appreciated in aesthetic terms, which assess the execution of the logic but do not contribute to the validity of the argument, although they may influence its persuasiveness. Lionel Trilling notes that systems of ideas have an "aesthetic effect," which poetry may emulate when it seeks "the authority, the cogency, the completeness, the brilliance, the *hardness* of systematic thought."[124] Such qualities are prized especially in metaphysical poetry. Other styles produce other dramatic effects. In *Reason's Double Agents*, Carol Johnson uses the phrase "reason reasoning" to describe the intellectual drama of metaphysical poetry. It displays a process of reasoning as it works its way from premises to conclusion, from doubt to certainty. The reader admires a line of thought conducted through the poem, for example, in

Donne's poetic syllogisms. In contrast, the neoclassical mode presents "reason reasoned." In this case the mind displayed in the poem is already made up, perfected, complete. It is confident of the truth and expresses itself, for example, in the maxims and epigrams of Pope.[125] The drama of "reason reasoning" suggests the enthymeme of Aristotelian rhetoric, that proceeds through induction from probabilities to an acceptable conclusion.[126] "Reason reasoned" suggests Aristotle's example or paradigm, which is already formed and exemplary. In view of the problematic criticism of the *aporia*, we require a third strategy: "reason confounded." This is the festival of reason, that uses logic aggressively to test itself, but does not thereby devise an independent mode of thought. The festival remains rational and illustrates the fate of reason from its beginning to its end.

The drama of argument is especially useful because it shows how the three functions are interdependent rather than exclusive, and because it suggests a practical approach to the poets studied in the following chapters. I have selected authors who offer varied approaches to common problems and thus illustrate the different ways in which logic, rhetoric, and drama compete and cooperate to fill the imagination and enlighten the reason. My approach will be to examine the origins, means, and ends of argument: to study how poetry argues and what it argues about, where poetic arguments arise and what they aim to achieve. I shall begin by focusing on a rupture between the authors' theoretical posture and poetic practice. They do not practice what they preach. They claim to argue in one way but in fact argue differently. More specifically they claim to rely on unreason, which they define in different ways, but always by appealing to the fruitful modernist tension between logic and rhetoric, discourse and figure, Jekyll and Hyde. In practice, however, they inevitably rely on the many resources of rhetoric, whose conceptual operations – substitution, conflation, variation, reversal, and even contradiction – inevitably remain logical, even when they seem unreasonable. My approach will be, first, to investigate their accounts of poetic unreason; then to exorcize these ghostly powers by demonstrating the rationality of their rhetorical and dramatic strategies; and finally to show how the poets' impatience with reason is of thematic and stylistic importance, as they argue about poetic reverie (Moore), about definitions of the self (Edward and Dylan Thomas), about the powers, conditions and limits of thought, and about the possibility of transcending those limits (Moore, Eliot, Stevens).

I wish to avoid the implication that my critical exorcism is reductive because I take the modernist tension between mental faculties and make it seem fruitless, or because I violate the mystery of the waking dream. If everything is logic and nothing but logic, what happens to the spell so deftly cast by modernist poetry – its transgressive and uncanny power? I have traced the history of this romantic spell and observed how it inspires symbolism, haunts the matter-of-factness of imagism, and lurks in the textuality of deconstruction. In response to it, I hope to teach Malvolio's lesson: that logic need not be frigid, tedious, or plodding, but can cause our arguments to cut strange capers, when they perform the dance of the intellect among words. Logic can be elegant, dramatic, mysterious, and festive as it follows all the twists of reason as well as the urgings of emotion.

In each chapter, after considering the claims for unreason, I shall organize my discussion further by concentrating first on the locus and then on the trajectory of argument. The first is the dramatic arena of argument, the point of inception and conception, the origin. In a dramatic sense each author enacts a poetic character through an appeal to the reader, and the line of argument appears as the movement of his or her thought. Our sense of the poet as a source of experience and as a presiding personality in the work derives from the drama of arguing. In Howard Nemerov's words: "a poem is not so much a thought, or a series of thoughts, as it is a mind."[127] If a poem displays a mind at work, then we can see the temper of that mind by the way it works. The mind is constituted by the drama and by the language of its argument. In the chapters on Edward Thomas and Dylan Thomas, I shall consider two ways of constituting and exploring a locus of argument and of seeking ways in which to enlarge its domain. Edward Thomas cultivates a sympathetic, imaginative understanding that radiates from and returns to a self, which, for all its arguments, remains essentially mysterious. In his case argument often takes the form of a puzzle. Dylan Thomas writes more in the tradition of the romantic egotistical sublime. His progress is a heroic adventure of the self as it voyages through the world, which it attempts to dominate by constructing a "monumental argument of the hewn voice."

The second subject is the trajectory of argument, and it too is dramatic. After a poet's thought moves away from its imagined centre, reference point, or locus of departure, it seeks an imagined destination. It projects a conclusion, that will fulfill the needs of the origin and provide a satisfactory perspective on the entire course of argument. In Langer's words quoted above, it moves between "the beginning and the end of logic"; or in Stevens' words, it aims at "The extreme of the known in the presence of the extreme / Of the unknown."[128] Inevitably at issue here is the problem of transcendence: the ability of the mind to presume its origins and to exceed its limits. As I trace the trajectories of their arguments, I shall consider this theme in Moore, but especially in Eliot and Stevens, who illustrate contrasting notions of transcendence.

Eliot wishes to pursue thought until it transfigures itself and rises "Into another intensity" ("East Coker"); whereas Stevens wishes to attain a comprehensive, shared understanding.

Before considering the two pairs of poets, however, I wish to continue my pursuit of Marianne Moore's toad, because she, in her own way, surveys the entire field of my argument.

CHAPTER TWO

Marianne Moore

An argument is an inferential pattern, a train of ideas that are logically connected and lead to a conclusion entailed by the premises originally accepted and unifying the preceding discourse into a meaningful, satisfying whole. When I first offered this definition, I noted how it reveals the motive and shape of poetic argument, as manifested in linguistic power and aesthetic form. However, in the light of the first chapter we can discern in it all the terms of our discussion. It suggests that an argument is an admirably logical, rhetorical, and dramatic structure, stretched vulnerably between a point of departure and a point of arrival. It suggests that through its premises an argument establishes a field of reference expressing both a faith and a need – a faith that certain things are axiomatic and can only be as they are, and a need to explain other things in terms of the abiding faith. In the imagery of modernism silence is the unspoken faith that precedes thought, as well as the confidence or doubt that follows it. The definition also implies that an argument is aggressive, because it is a venture or adventure of thought. It launches itself on a course whose trajectory is regulated by logic, but whose stability is not necessarily assured and whose destination cannot be final. The conclusion sought has a complex function: it composes thought in the sense of formulating, unifying, satisfying, and settling, but also unsettling it. As soon as a terminus to thought can be imagined, we feel a renewed need to discover what lies a step further. From this description, too, we can draw some of the characteristic themes and ambitions of modernism: the power, resources, and limitations of reason and language; the unified nature of poetic seeing, saying, and thinking; the problem of the self that is both formed and baffled by its thoughts; thought as alienation and redemption; transcendence; the waking dream.

The poetry of Marianne Moore offers a fine opportunity for studying the practical application of these grand themes and ambitions. Although it is easy to see what is unique or idiosyncratic in her work, recent studies have stressed how often and how keenly she touches on the central issues of modernism. I, too, wish to treat her as a representative figure, who shows how modern poetry aspires to argue, how it actually argues, and what it argues about. In her own remarkable way she shares all the interests that will occupy subsequent chapters. She reveals the locus, the aspiration, the trajectory, and the inconclusive end of modern poetic arguments. I intend to discuss the motive and shape of her arguments by using two of our conceptual models: the waking dream and the poetic of vision.

Traditionally, poetic argument begins and exercises its compelling power through enchantment: it cultivates an imaginary garden. The true poet dreams being awake, according to Lamb, or, reversing the emphasis, calculates being asleep. The waking dream is an image favoured by romantic theory to express the independence and interdependence of two states of mind and to combine reason and imagination, the visual and the visionary, in poetic discourse. As I indicated, the terms of the oxymoron both complement and resist each other, since they are diacritical (they require each other in polarity) but irreconcilable (they make opposite demands of consciousness). This contradiction, far from being a cause of embarrassment, is a source of pride for romantic poets and critics, who use it to celebrate the inspired faculty of unreason, whose enchantment guarantees the otherness, that is, the uncanny power of poetry. It performs a similar function in modern poetry, except that the site of the contradiction shifts, so that the state of wakefulness becomes primary, the allegiance to reality more taxing, and the role of reason more problematic. For Valéry, Cassirer, and Langer, the poet lives not in paradise, but in the waking world, to which he or she carefully summons the subtle resources of dream.

For Moore, too, poetry is a vigilant dreaming or "pattern of revery" (*CP*, 129),[1] by which unreason inhabits but never displaces reason. Poetry argues on behalf of reality in a special manner that seems to falsify reality and at times even to defy logic, but that ultimately permits a closer alliance with reality. The alliance, in which mind and world embrace, is the visionary goal toward which Moore carefully argues. To this end her real toad in the imaginary garden of art croaks in the voice of reason, not of Croce's or Eliot's autonomous, aesthetic logic. But it must be a subtle and supple reason, capable of designing "the absorbing / geometry of a fantasy" (*CP*, 231). Transposed into our terms, the absorbing drama of poetic argument arises from the rhetorical play ("fantasy") of logic ("geometry") and the wholly logical play of rhetoric.

Therefore, the pattern of reverie does not lull us to sleep, but sharpens our wits and makes us alert.

Although she respects both pattern and reverie, Moore is very much the modernist in stressing the former and treating the latter as the reward for orderly contemplation. Her work seems dominated by pattern and its rich details, but the more rigorous the thought, the more discriminating the attention, and the more patient the observation, the more powerful is the reverie. Insight is the "lion's leap" (*P*, 3) or toad's hop that springs from argument. This dramatic sequence of control and release recurs in her poems and is the very rhythm of poetic attention and thought. It confirms her often repeated dictum: "freedom in art, as in life, is the result of a discipline imposed by ourselves" (*P*, 20). Precision - which means precise arguing - permits vision, gusto, and enchantment, because it is in fact "a thing of the imagination" (*P*, 4). It is not a passive subservience to fact, but an active discerning and an eager receptiveness. It is imaginative because it is the effort by which the mind exercises, displays, and treasures its powers of tact and discrimination. "What is more precise than precision? Illusion" (*CP*, 151), she affirms in "Armor's Undermining Modesty," returning through her paradox to the refining energy of the mind that makes it alert and responsive, but that also makes it seem dreamlike. It reappears as the illusion or "imperishable wish" that concludes the poem. As I intend to show, this forceful yet impalpable energy helps to explain the origin, the motive power, and the conclusion of her arguments.

Poetry begins in and returns to unreason, but we must treat the word cautiously. Moore uses it to explain both the mysterious stimulus that incites thought and pushes it on its way, and the retreating destination that arguments continually cast before them. Beginning and end are not contrary to logic; instead, they are proposed by logic, whenever it tries to survey its course or to test its own basis and validity. Since they are preconditions of thought, however, they will always escape the mastery of thought. In that sense they remain unreasonable, and unthinkable, a condition we see dramatized in her poetry. Occasionally she uses the word "unreason" in the approved manner to mean a faculty contrary to reason, but in such cases the term really operates as part of a rhetoric of denial, like the strategy of silence. It suggests, first, not an alternative to reason, but the unaccountable impulse within reason that impels us to think and forces our thoughts to be argumentative rather than casual. It is the wish, faith, or desire that urges on our trains of thought and gives them form and purpose. It is what Stevens calls our "rage for order." Wishes may seem illusory, modest, or intangible, but they are forceful. They change the world. In a lecture on

Stevens, Moore explains: "For poverty, poetry substitutes a spiritual happiness in which the intangible is more real than the visible ..." (*P*, 43). She agrees with him that the intangible is not a poetic delusion but a commanding part of reality, invisible in its origins but felt strongly in its effects. Poetry as happiness and as discovery is also real. It is a precise wishing or disciplined dreaming that reveals both reality and humanity, the two objects of Moore's attention. She inspects both the world and the forces of the mind that engage with and illuminate the world. Secondly, as a negative, correlative term, unreason permits her to explore the philosophical dualism that complicates all seeing, saying, and thinking, whether expressed as an opposition between subject and object, word and thing, mind and matter, appearance and reality; or as the doubt lodged in all certainty; or as the duality of poetic vision, which illuminates reality with the light of the imagination; or as the complexity of poetic argument, which reasons itself into illumination. Unreason in the third sense imposes a hidden duplicity on thought, making it discontented, unappeased, and inconclusive – qualities found even in those poems that seem at first so confident.

With regard to the vigilance of the waking dream, we might say that poetic argument begins at the moment when we fall asleep, only to awaken within our dreams; and it ends when we lapse back into our customary, somnolent, waking state. To investigate such radical shifts in consciousness, Moore often turns to animals, which in a sense can live freely within the waking dream. Since the extremes of thought lie on the far side of the logic that they provoke and that, paradoxically, produces them, she can describe them only through analogy as natural power or instinctive certainty, as physical presence or the mere fact of being, as the elemental conditions of energy and substance. The toad, ambiguous emblem of the "genuine," is the most famous example,[2] but we find also a snake, suggesting a "train of thought" (*CP*, 58) that mesmerizes the onlooker. The elephant, "Melancthon," (*ClP*, 45-48) represents "black earth" (its name in Greek), physical power, brute substance, and "the indestructibility of matter." Yet it displays "spiritual poise," as it meditates eloquently, while its sensitive trunk reaches out with a contradictory, tactile awareness ("to see and not to see; to hear and not to hear"), that extends into the metaphysical "translucence of the atmosphere." Thus the poem covers the full range of thought, which begins with the brute fact of our being in the world and ends in, or aspires to attain, an ultimate wisdom. This wisdom would permit the heroic triumph of mind, as it reappropriates the reality it has forfeited through the process of thinking. Truth, for Moore, is comprehension and compensation, but of a special, puzzling kind. It is perfect knowledge that in our present, imperfect state we can only imagine as an ultimate mystery that mirrors the mysterious impulse that instigates the poem. Or, as she says elsewhere, poetry is a process by which "Mysteries expound mysteries" (*CP*, 142). Animating this whole project in understanding is the imperishable wish or "the beautiful element of unreason" beneath the elephant's thick skin. Its deeper, unreasonable need can be disclosed, not by regressing to mindless nature, but by musing philosophically with the "sinuously alert æsthetic sensibility" (*D*, 81:535) – represented by the magical "wandlike" trunk – that Moore favours in poetry.

"Melancthon" probes poetry's unreasonable point of origin by seeking a truth hidden beneath the "patina of circumstance" and imagined as a source of spiritual poise and power. Rhetorically, it proceeds by persistently asking questions about reality and identity ("What / is powerful and what is not?" "spiritual poise, it has its centre / where?" "the elephant is / black earth preceded by a tendril?"), so that it hints at unstated answers as it circles the centre where those answers might lie. The truth of the poem is never stated, only implied. In "Sun" (*CP*, 234) this hidden centre is a splendid "plan / deep-set within the heart of man." In "Then the Ermine" (*CP*, 160–61) it is "the power of implosion" (*CP*, 161), and the same inward-gathering strength is summoned here. For all its self-deprecation, "Melancthon" questions itself in order to assert the heroic principle of life: the triumph of mind. The pattern of reverie builds thematically from matter to spirit, dramatically from control to release, and logically from calculating patterns of thought to finding satisfaction and wonder in life. According to this argument, the tangible world is endowed with power by intangible forces, or as Moore says later, "The power of the visible / is the invisible" (*CP*, 100). Inspecting the world intently, uncovers its truths, which ultimately must be moral truths, because they justify our presence in the world.

The argument of "Melancthon" leads from the imagined beginning to the proposed end of thought. It works its way from pattern to reverie, from the visible to the invisible, from the inhuman to the human (although this point requires qualification) and from reason to unreason. But again, Moore's treatment of unreason is cautious. It is not irrational or contrary to logic; it is the fruit of logic, the extremity of thought that speculation proposes to itself. Like so many modern poets, she finds the idea of unreason attractive but dangerous, because it offers a way of accounting for the splendid force of poetic argument (Quintilian's aggression), but also recalls the mad, mystical, and transcendental legacy of romanticism, which she mistrusts. Accordingly, she cultivates a passion for precision and attains her insights through the intense concentration that precision enforces. She insists that, if poetry has "more elasticity than logic" (*CP*, 53), it nevertheless must be a " 'method of conclusions' " (*CP*, 85) that tries its truths "by the tooth of disputation" (*CP*, 66). It seeks conclusions and seeks them logically. Insight, intuition, and freedom are all products of reasoned and reasonable inquiry. She admires Lewis Carroll for his "precision of unlogic ... [which] is logic's best apologist" (*D*, 81:177) and William Carlos Williams for his "chains of incontrovertibly logical apparent non-sequiturs" (*P*, 136). She praises HD's poetry for exploring "that inner world of interacting reason and unreason in which are comprehended, the rigour, the succinctness of hazardous emotion." Rigour and hazard, the orderly and the fortuitous, combine in the "fastidious prodigality" of "controlled ardour," and all are properties of argument – "a secure, advancing exactness of thought and speech" (*D*, 79:170).

Moore illustrates the impulse, the ambition, and the fate of poetic argument in a second elephant poem, which covers the range of my own discussion in this chapter. "Elephants" (*CP*, 128–30) is about knowing, and it, too, combines bulk and delicacy in exploring the theme of reason and unreason by following a parade of thought to its limit. It begins modestly but bravely with a daring comparison, the terms of which link remote and unlikely things: the wistaria-like trunk. This simile establishes an ironic pattern of opposition that runs through the poem: massive/feather light, serenity/fear, sweetness/gravity, worship/mourning, "carefullest unrehearsed/play." The opening simile establishes the dual nature of the elephants, whose "matched intensities" produce "tranquillity" rather than "deadlock," because they cooperate with rather than combat each other. They are "opposing opposed," yet in concert. It also indicates the dual nature of thought, which depends on the same dialectic of cooperation and resistance. The mind argues with itself. It develops by proposing analogies that seek out resemblances and differences: "As if, as if, it is all ifs; we are at / much unease." As Randall Jarrell observes, Moore "shows that everything is related to everything else, by comparing everything to everything else; no one has compared successfully more disparate objects."[3] These analogies and hypotheses are the means by which thought restlessly propels itself toward a receding and unattainable goal. The passivity and resignation advocated in "Elephants" conceal an inner tension calmed only by the prospect of an ultimate "repose," which corresponds to the centre of spiritual poise in "Melancthon" and is the end of the unease of thought in serenity.

Thought aims at totality, which is the unity of all understanding, the truth of all analogies that obliterates all differences by reconciling all opposites. Even as thought follows a "path enticing beyond comparison" (*CP*, 186), however, it relies on the logic of analogy and its implied differences, since only different things can be analogous. Following the same argument in "Style" (*CP*, 169-70), Moore tries to imagine perfect grace by proposing a series of comparisons, only to conclude: "There is no suitable simile. It is as though / the equidistant three tiny arcs of seeds in a banana / had been conjoined by Palestrina." The rejection of simile requires us to think in ever more provocative similes. For Moore, thought, when it grows most provocative, often becomes religious in range and vocabulary, though not necessarily so in substance. In "Elephants," thinking is a "religious procession without any priests," an inconclusive, secular pilgrimage toward Truth. It is secular because, even though elephants are "toothed temples," they are unaided by revelation and are "not here to worship" at the shrine. Like Melancthon, they are "life prisoner[s]" confined but reconciled to the painful shortcomings of existence. Like Moore, they accept "Life's faulty excellence" (*CP*, 35). Their understanding is Socratic, not hieratic, and they offer a "pattern of revery not reverence." They are poets, not mystics. Because they merely carry the cushion that carries the casket that carries the relic, Buddha's Tooth, their argument is a procession that sustains and anticipates a distant truth. The holy object is symbolic of a still higher wonder that must be broached elaborately and indirectly through the tooth of disputation. Poetry is a ritual that aims at radiant knowledge, or, in the holy language of Sanscrit, "the / small word with the dot, meaning know, - the verb bůd." Translating the word is another way of endowing it with power by holding it at a distance. This distance, which is aesthetic as well as philosophical, confers the sense of mystery demanded by complete knowledge, or the mystery which *is* complete knowledge. But knowledge so total and so unattainable to fallible humanity (the sleeping mahout) can only be imagined through paradox as silence, unreason, or unknowing: "the wisest is he who's not sure that he knows."

"Elephants" can be read, therefore, as an account of poetic thinking as it argues with itself. It exhibits an ungainly/graceful parade of thought that is rooted heavily in nature (the animals) but imaginatively proposes the supernatural and an ideal of perfect wisdom (Buddha). Nevertheless, the prospect of transcendence is entertained cautiously and soberly, not celebrated ecstatically as a religious mystery. It is meditation imagining its own fulfilment. The elephant is the "child / of reason," not only because it has been tamed, but because it illustrates the confining conditions of human thought, against which thought itelf strains. Elephants are "knowers" whose knowledge is incomplete. Wisdom is the sublime goal - "magic's masterpiece" - cast up by the process of thinking, but no one caught up in that process believes he has mastered it completely. Like the elephants, he is both its master and servant. We might draw from "Elephants" the same conclusion that

Lisa Steinman draws from "The Student" (*CP*, 101–2), another poem about studious, enlightened thought: "Absolute knowledge, presumably, precludes the necessity of continued investigation. Thus 'The Student' maintains its valorization of process and imagination in refusing to settle the questions it raises. On various levels, the poem courts the uncertainty that sparks the imagination and intellect. It suggests we can neither separate nor wholly merge the terms of Moore's dialectic; we can neither give up trying to get things right, nor – it is suggested – will we ever finally get things right."[4]

To sum up: Moore's arguments dramatize human thought as puzzle (like Edward Thomas), as adventure (like Dylan Thomas) and as ritual (like Eliot). She regards poetry as a waking dream, but stresses its rational character, whose precision yields imaginative insight into reality and its relation to mankind. The insight gained may be ecstatic, but "Ecstasy affords / the occasion and expediency determines the form" (*CP*, 88). It is a controlled, achieved enthusiasm. Her motto is "*Festina Lente*. Be gay / civilly" (*CP*, 26). Poetic reverie is civil, not irrational, and unreasonable only in the sense that it articulates a series of mysteries. As noted above, unreason involves, first, the enigmatic resistance of reality to the thought that it stimulates and puzzles: reality conceived as mere being or feeling, as fact or stimulus. Secondly, unreason is the spiritual or mental power that marshals our experience: the invisible wish interpreting the visible world. And thirdly, unreason is the problematic of reason: the propensity of reason to entangle itself in argument. In a review of George Moore Marianne Moore approves "that pleased contemplation of the resolving of a promised climax into contradiction" (*D*, 78:223). In poetic contemplation this is not the defeat but the fulfilment of reason, as it aspires to complete understanding and discovers the uncertainty that sparks the imagination and intellect.

Mysteries expound mysteries. Moore's arguments begin in unreason in the first sense, and through a precise pattern of logic argue their way toward unreason in the second sense. They begin with the basic reality of facts and experience and end in sovereign ideas that would rule those facts and sanction that experience. To examine this course of development further, we must consider unreason in the third sense, as the problematic of reason, to see how it functions in a poetic of vision.

The problematic of reason is illustrated succinctly in the enlightened confusion of "The Mind is an Enchanting Thing" (*CP*, 134–5), a poem that teases us by challenging its own power of enchantment. Following the rhetorical strategy already noted in "Elephants," it describes the mind in antagonistic terms as "animated by / sun," brilliant, luminescent and iridescent, yet also "feeling its way as though blind." It is an airy bird "with its eyes on the ground." Poetic understanding is "unequivocal / because trued by regnant certainty" – the reigning monarch of the poem being the sun, radiant vision, perfect comprehension. Yet poetry is also "conscientious inconsistency." It both enchants and disenchants: "Unconfusion submits / its confusion to proof." Unconfusion is totality: the prismatic clarity of a unified, harmonious art. It would be a sleeping dream, an imaginary garden containing only imaginary toads. But the negative form "unconfusion," suggests that this garden must be entered by perversely denying reality, and Moore refuses to do so. She considers it a privilege to see so much confusion in the world (cf. *CP*, 5). She dissipates the mist obscuring the vision of the heart and reveals that even our dreams of perfection are inconsistent, but artfully vital in their inconsistency ("the / inconsistencies / of Scarlatti"). Perfect consistency would be, like Herod's oath, a death sentence. Reality is a lively confusion that must be submitted to inconclusive proof. It must always be felt, tested, argued.

Moore does not recommend obscurity or inconsistency, but she recognizes their role in pressuring and testing logic. Through its imagery of light and sight, the poem proves that thought at its most strenuous must always be a problematical, enlightened confusion. This necessity becomes clearer, if we recall how much Moore is in the imagist tradition when she associates poetic language with vision and insight and when she expresses the goals of poetry in visual terms. "Poetry is a way of looking, various because vision is irregular, reasonable because, irregular, it is not indiscriminate."[5] It rules the irregular, though imperfectly; it reasons the unreasonable, though inconclusively. This poetic based on sight provokes a series of logical complications that are inherent in its formulation, complications that we encountered earlier in the imagists' dedication to vision and factuality and that explain the obscurity of the origins and the truths sought by Moore's arguments.

As we saw in the previous chapter, when poetry is treated as a kind of seeing and meaning is understood as accuracy of vision, then the freshness of direct sensation – the imagists' declared goal – subtly turns into unreason and the indirection of argument. For Edward Thomas, this transformation can be painful, since it marks a disjunction between himself and the object of his vision, nature; for Dylan Thomas, it can be exhilarating, since he casts himself into the drama of metamorphosis. For Moore, who is more dispassionate, it is only logical that the simplicity of seeing should turn into the complexity of arguing, that precision should turn into illusion. How does this transformation occur, and what does it entail? A. Kingsley Weatherhead stresses the virtue of simplicity when he examines the kinds of vision and perspective in Moore's work. He claims that she is best when a realistic view, wary of sentimentality and universals, confines itself to specifics and careful moral judgments. She then offers only "a very particular truth firmly attached to the percepts which gave rise to it."[6] Immediate experience is the guarantee of truth. But the very intensity of her vision and the aggressiveness of her attention inevitably push her beyond these limitations. Any natural object, artifact, or form of life seems amazing if examined intently. It discloses an intent; it pushes one to unforeseen conclusions. "Enigmas are not poetry,"[7] Moore warns, but poetry casts up enigmas, even when it tries to be factual, because of the regular/irregular way it looks at the world and because of the recalcitrance of the truths that it seeks.

A poetic based on vision and factuality must call both goals into question, as soon as it considers the relationship between them. Poetic vision inevitably turns visionary and argumentative. It celebrates but is not content with the literal, because "it must be 'lit with piercing glances into the life of things'; / it must acknowledge the spiritual forces which have made it" (*CP*, 48). More specifically, as we have seen, it seeks insight into reality (the essence of the actual, the purity and otherness of the object, the prime conditions of being); into humanity (consciousness, the purity and fullness of the subject); and into the relationship between the two, the way the one requires or forbids, invites or resists the other. If enigmatic reality provides the impulse for human thought and if the ideal reappropriation of reality by consciousness is its goal, then the course of argument between them depends on how beginning and end are reconciled. Traditionally, thought masters reality by proposing a union of object and subject through some higher vision, synthesis, or transcendent unity. Dialectic should, like the ideal marriage, be "that striking grasp of opposites / opposed each to the other, not to unity" (*CP*, 69). An argument should be unified by virtue of its premises, which forecast certain acceptable inferences, and by its conclusion, which retrospectively embraces the sequence that produced it. But "Elephants" and "The Mind is an Enchanting Thing" have shown that, for Moore, any appeal to unity is problematic.

The problem begins at the beginning and, earlier still, at what precedes a train of thought. Critics differ about her treatment of factual reality, although all agree she has a highly cultivated "capacity for fact" (*CP*, 76). Like Graves, she prefers the common asphodel. Kenneth Burke was the first to call her an "objectivist," although he qualified the term, and others have praised her "minute obligation to fact," her skill at "invading reality" and granting fact "its proper plenitude."[8] Her respect for and delight in facts is evident in the abundance of lists, exotic details, hyphenated words, and alternate names – an abundance she relishes as aspects of things and of a world full of things. It is evident in her epigrammatic style, which she calls "Authentically / brief and full of energy" (CP, 89). Authentic and energetic because brief, the polished concision of her words seems to pierce directly to the heart of things. Following Coleridge's advice, she tries to treat words as the very things they symbolize, as if to make them the equivalent of immediate experience by eliminating the conceptual distance between symbol and referent. She cleans soiled words in order to uncover the objects they represent and obscure.[9] The jerboa is "untouched," "free-born," and, like the blacks, "with an elegance / ignored by one's ignorance" (*CP*, 13). It is independent of human knowledge and judgment.

But devotion to the object has unexpected results and twists the argument of a poem back upon the arguer, complicating Moore's effort to see things simply and directly. For this reason, it is misleading to say that she argues from the inhuman toward the human, or the reverse. She vacillates between the two, as one involves the other. Respect for facts leads to an ideal of the purity of facts, and purity is not a property of things, but a product of judgment and exclusion. Objectivity perfected becomes an act of imagination, the imagining of an exclusive, untouchable otherness. In this way precision becomes illusion. In "A Jelly-Fish" (*CP*, 180), the reality of the animal is "Visible, invisible, / a fluctuating charm" that is best left alone. In "The Monkey Puzzle" (*CP*, 80), reality is an exotic tree – defiant, dignified, independent, and fierce, a tiger or a lion rather than a domesticated dog. Our ignorance of it is complete ("society's not knowing is /colossal"), but it will "not come out" or present itself to us, and it bewilders our efforts to invade it. Consequently, what at first seems clear, beautiful, literal, and stark turns into a puzzle. Reality can only be imagined through puzzles and artifices, entanglements of thought that we rely on, but know to be false. We require fictions, such as the fantastic world of "Flaubert's Carthage," and an elaborate rhetoric of metaphors, analogies, and oxymorons. Ironically, the argument of the poem ("this bypath of curio collecting") turns around and treats the elusive reality as an imitation of art, rather than the reverse. The tree is "A conifer contrived in imitation of the glyptic work of jade / and hardstone cutters." Like a monkey, the inhuman world mimics and mocks human efforts to grasp it. The thing-in-itself at its imagined point of origin remains enigmatic. However, Moore finds comfort in the conclusion, "we prove, we do not explain our birth." The argument ends unreasonably, in so far as it attains only a problematic understanding of the presence of reality, felt as that originating power of our experience which is not itself subject to experience. Only in that inconclusive sense do we prove (sense, feel, experience, approve) our birth (the inception of consciousness).

Similarly, "In the Days of Prismatic Color" (*CP*, 41) offers a myth of lost origins: the pure, unfallen being of the world that precedes and baffles our intellectual efforts to understand it. Turning in the opposite direction, "A Grave" (*CP*, 49–50) tries to look death in the face, only to discover that it has no face, volition, or consciousness, because it is an absence rather than a presence. Both poems try to see precisely, but discover that the "other" – birth, being, death, origins, ends – is precisely what we do not see, what the ocean cannot mirror, what the eye fails to distinguish. The genuine object eludes us when we try to see with perfect objectivity. For this reason, as several readers have noted, contact with reality in Moore's poems is remarkably indirect, mediated by quotations, museum catalogues, guidebooks, and pictures. We require stepping stones to the truth, even to the truth of facts. Through indirection she reminds us that insight into things requires a devious course. In "A Grave," the poet addresses a man looking into the sea; she does not look herself. In "Apparition of Splendor" (*CP*, 158–9), she celebrates the prickly reality of a porcupine by approaching it obliquely, first recalling Dürer's drawing of a rhinoceros that partakes "of the miraculous / since never known literally." The literal, like objectivity, is an ideal of saying, seeing, and understanding. Or, since vision in poetry is really a consequence of argument, the literal is an arguing that ignores itself, a rhetoric that overlooks its figurativeness, so that word and thing seem to concur splendidly, making us forget that splendour is an apparition, not a fact.

The same complication applies to another of Moore's poetic values associated with sight – gusto. It seems to be the exuberant force of being, the energy with which things proclaim themselves to our senses, but it, too, proves to be a matter of imagination and judgment. William Hazlitt calls gusto in art the "power or passion defining any object." He emphasizes its tangible qualities, the sting of sensation, the "internal character, the living principle" in things. It seems to be a property of objects but quickly becomes a feature of consciousness through its appeal to imagination. It is an idea of strength and moral grandeur, an "energy of will." Claude's landscapes lack gusto because "his eye wanted imagination," whereas Milton "grapples with and exhausts his subject."[10] Vision must not be passive. Mere seeing is uninformed, in the double sense of being ignorant and of being unshaped and uninspired by a powerful principle – the invisible directing the visible. That principle, which for Moore is at once moral and aesthetic, combats the world, and gusto is the energy of their encounter. The poet disputes reality in order to approve its truths.

These arguments about the elusive nature of reality as fact and stimulus point to a common preoccupation with truth, conceived of as something not palpable and evident, but obscure and recalcitrant; as something invisible, which we must nevertheless try to see. That truth is by nature hidden, is a consequence of the view that poetry is a special kind of vision or dream-thinking.

> Sun and moon and day and night and man and beast
> each with a splendor
> which man in all his vileness cannot
> set aside; each with an excellence! (*CP*, 118)

We need to look with piercing glances into the life of things, because their splendour and excellence are lodged somewhere within. We need a "hyperprecise eye" (*MMR*, 226) to see beyond appearances, because truth is hidden beneath the texture of things and must be elicited through intellectual effort. We need to argue because truth must be proven. Moore's fastidious attention to appearances confirms that they are superficial, not substantive, and become splendid only when illuminated from deeper sources and "brimming with inner light" (*CP*, 9). The pedantic literalist is insubstantial because his meditation fails to reach the "spontaneous core" (*CP*, 37). In her reading diary Moore recorded a comment by W.H. Wright: the "artist sacrifices minor scientific truths to his creative inventiveness because he is ever after a profounder truth than that of accuracy of detail."[11] Although she was less willing to sacrifice factual or scientific truths, Moore agreed to the principle of ranking kinds of truth. This division accords with the familiar metaphysical dualism of phenomenal and noumenal worlds, whereby the haphazard diversity of appearance is contrasted with the presumed unity of reality, or conversely, the orderliness of appearance is contrasted with the amorphous flux of reality. In either case, truth, essence, or reality is conceived of as inner, other, or transcendent. This dualistic ontology is summed up in a biblical passage which Moore quotes in "Blessed Is the Man" (*CP*, 174): "By faith we understand that the world was created by the word of God, so that what is seen was made out of things which do not appear" (Hebrews 11: 3).

Human consciousness is divorced from truth which it pursues through the self-discipline of philosophy. The philosopher solves the riddle of reality, because, according to Hegel's optimistic dictum: "The initially hidden and precluded essence of the universe has no strength to resist the courage of knowledge."[12] Courage and clear thinking are virtues for Moore, too, but she is less optimistic about the efficacy of thought. I suspect that, in the same spirit, she would also disagree with Hazlitt's assurance that Milton "exhausts" his subject, since the world as she views it is inexhaustible and consciousness is tireless. Because truth is hidden and enigmatic, its resistance to thought can never be overcome and remains one of its defining features. Truth is what can never be known or thought directly. It is unreasonable and can only be implied obliquely through poetic argument, that is, rhetorically through fiction, symbol, and analogy. As we saw in "Elephants," thought advances by discovering significant similarities and differences, and it envisions a complete truth discoverable by a perfect wisdom. In other poems truth is a monkey puzzle, a riddle about ourselves and our origins. It is the "Slim dragonfly / too rapid for the eye / to cage" (*CP*, 220). It is the inconceivable accuracy of the quartz crystal clocks," 'instruments of truth' " (*CP*, 115) so precise that they announce the truth of the instant only after it has passed.

In another metaphor of vision, truth is the prismatic colour of an original world whose splendour was an immediate reality rather than an apparition to be coaxed forth. Thought then was direct, not oblique: "obliqueness was a variation / of the perpendicular, plain to see and / to account for" (*CP*, 41). Civilization complicates, sophisticates, and refines thought, but in the process obscures truth, a development marked in the poem by the darkening of the imagery: smoke, mist, murkiness, darkness. The belief "that all / truth must be dark" is condemned as a "dismal fallacy," since truth is conceived through imagery of light, brilliance, and luminescence. But the mythical perspective of the poem ensures that truth can no longer be incandescent as it once was. This is Moore's version of the myth of the Fall into language and intelligence. Corrupted by civilization, we can never see with the simple purity of unfallen Adam. Even proposing Adam as the model of primal understanding, illustrates our need for allegory. In a characteristically double argument, Moore assures us that the truth is, or should be, simple and manifest, but perversely demonstrates that it is not, that indeed the very ideal of simplicity is a sophisticated one. According to Costello, the poem offers both "the illusion of truth's presence and the awareness of a proxy" for it, because there are two impulses competing in the poem, offering rival visions: "Moore's satiric impulse is to tear the veil, to expose motives and break through pretensions, to penetrate a mist of confusion to simplicities and primitive truths. But her allegorical impulse is to veil and mask those truths, as the only way of bringing them forward into art. The genuine must be figured to be known, though the figure at once reveals and conceals it."[13] Consequently, the pronouncement at the end sounds reassuring but proves puzzling. The first image of the statue suggests that we should continue to think of truth in terms of vision, as a perfection of sight, an object clearly seen. But in a pattern that I have disclosed several times now, vision yields to argument. Finally, truth speaks to us, making its appeal through language that is figurative and ambiguous:

> Truth is no Apollo
> Belvedere, no formal thing. The wave may go over it if it likes.
> Know that it will be there when it says,
> "I shall be there when the wave has gone by."

The conclusion raises more questions than it answers. Is truth the fixed object or the wave that passes over it? In an earlier version of the poem Moore suggested that it could be either dynamic or static at will, though at whose will is unclear: "Truth, many legged and formidable also, / is stationary by choice."[14] Or is the wave an image of consciousness and art sweeping over reality, touching it only in passing? If so, there is a formal incompatibility (solid / fluid, static / dynamic) between world and mind. Is art, through which we imagine truth, false because of the unyielding perfection we admire so much? The effect of the conclusion is to leave these questions unanswered.

The argument is inconclusive in the obvious sense that the answers it offers raise further questions, but also in the sense that the thirst for posing questions is unappeasable. The desire for appeasement or satisfaction, however, remains urgent in the poem, and for this reason the magisterial tone at the end is countered by a subtle, vital discontent. The need for an authoritative conclusion persists ("'I shall be there when the wave has gone by'"), and demonstrates that the act and art of questioning have moral as well as aesthetic implications. For Moore, to argue cogently and to see clearly are also to think and to see rightly. Her ethical resolve ensures that the inconclusiveness of her poems reflects what I earlier called the modernist argument of reappropriation, rather than the postmodernist argument of *différance*. That is, she aspires to a complete understanding that will also be a moral fullness, since she regards truth as ethical as well as logical. In older, theological terms this higher state was called right reason. In "Elephants," it is denoted by the Sanscrit word meaning "know." Later she calls it "sublimated wisdom" (*CP*, 47), an ideal that she realizes must always lie beyond her reach, but whose existence she does not doubt. She does not treat it as a philosophical fiction or a linguistic fantasy. Therefore, the formal incompatibility of mind and world is a dilemma to be met by force of character, rather than a condition of language to be aggravated through rhetorical indeterminacy. We need to argue in poetry in order to dispute for the truth, to win our way to it, and that combat tests and improves our character. It teaches wisdom.

We think our way to truth by deploying intelligence, but we must also earn our right to truth. In this respect the impulse to argue is a moral resolve as well as a physical need and a philosophical restlessness. It manifests itself in the personality of the poet and of her subjects.

"To a Steam Roller" (*CP*, 84) condemns a half-witted, heavy-handed thinker for lack of discrimination and humility - flaws in character that inhibit understanding. When the butterfly flutters out at the end of the poem, it represents truth as gift and reward for those who attend it in the proper spirit. The moth that startles the poet at the beginning of "Armor's Undermining Modesty" (*CP*, 151) serves the same function. The spirit recommended is at once forceful and humble, combative and modest, resilient and submissive. It is illustrated by jerboa, pangolin, elephant, and ostrich. Many of Moore's poems are concerned with cultivating the proper attitude and promoting the correct sort of attention in both poet and reader. Their subject is propriety, and through tone and argument they dramatize the proper attitude. These poems are instructive in two senses. First, they offer instructions on how to observe, to improve taste, to form judgments, to welcome and respond to experience. Their "theme is almost always the Good Life"; they are "exempla of rightness"[15] that make a show of being didactic. They instruct, exort, caution, or reprimand the injudicious reader. Secondly, they provoke an interest in the basis of these instructions: the standards of correctness, the nature of propriety, the decorum of judgment. Thus they both moralize and offer a critique of morality, two tasks that, when they conflict, lead a poem into logical and ethical ambiguity.

As they moralize, Moore's poems are authoritative or proper, but as they criticize, they are sceptical or improper. The tension between the two reflects the ambiguity of her arguments, since judging and understanding are often at odds. Judgments generalize, unify, and affirm a consistent standard, while criticism particularizes, fragments, and casts doubts. We can appreciate her inconclusive conclusions only if we recognize the urgency of their moral purpose as well as their logical subtlety. On the one hand, her decorous standards (her refusal to say "water-closet," her objection to Pound: "Unprudency is overemphasized and secularity persists")[16] are well known. In "An Octopus," she associates decorum with restraint, "the love of doing hard things," "Relentless accuracy" (*CP*, 76), and hence with the freedom that comes from self-control. Instruction in moral and critical propriety also appears in "Efforts of Affection" (*CP*, 147) through Jubal and Jabal, the inner and the outer life, the man of art and the man of action from Genesis 4: 20–1. The object of the poem is to "attain integration too tough for infraction," that is, to gain a vision of totality through love and humility and represented by the jubilant sun. Totality is expressed morally as "wholesomeness" and critically as "wholeness." On the other hand, the sun is dangerous: it "can rot or mend." Love can set free or enslave, integrate or disintegrate. It too can be either proper or improper.

"Propriety" (*CP*, 149–50) argues in greater detail about the virtue which, through a dramatic display of discretion and tact ("Brahms and Bach, / no; Bach and Brahms"), it also illustrates. Again the insight is prompted by a sign from nature – the singing bird and spiralling woodpecker – not by the naked truth, but by a lovely promise of the truth yet to be achieved. Birds and music indicate the correct attitude and conduct which, once again, combine diverse features: "cheerful firmness," strength and flexibility, humility and resistance. It is central to Moore's argument that these are moral as well as aesthetic virtues. They govern the way we look at and admire the world (the fir trees, the crescent moon), as well as the way we behave. But they also permit a critical awareness of the grounds of propriety: what makes propriety proper. As in "Efforts of Affection," this truth depends on integration and love ("an owl-and-a-pussy- / both-content"). They grant a harmonious vision of man and nature, in which the proper accord between them derives from an unseen but vividly imagined source of strength, expressed variously as "the root of the throat" from which music springs, the root of the tree, the "strength at the source" of nature, the sea that wears the rock, the moon that moves the sea. The source is also the inborn genius of Bach and Brahms, something that can only be implied negatively as "unintentional" and "uncursed by self-inspection." In each case the truth is powerful and hidden, an unseen source of energy with which, all things being proper, we can reach an accord. The same condition appears in "People's Surroundings" (*CP*, 55–7) as a world well furnished: nature, artifice, and man "in their respective places" are at ease together. It appears in "Enough:1969" (*CP*, 245) as a stone wall whose natural fit requires no mortar. Ideally, then, propriety is the state of being at home in the world and in touch with its essence.

How does one touch that essence? In other words: how does one reach the end of thought, the end that thought promises itself? When examining the American character, Moore cautions that, "To have misapprehended the matter is to have confessed that one has not looked far enough," but then hints that we can look further with the aid of "sublimated wisdom" (*CP*, 47). In "Propriety," as in "Elephants," the direction of her thought is toward sublimation and transcendence, toward an unreasoned seeing or enraptured thinking. In this respect, too, her arguments are modernist rather than postmodernist, but they are also cautious. They mistrust or restrain their own enthusiasm. Several critics mention Moore's Christian, specifically Presbyterian, character and treat her optimism as an aspect of her faith. Andrew J. Kappel calls her a "good Christian poet," who regards the confusion of the world as a necessary evil to be overcome. She "does not seek to escape from the tormenting chaos of the world but accepts it as a good which must be preserved if we are to fight against it the good fight God planned for our edification." If the world seems bad or worthless, it nevertheless serves a good end: "To the Christian the world is not of value in and of itself; what matters is what we make of it...." In this view transcendence is the edifying process by which we rise above the wicked, the physical, and the merely secular, and aspire to a higher source of truth: "[The mind] is greater than the world's confusion, which it 'sees' or comprehends within its desired larger vision of the Order of Things. The Christian mind 'sees' the world's confusion as in the process of achieving the order of its creator."[17]

Although Moore often draws on biblical imagery and diction to express Christian sentiments, it is hard to find in her poetry the theological struggle that Kappel describes. Whatever her personal belief, the poems do not dramatize a pilgrim's progress toward salvation, although they do argue for self-improvement by refining morality, intellect, and sensibility. She struggles to apprehend reality and depicts both physical and mental combat, but she does not fight against or surmount an inherently worthless world. On the contrary, she tries to live in accord with it and treats nature as a model of propriety. Nor does she convey a strong sense of evil, although especially in her war poems she is certainly aware of evil. One can be Presbyterian as a matter of temperament, sentiment, instinct, moral preference, or even taste without being specifically doctrinal or orthodox. Donald Hall, who acknowledges her life-long religious belief and practice, claims that "traditional Christian doctrine is not clearly apparent in her poetry" and concludes: "One gathers from the poetry that Miss Moore's religion involves an adherence to the spirit of Christianity and the practical application of its values to living without necessarily including belief in the efficacy or even existence of God."[18] One can secularize Kappel's argument even further, as does Ralph Rees. He offers an idealist interpretation when, in contrast to the objectivists, he claims: "Moore finds a more immediate reality in thoughts than in facts and the things that arouse the senses. The imagined, because it is more individual and more personal than the other phenomena, seems to her the very essence of reality." Through imagination Moore finds not religious salvation, but a more compelling, phenomenological truth: "A truer actuality exists in mental experiences than in sensuality."[19]

Michael Edwards explains the transcendent impulse in Moore in slightly different terms, which I find more congenial and which prepare us for the arguments on behalf of transcendence offered by Eliot and Stevens. Edwards distinguishes different levels of awareness in her poems as sight deepens into insight. The first level is superficial in the wholly laudable sense that "Surfaces do not give way to depths;

appearances are not erased by hidden reality." The second detects and respects the otherness of a world with a life of its own. The third is "unemphatically Christian," because it hints that "presence becomes religious presence" but permits only what Moore calls "transcendence, conditional" (*CP*, 215). The divine, heroic, and fabulous attend but do not displace the real, and "objects are sometimes seen on the near edge of an unseen hinterland," which Edwards recognizes as religious but discusses mainly in aesthetic terms. Art argues about itself. It reflects on its own relation to the world, on its power to discern meaning, to distinguish, and inscribe the real through fiction, and to transpose the world "if not into a state of grace, at least into one of elegance and newness."[20]

In my terms transcendence is a logical, though ambiguous consequence of Moore's arguments, an implication of her poetic based on vision and the waking dream. Her observations and meditations begin modestly, but later try to stretch beyond sight and reason to reach a sublimated wisdom. Precision, concentration, and adherence to literal facts prompt a dramatic expansion of thought in an inductive pattern, whereby the humblest thing, when examined intently, can testify to a larger significance. It promises the purity and integrity of the thing-in-itself and the plenitude of the all-knowing, authoritative subject. In Moore's scheme of things, it also proposes a moral fullness or rightness, a vision of the world subsumed by "love undying" (*CP*, 148). Love too is a deep-set plan and power of implosion. It permits poetic vision as it argues against death, cements faith (*CP*, 188), and affirms life. According to one argument, proven by both nature and art (the maternal cephalopod paper nautilus and Mozart's *Magic Flute*), love constructs an unreasonable but resilient ethic: "as if they knew love / is the only fortress / strong enough to trust to" (*CP*, 122); "Trapper love ... illogically wove / what logic can't unweave" (*CP*, 171–2). In a second argument love cannot resolve the tangled problems of reality, but suffuses a spirit that allows us charitably to accept them: "The problem is mastered ... The Gordian knot need not be cut" (*CP*, 216–17).

The goal of Moore's waking dreams, visions and arguments, therefore, is philosophical, aesthetic, or moral comprehension. They aim at wholeness or wholesomeness, but in each case it is really the intensity of vision and the rigour of reason that permit us to imagine the final transcendence. Propriety, perfection, purity, wholeness, eternity, love – these ideals emerge at the end of Moore's arguments where they indicate the vanishing point of thought. Her poems are not simple affirmations or celebrations of faith. They do not record mystical experiences. They are not devotional meditations of the kind studied by Louis Martz in *The Poetry of Meditation*: the disciplined, attentive thought that gives a taste of divinity. Rather they are exercises in seeing and thinking about the world, and it is the problematic process of reasoning that creates those absolutes she handles so discreetly. She is an "Almost / utmost absolutist" (*CP*, 188). Her poems are "imaginatively inconclusive" (*MMR*, 183) because they follow reason to the hinterland of unreason: to the inner silence where the deepest feelings lie (*CP*, 91); to the invisible sources of desire and imagination; to the moral imperative that defies circumstance; and to the logical confusion that is also enlightenment. Consequently, transcendence remains conditional, a logical hypothesis and a felt need. This means not only that her arguments are hypothetical, but that they cautiously inspect themselves in order to question the conditions of transcendence, just as they examine the grounds of propriety.

In "The Pangolin" (*CP*, 117–20), for example, Moore considers grace as aesthetic virtue and gift from God, but leaves unanswered her puzzling question about eternity: "If that which is at all were not forever, / why would those who graced the spires with animals ... have slaved to confuse grace with a kindly manner ... ?" She remains silent just when she should be most eloquent. Her tone conveys wonder and uncertainty, as does her pun on "confuse," meaning both to mistake and to blend the divine (grace) with the human ("a kindly manner," graciousness). Her argument, too, is nicely confused. Man's ingenious, graceful art (ornamenting a mediaeval church) is taken as proof of immortality, when it really only confirms his faith and determination: "Beneath sun and moon, / man slaving / to make his life more sweet." As in "Elephants" and "Spenser's Ireland," man is both the master and slave of thought, a predicament which ennobles him by granting a vision of freedom and eternity: "you're not free / until you've been made captive by / supreme belief" (*CP*, 113).

In the title of "What are Years?" (*CP*, 95), we have another enigmatic question: "the unanswered question, / the resolute doubt, – / dumbly calling, deafly listening." The mute answer is associated wth courage, understood as unreason: the unfathomable source of human will and resistance. Moore agrees with C.S. Lewis: "Courage is not simply *one* of the virtues but the form of every virtue at the testing point, which means at the point of highest reality."[21] To summon courage in the midst of World War II is to discover our essential humanity. But to discover humanity is to accept our imperfect, paradoxical nature, whereby freedom can be asserted only in the midst of captivity, like the sea in one of Moore's favourite images, that rises upon itself and "struggling to be / free and unable to be, / in its surrendering / finds its continuing." We transcend our confinement only by accepting it. We affirm dignity, purity, and joy in the same way, like the caged bird whose song announces "how pure a thing is joy. / This is mortality, / this is eternity." The conclusion to this argument is characteristically ambiguous. Like "The Pangolin," it seems to proclaim our immortality, but may prove only the importance of faith, determination, and courage, our mighty needs which we realize imaginatively through art (the bird's song). The last two lines suggest that the ideal of eternity is conceivable only within our mortality, that is, only by accepting the absoluteness of death; just as freedom was only conceivable within our imprisonment.

The same ambiguity darkens the final words of "By Disposition of Angels" (*CP*, 142), in which the steady, inviolable stars express the poet's hope for transcendence. Elizabeth Phillips reads this poem as an elegaic meditation on "the active presence of God in the world,"[22] but the divine seems rather to be absent, remote, and accessible only through "Messengers" which, like all symbols, are equivocal: "Mysteries expound mysteries." The angels - figures of the imagination, perhaps - are agents of fallible understanding. Again the poem opens with questions indicating that perfection is conceivable only indirectly through signs set in the context of imperfection and death ("Steadfastness the darkness makes explicit?" "How by darkness a star is perfected"). Again at the end the assurance of immortality is subtly set in doubt: "Steadier than steady, star dazzling me, live and elate, / No need to say, how like some we have known; too like her, / Too like him, and a-quiver forever." Phillips suggests that the unnamed people are Moore's mother and maternal grandfather, yet their anonymity makes the lament at once personal and general, a contemplation of death as such. The brilliance of the stars reminds her that the man and woman once were "live and elate," but does not confirm that they still are so. The regretful tone ("too like her") expresses, if not despair, at least an unwillingness to accept their loss, and suggests a contrast between the stars, which are "a-quiver forever," and the people who are mortal and now consigned to darkness. The stars' winking signals their absence.

One final example will illustrate how transcendence is both conditional in and a condition of Moore's poetic arguments. "To a Giraffe" (*CP*, 215) combines many of the themes and techniques discussed in this chapter. It offers moral and critical instruction, by using an animal as a model of behaviour. Like the toad, the giraffe is familiar but grotesque enough to capture our interest and emphasize its difference from us. Unlike humans, it lacks the psychological complexity of an "emotionally-tied-in-knots animal." It is well suited to its environment and has little trouble reaching its remote, select food. It is "unconversational" and so testifies to a mute or ineffable truth. The poem opens with perplexing questions about the basis of propriety: what is permissible and desirable? Who grants permission and by what standard? As the giraffe illustrates, propriety means being adapated to and at home in the world; but we, who are short, neurotic, and conversational, are improperly at odds with existence. We aspire to see "profound" truth, but discover that "the eye is not innocent" and that "existence / is flawed." Consequently, we stretch for the lofty boughs of philosophy in an effort to understand and transcend our fate.

The argument of the poem follows the logical structure: if ... what? It begins with a hypothesis ("If it is unpermissible") and questions its implications. If we are no longer innocent, in touch with literal reality, or adapted to the world like the giraffe, then what should we do? What is proper? The questioning then opens out in a manner that offers hope for transcendence. Since we are defined in contrast to the giraffe by our power of discourse, the argument is plotted by word-play through a sequence of words ending in -ible, -ble, and -al. There are twenty-four such words in only nineteen lines of poetry. The goal of the argument is totality, the transcendent "all." We advance from the undesirable to the desirable, from the unpermissible to the irresistible, from the unconversational animal to the eloquently metaphysical, from the literal to the exceptional, from the fatal to the perpetual. The argument stretches beyond the reach of the longest neck, above the imperfect conditions of earthly existence, toward redemption. However, this triumphant ascension of need, desire, and hope is undercut by a critical counterargument. The elaborate display of words and sounds suggests detachment, an amused reserve, and a restrained enthusiasm that encourage us to look more closely at the terms of the poem. The "consolations of the metaphysical" are profound and irresistible, but this does not make them true, only psychologically valid or compelling. The ground of judgment and propriety turns out to be our emotional need, not objective truth. What is perpetual is the *journey* from sin, our desire to escape it and to redeem our flawed lives. In this way the argument twists back into the Gordian "emotionally-tied-in-knots" pattern that it sought to escape. This interpretation does not mean that Moore was not religious or that her faith was imperfect. It means that her argument, derived from a poetic based on the dual and antagonistic demands of the waking dream and of poetic vision, inevitably questions itself. Transcendence is conditional, because it is permitted and thwarted by the conditions of thought displayed in the poem.

In this chapter I have studied the beginning, the course, and the end of Moore's arguments, and I have discovered not that they are irrational or antilogical, but that they are intricately and rigorously logical, and that through their precision they question themselves in an energetic play of argument and counterargument. Her arguments are so complex because of her sophistication, because of the density and intensity of her rhetoric, but especially because of the ambiguity of her formative terms and values – the waking dream, poetic vision, propriety, conceptual unity or wholeness, moral wholesomeness, wisdom, mystery, transcendence. Lurking behind and within all of these ideas is a productive, restless and ghostly fiction – unreason, understood variously as a mental faculty, as a special process of thought, as both the mysterious origin and goal of thought, and as the problematical character of reasoning. These are the terms that I now wish to examine in other poets by retracing my course and by noting further complications found along the way. I start by returning to the beginning or locus of poetic argument.

CHAPTER THREE

Edward Thomas

If poetry is the "lion's leap," where is its lair? In other words: in poetic arguments, where is the dramatic stage on which the rhetorical festival of logic is performed? The poetry of Edward and Dylan Thomas offers two contrasting ways of providing an unstable but productive locus for argument. I have shown in the first chapter that modernist theories must propose a poetic context or scene of writing in which arguments can arise and in which they can operate in their aggressive fashion. That field can be expressed in various ways, depending on the poet's manner of systematically defying reason and language. If poetry continues to occupy a transcendent realm of gold, it may be lodged in a garden of the imagination, waking dream, or ineffable state. If, as is more common in modern poetry, it inhabits a world of inner truth, its inwardness may be defined in different ways - subjective, psychological, aesthetic, or linguistic. It may be a quality of the imagination, a synthetic vision, a vigilant wakefulness, a subconscious instinct, a silent intuition, a rhetorical waywardness, and so on. In each case the motive and goal of arguing depend on the ground selected. As we have seen, in each case (with the exception of deconstruction) the aim is totality, the fullness of mind in accord with the truth of reality, a concord of being, seeing, saying, and knowing, once lost and now to be recovered through daring intellectual effort. This plenitude may be expressed as Yeats's unity of being, Eliot's integrated sensibility, Pound's vortex, Edwin Muir's fable, Allen Tate's vision of the whole life, or André Breton's surrealism; but in any case it is a condition to be won through a refined discipline of mind that paradoxically is held to be unreasonable and yet effective because unreasonable. All attempts to provide a distinctive locus for poetic argument are therefore attempts to define unreason.

As we also saw, however, to abandon reason is to pursue a phantom.

Since, according to modernist theories, discourse can never fully master unreason and must entice it through paradox, negation, and silence, unreason proves to be a dangerous ally. The poet is like the sorcerer's apprentice or like Malvolio in gaudy clothes: both are overwhelmed by wild forces that they release but cannot control. As the domain of poetry retreats further inward and becomes a hidden property of consciousness or unconsciousness, it grows more intimate yet more elusive and problematic. One of the chief aims of the argument, then, is to re-establish and reassert the self, which is increasingly felt to be in jeopardy. The self is the locus of argument and is generated by its arguments, yet it cannot fully direct them or depend on them. Instead, it is perplexed by them, because it relies on powers – like Graves's Mr Hyde – which it cannot trust to sustain the project of self-definition and discovery. Hence the recurring modern theme of the disappearance of the self, studied by Sypher and others.[1] Marianne Moore reveals, moreover, that this dilemma is a moral one. For all the scandal and irresponsibility of their techniques, the modern poets' demand for intelligibility is ethical as well as logical, and their challenge to logic produces a corresponding affront to moral judgment. Their need to restore the self is thus also a demand for moral integrity or wholesomeness. In this respect their arguments, even when they prove enigmatic, are not truly deconstructive, because they remain loyal to integral principles ("transcendental signifieds"), notably the self, understood as a rational and ethical centre, whose fragile unity they still hope to reaffirm. In Edward and Dylan Thomas, we find two attempts to establish the self as a viable basis for argument, both of which end in the discovery that it is unstable.

I have contended that the proper way to exorcize the ghost of unreason is to find its "lair," and to trace the operation of logic in poetic arguments that appear to be unreasonable but which, through their rhetoric and drama, disclose a prevailing rationality. The poetry of Edward Thomas is logically and rhetorically sophisticated, and this quality contributes to the formulation of arguments that seem inconclusive, because they take the form of puzzles that the poet attempts, with or without success, to solve. But he is not simply bewildered; his poems do not reach a dead end. Rather, his bewilderment becomes a factor in an argument that displays "lucid uncertainty,"[2] as it entangles itself in what he calls "reverie" and we have been discussing as unreason. The puzzle lies partly in Thomas's complex personality and partly in the problematic nature of thought. His work illustrates the interdependence of argument and character: each can be seen as an aspect of the other. The style of his arguments is not only the index of a given personality, an expression of his complex sensibility; it also creates the personality that appears in individual poems and presides over his entire *oeuvre*. Style is a dramatic exhibition of personality, or, conversely, personality is a rhetorical effect of style. Thomas's character is especially interesting because it is registered in arguments that strive to triumph over argument, since arguing is treated as a frailty. He would love to be thoughtless and unselfconscious, effortlessly blending with the natural scenes in which he delights, savouring a vitality that requires no calculation or proof. Instead he displays a restless, introspective, self-critical temperament, which questions its own powers of perception and conception. He portrays a complexity that yearns for simplicity.

Thomas's personality is displayed in his essays and letters and described in the books by his wife and in memoirs by his friends. While it is impossible to ignore these sources, I am more concerned with the poetic personality that emerges as both the source and the product of his arguments. It is what Paul de Man calls "the self that reads itself ... the author as he is changed and interpreted by his own work."[3] It is also the self that argues with and about itself, with the perplexing result that it is at once constituted and obscured by its arguments. This difficulty, while certainly true to Thomas's experience, is also the legacy of English nature poetry, both of the grand "Greater Romantic lyric" derived from Wordsworth and Coleridge, and of the more modest rural tradition studied by W.J. Keith in *The Poetry of Nature*.[4] In both traditions the poet considers himself by examining a natural setting from which he feels estranged and in which he seeks consolation or a solution to his problems. Thomas was well aware of these traditions and proud to be part of them. He accepted "the commonplace about the importance of Nature in all great English poetry" (*LGB*, 128)[5] and insisted, "there is no great poetry which can be dissevered from Nature" (*SC*, 43), although his own severance from it prompts his most troubled arguments. He continually uses nature to provide occasions to think about himself and to propose a standard for testing himself and debating his feelings. His best poems are meditations in which we watch a mind as it entertains ideas, inquiring, disputing, following its own emotional rhythm. "After all," he wrote, "in matters of the spirit, men are all engaged in colloquies with themselves. Some of them are overheard, and they are the poets" (*W*, 80). We overhear colloquies in which he presents an elaborate counterpointing of himself and nature, through which he winds himself into his own thoughts, drawing images of the natural world into his dispute. Following the traditional pattern, his poems usually begin in a natural setting but shift, as F.R. Leavis notes, until the "outward scene is accessory to an inner theatre."[6] I wish to examine first the relationship between outward scene and inner theatre, by which a dramatic locus of argument is established, and then the rhetoric through which the arguments are conducted with a rigorous but disturbing logic.

Thomas's treatment of the outward scene provides a basis for the colloquies that follow, by establishing his first, purest contact with reality. The self becomes a locus for argument only when it defines itself in relation to its surroundings. In his prose he often explores with great sensitivity the varying relations between the poet, the world he describes, and the world he creates. He places William Blake at one end of a spectrum of such relations. Blake creates a personal world out of his surroundings, his reading, his temperament, an imaginative landscape quite apart from everyday reality: "What he saw and read to any purpose made equal and similar impressions on him, and he combined the two with beautiful freedom ... he had made for himself out of the streets of London, the churches and shops, the fields of Dulwich, and out of ruminations among all sorts of books and pictures, a system of the world." Of certain descriptive passages Thomas comments, "these are magnificent, but not Sussex," and again, "Even South Molton Street is but three words in his writing, and not a reality of any sort" (*LPE*, 13, 20, 22). At the other end of the spectrum are John Clare, who describes flowers "in a manner which preserves them still dewy, or with summer dust" (*LPE*, 225), and Lord Byron, who feels the pulse of reality: "It was part of Byron's power, not as so many poets have done, to create a world of their own not subject to earthly laws, but to keep his verse always in touch with the actual world of his own time, to allow the circulation of blood between his poetry and his world of flesh, shone upon by the very sun and blown across by the living winds" (*FI*, 315). Thomas is eager to admit sun and wind into his own poetry, which clearly falls at the Byronic end of the scale. He finds the earth "lovelier / Than any mysteries" (*CP*, 363), because it is more mysterious and challenging than a world of dreams. He counters escapist illusions by an appeal to the world of flesh, to "Mother Dunch's Buttocks" (*CP*, 163), and to the waking call of the trumpet or the cock. His descriptions of the countryside in Wiltshire and Hampshire are accurate, since he was "an exact and informed naturalist."[7] In a letter to Eleanor Farjeon he shows how much he valued precision and how much he thought accurate observation validated his poetry: "I am pleased you like 'After Rain' best. I wonder whether I can do anything with 'inlaid' and 'played'. The inlaid, too, is at any rate perfectly precise as I saw the black leaves 2 years ago up at the top of the hill, so that neither is a rhyme word only" (*LFY*, 111). The words are justified because they are true, not because they happen to rhyme. In contrast, he criticized Swinburne for the mere "appearance of precision," noting that "Swinburne's style touches actual detail at its peril" (*ACS*, 15, 153).

Accurate observation is important, because Thomas respects the separateness of the natural world. He has a naturalist's love of the land, which permits him to leave it alone, to refrain from imposing his feelings on it. One of his favourite poses is that of the "watcher": the solitary traveller, curious and observant, who passes through a scene without disturbing it. This dramatic perspective serves as a logical point of departure for his meditations, because it permits him to define himself in concert with and in opposition to nature. Detachment permits him to focus on the scene by isolating himself and by minimizing the intrusions of thought, so that, like D.H. Lawrence, he can savour all that is separate and nonhuman in nature. In this way he can pretend that thought is intrusive and unnecessary. He can make a show of not arguing. For example, he admires the dust on the nettle because it proves that no one has meddled with the scene in fact or in thought: "As well as any bloom upon a flower / I like the dust on the nettles, never lost / Except to prove the sweetness of a shower" (*CP*, 307). The sweetness of the shower is really a quality of perception, not a feature of the land, but the perception is felt to be immediate and thrilling. To be thrilling, however, nature cannot really be immediate. It must be alien. Thomas responds so intensely to the voices of nature - wind, rain, birds - precisely because he recognizes that they do not speak a human language and cannot speak to him. He listens to silence, "an empty thingless name ... a pure thrush word" (*CP*, 221); or he declares, "This was the best of May - the small brown birds / Wisely reiterating endlessly / What no man learnt yet, in or out of school" (*CP*, 211). The personification here is whimsical, ascribing to the birds a peculiar wisdom that is not human and so, properly speaking, not wisdom at all. The calculated inappropriateness of the personification is a strategy in his argument. It expresses the fanciful attempt of understanding to transgress its own boundaries, to think the unthinkable. It illustrates, too, how clever and disciplined thought must be to give the impression that there is no thought at all and that poetry is unreasonable. The sounds and songs of nature are fascinating precisely because they defy comprehension: "Beautiful as the notes are for their quality and order, it is their inhumanity that gives them their utmost fascination, the mysterious sense which they bear to us that the earth is something more than a human estate, that there are things not human yet of great honour and power in the world. The very first rush and the following wail empty the brain of what is merely human and leave only what is related to the height and depth of the whole world. Here for this hour we are remote from the parochialism of humanity." (*SC*, 34).

Samuel Hynes reports how a reviewer of the six poems published under the pseudonym, Edward Eastaway, objected that they concentrate too much on "natural fact" and too little on "human things," but Thomas responded, "I don't mind being called inhuman."[8] He respects natural facts for their mysterious inhumanity, and in his writing he explores the relation between the natural and the "merely human," which desires to overcome its parochialism and share the "honour and power" of the world. His alienation from nature is therefore implicit in his very admiration for it. The harmony between human and natural orders, which he promotes through patient, precise observation, is so precious because so elusive. There are two figures in "The Watchers" (*CP*, 309): the carter who blends peacefully with nature; and the watcher in the inn, trapped indoors amid "stuffed fish, vermin, and kingfishers." Thomas strives, sometimes successfully, sometimes not, to advance from the condition of the watcher to the condition of the carter. He searches for a coexistence with nature, a condition which he sometimes calls "home": " 'Twas home; one nationality / We had, I and the birds that sang, / One memory" (*CP*, 177). The troublesome paradox, which turns his poems from celebrations into arguments, is that he is alienated from the natural world that gives him his greatest peace: "This is my grief. That land, / My home, I have never seen" (*CP*, 117). If "home" is the authentic ground of his being and he has never seen it, then the mystery of nature is mirrored by an inner mystery of the self that does not know itself. He is drawn to nature by the very wonder that divorces him from it, but that also promises to reveal his true being: "This is the beginning of the pageant of autumn, of that gradual pompous dying which has no parallel in human life yet draws us to it with sure bonds" (*SC*, 272). He detects this dilemma in the work of Richard Jefferies, W.H. Hudson, and Maurice Maeterlinck; the last "sees man as part of Nature, yet with that in them which seems to make their best achievements something apart from Nature and in spite of it ... Man, now as a part of Nature, and now as distinct from Nature, is his never-forgotten subject" (*MM*, 204, 210).

The conjunction "in spite of" expresses the logical twist taken by many of Thomas's poems as they consider his never-forgotten subject – the ambiguous relationship between man and nature. This ambiguity, which produces the self-defeating human achievements mentioned in the previous quotation, is summed up neatly in "Women He Liked" (*CP*, 339). Bob Hayward loves living things "For the life in them," and he plants elms along a country lane. But now "None passes there because the mist and the rain / Out of the elms have turned the lane to slough / And gloom, the name alone survives, Bob's Lane." Bob's act of sympathy with nature has the unforeseen effect of making the track impassable. His effort to be close to nature now keeps people away. The irony is enforced by the manner in which the path, previously unnamed, is now known as Bob's Lane, so that the scene is humanized in name or claimed through language, only when humanity is banished from it. Bob's triumph is also his failure: "To name a thing beloved man sometimes fails." The poem concludes logically, but with a puzzle stated so epigramatically that it is easy to overlook its dangerous implications. To name a thing beloved is the aim of Thomas's poetry, but frequently his achievements - his acts, thoughts and arguments - make inaccessible the very "home" that they seek to capture.

When Thomas feels himself banished from natural beauty, his colloquy becomes more aggressive and starts to turn on itself. He asks: "Why does Nature make these beautiful things so carelessly & then one wonders whether all beautiful things are not of this careless inevitableness and yet long wrought out too & then one has to earn one's living" (*LGB*, 155). In this letter we see, albeit humorously, the characteristic course of Thomas's thought. He moves from the outward scene, to the human world (the consideration of beauty), to his own intimate, pressing problems (the need to earn a living). His poems follow the same pattern when he observes nature "with a worried heart and a notebook" (*LGB*, 158). The notebook suggests accurate observation, the precise, earthy details which delight him - the dust on the nettle, the solitary fly that buzzes in "The Manor Farm" (*CP*, 49), the black leaflets inlaid on the road in "After Rain" (*CP*, 35). The worried heart suggests the inner theatre where his arguments are conducted. After describing the scene, the poetic watcher gradually makes his presence felt, hesitantly at first, by introducing a human faculty, emotion, or artifact. In "Fifty Faggots" the faculty is fancy, which fancifully weaves itself into the setting: "Now, by the hedge / Closed packed, they make a thicket fancy alone / Can creep through with the mouse and wren" (*CP*, 207). Fancy suggests the consciousness which must now contemplate and interpret the scene. In "Rain" (*CP*, 259) it is memory that introduces the human element, but more precisely: "Remembering again that I shall die." This memory looks back to a repeated past event (remembering again) and ahead to the future (that I shall die). In one deceptively simple line Thomas evokes that complex, temporal awareness which he finds so tormentingly human. In "The Signpost" (*CP*, 23) it is the sign and the choice it prompts; in "Health" (*CP*, 179) it is the exuberant appeal to the eye and to the "desire of my heart"; in "The Thrush" (*CP*, 251) it is the "sweet names" of the months, which add to natural fact the complications of human awareness.

With the introduction of a human faculty, the watcher begins to watch himself and to argue. The dramatic strategy employed most often is one mentioned in the first chapter: "reason reasoning." We watch the poet's mind at work as it argues toward a conclusion that it may attain or that may be displaced by an unforeseen realization. Although Carol Johnson calls it the metaphysical strategy, only a few poems such as "Song: The Clouds that are so Light" (*CP*, 261), "At Poet's Tears" (*LFY*, 132), and "These Things that Poets Said" (*CP*, 275) argue in a polished, witty manner. In the last, Thomas compares his own experience of love with the accounts of poetry and concludes:

Only, that once I loved
By this one argument
Is very plainly proved:
I, loving not, am different.

This poem exhibits the conflicting needs of a complex personality, because, as it apparently proposes one, precise argument, it actually dramatizes another more unruly one. Thomas's attempt to construct a balanced argument, contrasting art and life, reveals his need to master inconsistent experience by making it orderly. But his "plain" conclusion does not succeed in defining love, only in proving that he has suffered and been changed by love and in trapping him in an ambiguous state of "difference." His final emotional and intellectual uncertainty is not illogical, but it plays against the neat form of the poem and the apparently confident tone. The force of this interplay is whimsical and wry. By examining himself rationally, he proves that he is confused. Nevertheless, he observes the whole procedure with some detachment and considerable wit, for example, when he parodies the literary style he has just found inadequate: "Between us / Decide, good Love, before I die."

The complexity of this argument is typical of his poetry and indicates how the reasoning of reason proves disconcerting. Instead of reaching a satisfactory conclusion, he may argue himself into whimsy or discontent. Instead of feeling at home in natural beauty, he may lose himself in disturbing thoughts and feelings. The darker side of reason is illuminated by another remark to Gordon Bottomley: "I read de Musset's "Confession d'un Enfant du Siècle.' Have you read that book? The magniloquent way in which he mistakes reverie for thought reminds me of myself, as also his glorious and elaborate sorrow at nothing at all" (*LGB*, 62). This comment of 1904 looks ahead to the poetry, that sets thought against feeling, combining logical form and emotional rhythm. Although Thomas does not say that "reverie" is illogical, we can detect the ghost of unreason in its opposition to "thought," a contrast that repeats the familiar configuration of modern poetic argument: thought and reverie, reason and unreason, sometimes cooperating, sometimes at odds, combine in his version of the waking dream. But we can also see his determination to remain vigilant. He refuses to make the mistake of abandoning thought and condemns himself – unfairly – for elaborate emotion. This resolve is both reflected and contested in poetic monologues, colloquies and meditations, all of which argue through a bewildering combination of logic and emotion. Reason is not necessarily an ally. It produces an argument that may turn into a puzzle, which the poet fails to solve. His difficulty comes both from emotional complexity and from an unruly logic that makes it difficult for him to master his own thoughts and feelings.

Commenting on the problem I have just noted, Michael Kirkham suggests that the paradoxes, tensions, shifting perspectives, and analogies in some of Thomas's poems permit "analogical thinking," that provides a unified, transpersonal vision and that intimates we might even transgress the limits of conceptual thought and speech.[9] I have argued at length in the first chapter that such thinking, while it may seem unreasonable, cannot really be contrary to logic, and that the techniques adduced confirm rather than disprove its rational structure. Although the poems display the darker side of reason and the involutions of thought, they do not cease to be rational. Consider, for example, the argument of "Liberty" (*CP*, 255), an inconclusive meditation by a precise mind whose thoughts both liberate and confine it. The speaker sets himself in a moonlit scene of memory and mourning, where he entertains conflicting ideas of freedom and constraint, desire and loss. He displays an acute intelligence, but the way he entertains ideas – his reverie – is as revealing as the ideas themselves. The way he thinks about liberty proves to be a dramatic example of his equivocal freedom, since liberty is ultimately a state of mind. His argument recedes to a place deeper within his consciousness, where, like freedom, it grows more tenuous. Both he and the moon "have liberty / To dream what we could do if we were free / To do some thing we had desired long." This notion of imaginative freedom in the midst of confinement teases and fascinates him, but he does not follow it through to a conclusion. Instead, the play of thought produces paradoxes ("I should be rich to be so poor"), which express his puzzled discontent and self-consciousness. He finds that to be intensely aware of oneself is to be aware of one's limitations and losses. It is to brood over all that is "unforgotten and lost." Yet even in this state he asserts the liberty of a mind which is constantly active, dissatisfied and free to dream.

There's none less free than who
Does nothing and has nothing else to do,
Being free only for what is not to his mind,
And nothing is to his mind.

The reverie is darkened by negatives, but the thought remains acute. Freedom does not lie in mindlessness, and to be carefree is not necessarily to be free. His own life is rich because he can "wonder whether I was free or not," and even the present moment of confusion and regret contributes to that richness. To wonder, in this sense, is both to claim one's freedom and to discover its limitations. Nevertheless, in the end Thomas has not relieved the sombreness of the scene which prompted his meditation. The poem ends in darkness, with the moon less an ally than the mysterious sign of an unattainable ideal that contrasts with his own "imperfection." Confusion and regret are not dispelled, and despite the tentative affirmation he never succeeds in defining or asserting his freedom. In this argument, therefore, he entertains ideas which fail to satisfy him, but by wrestling with them he dramatizes the rich though painful awareness that he claims as the basis of liberty:

> And yet I still am half in love with pain,
> With what is imperfect, with both tears and mirth,
> With things that have an end, with life and earth,
> And this moon that leaves me dark within the door.

In this conclusion he displays a divided mind that has been the subject of critical disagreement ever since D.W. Harding suggested that, because Thomas never understood the cause of his melancholy, he failed to "probe his unhappiness." Kirkham argues just the reverse and, using "The Other" as test case, claims that Thomas's self-knowledge is clear and penetrating and that through sceptical self-mockery he diagnoses his problem as an inability to join a stable, human community. He probes but cannot solve this dilemma, because he understands but cannot relieve his distress: "The solitary, whose *sickness* is impoverishment of the social instinct, cannot (by definition) know inwardly the social disposition he is seeking, only that he lacks that disposition and suffers for it"; he "recognizes equally the inescapable compulsion to search for social gratification and the impossibility of success." Thus his argument remains in one sense inconclusive, but in another affirms "the human values by which he himself is judged to be a failure."[10] Andrew Motion draws a similar moral from the poem, but offers a more optimistic portrait of the artist. Where Kirkham diagnoses "the *pathology* of questing," Motion concludes, "the journey and not the arrival provides him with the wholeness he seeks, because it is there that self-consciousness is at a mimimum." In his poetry generally, Thomas displays "a capacity to see the potential for gain in the certainty of loss"; he manages "to comprehend failure and fulfillment simultaneously."[11]

What is Thomas's true character? These interpretations illustrate the difficulty of abstracting a clearly defined personality from specific poems or from a poet's work as a whole. To the literary critic, personality is a characteristic pattern of human needs, responses, and preferences, a design which we analyse and then systematize as Thomas's "frame of mind" or "philosophy." Thus Edna Longley judges the conclusion to "Liberty" (composed in 1915, but based on a passage from *The Heart of England*, 1906) as "perhaps Thomas's most complete statement of his mature philosophy, which recognises that the benefits and limitations of earthly existence are inextricable."[12] But we have no way of independently identifying a personality that precedes and finds suitable expression in his style. Instead, we must infer the personality from the style and argument of the poems. It emerges from our interpretation, from our decisions about which poems are exemplary, in what order they were written, what influences they reveal, and so on. Kirkham regards "The Other" as typical, not exceptional. Longley regards "Liberty" as mature, not juvenile. All the critics cited agree, however, that there is a basic division in Thomas, whether between understanding and belief, fulfilment and failure, or benefit and limitation. Stan Smith traces the opposition to Thomas's Welsh/English upbringing and to the contradictory social ideology of late Victorian and Edwardian England;[13] while H. Coombes contrasts "precision of feeling," at which Thomas excels, with "complete self-knowledge," which he lacks.[14] Following the same pattern, I have distinguished between thought and reverie as properties of both his character and his style. This duality is the formal principle by which we reconstruct his personality, and it arises, as the detailed analyses of Kirkham and Motion illustrate, from the ambiguity of his poetic arguments.

By arguing with ideas and with himself entertaining these ideas, Thomas dramatizes a temperament that understands itself but is not content with self-knowledge. Understanding his dilemma does not solve it. Probing his unhappiness may offer relief but may also complicate his melancholy. He argues in pursuit not so much of self-knowledge as of self-possession, an intellectual-emotional balance that finds its model in the harmony between man and nature. Self-possession is the fusion of seeing, knowing, and being that was proposed by the imagists and that serves as the perfectly constituted locus for poetic thought. For Thomas, it is the state of "health," when a well-integrated personality, its various faculties all balanced, falls into accord with the natural world. It is "unthwarted intensity of sensual and mental life, in the midst of beautiful or astonishing things which should give that life full play and banish expectation and recollection" (*HE*, 84). Thomas never abandons this sensual-intellectual-moral ideal, even when it is sorely tested. When he feels at home and at ease, he enjoys a continuity between himself and natural beauty: "and now I might / As happy be as earth is beautiful" (*CP*, 247). These lines from "October" sum up his desire, and in the hesitant verb tense hint at the difficulties he encounters. As we have seen, he recognizes that human and natural orders are essentially alien. Mind and world are incongruous because, as Richard Jefferies taught him, the "balance of logic does not correspond with life." Our neat reasoning cannot cope with exuberant, natural disorder: "Our symmetrical and regular thought is not fit for this unruly universe" (*RJ*, 184). Or, conversely, our unruly emotions exclude us from natural orderliness. In "The Glory" (*CP*, 199) Thomas finds:

> The glory invites me, yet it leaves me scorning
> All I can ever do, all I can be,
> Beside the lovely of motion, shape, and hue,
> The happiness I fancy fit to dwell
> In beauty's presence.

As in "October," it is through happiness rather than knowledge that he hopes to match the glorious occasion, but again his scornful doubts intrude.

As all Thomas's friends and critics observe, there are fortunate moments when man and nature fall into accord and the watcher blends with the scene, a condition Thomas calls liberty, content, home, glory, joy, health. In his prose he often evokes the richness of being when natural beauty gives full play to life: "And in our own muscles and hearts the evening strives to form an aspiration that shall suit the joy of the hills, the meadows, the copses, and their people" (*HE*, 31); "I sat down under a roof, I remembered little, thought of nothing, but I glowed and was at ease, trembling and tingling from the indescribable intimate contacts of the day" (*LT*, 73–4). In his poetry, too, he celebrates those spots of time when the watcher is transformed by his perception. They are "moments of everlastingness" (*CP*, 31) that are "out of the reach of change" (*CP*, 227) in "a season of bliss unchangeable" (*CP*, 49). Usually this precious vision comes unexpectedly and unsought, the gift of a sudden intensity of awareness. Often it is associated with music, nursery rhymes, bird songs, or folk songs:

> The song of the Ash Grove soft as love uncrossed,
> And then in a crowd or in distance it were lost,
> But the moment unveiled something unwilling to die
> And I had what most I desired, without search or desert or cost. (*CP*, 269)

Thomas may enjoy this joyful moment without examining it, or he may, in the midst of his reverie, wonder at his ability to feel such delight. Indeed the mere fact of writing about it testifies to his wonder and makes him self-conscious. He then asks: "How can our thoughts, the movements of our bodies, our human kindness, ever fit themselves with this blithe world?" (*SC*, 55). How can we be as happy, wise, or free as the earth is beautiful? Similarly in *The Heart of England*, he is daunted by the beauty of the poppies he so admires: "Had they been reported to me from Italy or the East, had I read of them on a supreme poet's page, they could not have been more remote more inaccessible, more desirable in their serenity. Something in me desired them, might even seem to have long ago possessed and lost them, but when thought followed vision as, alas! it did, I could not understand their importance, their distance from my mind, their desirableness, as a far-away princess to a troubadour" (*HE*, 72). When thought follows and dispels vision, the arguments of poetry prove unsatisfying. Desire, sensation, and understanding are now in conflict rather than harmony. Immediate enjoyment of the poppies turns into a literary experience that occurs on the page rather than in nature. What Thomas most desires comes effortlessly "without search or desert or cost." When he seeks his vision more thoughtfully and when he argues about its validity, he often finds that it eludes him at great cost. In his confusion he suffers a double loss. He becomes so self-conscious that the palpable reality, which prompted his meditation in the first place, eludes him; and he finds as a painful corollary that even his own feelings puzzle him.

As I have said, Thomas's colloquy begins when he questions his relation to nature, often by introducing an inquiring human faculty – fancy, memory, the observing eye, or the worried heart – into the scene. His rhetorical strategy is then to propose a set of balanced contrasts through which he sets his thoughts and feelings in order.[15] This is the balance of logic and life, that he wishes to maintain:

> Downhill I came, hungry and yet not starved;
> Cold, yet had heat within me that was proof
> Against the North Wind; tired, yet so that rest
> Had seemed the sweetest thing under a roof. (*CP*, 119)

Through such contrasts he sets himself within the scene and illustrates how man and nature are familiar yet distinct. In "The Mill-Water" (*CP*, 235):

> Solitude, company, –
> When it is night, –

Grief or delight
By it must haunted or concluded be.
...
Sometimes a thought is drowned
By it, sometimes
Out it climbs;
All thoughts begin or end upon this sound ...

The contrasts give the impression of a well-ordered mind, master of its subject. But the thought that climbs from and returns to the sounds of nature soon loses its confidence. Qualifying words and phrases - perhaps, maybe, almost, nearly - subtly intrude to challenge that mastery and to replace it with the hesitancy characteristic of Thomas's assertions. He begins to question himself: "And I am *nearly* as happy as possible / To search the wilderness in vain though well" (*CP*, 315); "And yet I *almost* dare to laugh / Because I sit and frame an epitaph" (*CP*, 97); "But I am *almost* proud to love both bird and sun" (*CP*, 181; all my emphasis). His doubts grow as he pursues his thought. He may pose a series of unanswerable questions ("The Glory"). He may try to sort out conflicting ideas ("Liberty") or conflicting feelings ("Rain"). He may seek a new perspective on his problem by searching through memory ("Old Man") or through fancy ("The Signpost"). In each case he challenges himself, winding himself into uncertainty, setting himself ever further apart from the natural scene that was his place of departure.

At this point his argument takes an interesting rhetorical turn. In an attempt to set his feelings in order and to bridge the widening gap between himself and nature, he resorts to a daring metaphor or, more often, simile. Like Marianne Moore, who uses a similar technique for a different effect, he looks for persuasive and instructive analogies:

But head and bottle tilted back in the cart
Will never part
Till I am cold as midnight and all my hours
Are beeless flowers. (CP, 175)

In this example, from "Head and Bottle," the fusion of man and nature is comical because the communion, signalled by the comparisons, is really a drunken stupor. The drunkard merges peacefully and mindlessly with the scene:

He neither sees, nor hears, nor smells, nor thinks,
But only drinks,

Quiet in the yard where tree trunks do not lie
More quietly.

The shift from first to third person suggests that the poet is observing the drunkard and is not himself keeping company with the tree trunks. He is still a watcher. He does merge with the trees, however, in "Aspens" (*CP*, 233), where a counterpoint of human and natural sounds (wind, rain, songs, the sounds of the blacksmith) at first suggests a separation of man and nature: "Aspens must shake their leaves and men may hear / But need not listen, more than to my rhymes." The words "must" and "may" subtly confirm the distinction between the two orders, but then a metaphor, suggesting the whole enterprise of poetry, successfully unites the poet with the scene:

Whatever wind blows, while they and I have leaves
We cannot other than aspen be
That ceaselessly, unreasonably grieves,
Or so men think who like a different tree.

In his grief and in his poetry he finds company with the trees but not, the last two lines hint, with the other human figures in the poem. As in "The Other," he finds solace in nature but not the full, sociable comfort he desires.

In "Beauty" (*CP*, 97) Thomas adopts a whimsical tone that permits him to play with similes until he settles on one that satisfies him. At first, "tired, angry, and ill at ease," he feels like a cold, dark, river, but he then finds consolation in a comparison with birds: "Not like a pewit that returns to wail / For something it has lost, but like a dove / That slants unswerving to its home and love." Thomas is comforted by the very process of considering these comparisons. He discovers beauty by proposing, rejecting, and finally adopting a simile appropriate to his varying moods. The subtlety of his feelings is conveyed by the precision of the image: the pewit, because of its character, is not a suitable bird, but the dove is. Thomas reverses his customary procedure in this poem: instead of beginning by observing a scene, he gradually creates one through figures of speech and then takes comfort in it.

He follows the same strategy in "After You Speak" (*CP*, 329), where another bird simile, gradually extended, offers an image that permits him to express his feelings for his wife. This lovely poem is based on one elaborate simile which interprets the dark, silent gaze that follows her words.

Even so the lark
Loves dust

And nestles in it
The minute
Before he must
Soar in lone flight
So far,
Like a black star
He seems –
mote
Of singing dust
Afloat
Above,
That dreams
And sheds no light.
I know your lust
Is love.

The technique is imagistic: intangible emotions are given substance through an analogy whose basis slowly becomes clear. Through the image of the lark taking flight, a series of opposites – earth and sky, dust and air, dirt and purity – are combined in the paradoxical "black star," in the "mote of / singing dust" with its suggestion of joy and mortality, and in the dark, inward illumination of "dreams / And sheds no light." The last two lines return to the inner, emotional theatre and imply a comparable contrast and reconciliation of love and lust, spirit and flesh. The poem distinguishes these pairs, while demonstrating the intimate connection between them. The intimacy of the connection and of the emotions they arouse depends on the precision and beauty of the imagery.

In other poems, however, Thomas's similes prove inadequate because the analogies they propose fail to satisfy his doubts or to lead his arguments to a satisfying conclusion. For example, in "Blenheim Oranges" (*CP*, 355–7), after examining a dark, decrepit, but dignified house, which he hopes to use as an image of his despair, he notes: "I am something like that; / Only I am not dead." The analogy is imperfect, and, as his brooding continues, it leads him beyond the gloomy, companionable house toward feelings he cannot share with anyone or anything:

Only I am not dead,
Still breathing and interested
In the house that is not dark: –

I am something like that:
Not one pane to reflect the sun,

For the schoolboys to throw at -
They have broken every one.

This poem uses the same dual technique that Keith finds in "Over the Hills," where visual simile and logical argument - or, more correctly, competing arguments - are in conflict. The simile, which has been declared inappropriate, nevertheless supplies a "pictorial movement" that allows Thomas to envision another house, one which is not dark and contains his own living despair. In another dark house, in "The Long Small Room" (*CP*, 369), he again seeks the companionship of nature to relieve feelings that he cannot understand or control: "When I look back I am like moon, sparrow and mouse / That witnessed what they could never understand / Or alter or prevent in the dark house." But again the analogy proves treacherous. It offers no comfort, because it fragments rather than unifies awareness. It not only confirms the rift between the poet and the world, but enforces what Stan Smith calls an inner "discrepancy between witnessing and understanding." It "arises precisely from the looking subject's inability to make sense of something he looks at, in self-division, as the meaningless activity of an alien object."[16]

One thing remains the same - this my right hand

Crawling crab-like over the clean white page,
Resting awhile each morning on the pillow,
Then once more starting to crawl on toward age.

His curiously detached hand writes, as he tries to remember and express his feelings, actions which distinguish him from moon, sparrow, mouse, and even crab, by reminding him that he is tormented by time as they are not.

As these examples show, Thomas uses similes as a means of both discovery and failure to discover. The images they supply may or may not satisfy his argument. Satisfaction is most clearly at issue in "Health" (*CP*, 179-81), where simile prompts simile, weaving a net of analogies with which to capture complicated ideas and emotions. He explores the dilemma, whereby "I am not satisfied / Even with knowing I never could be satisfied," by multiplying comparisons:

I could not be as the wagtail running up and down
The warm tiles of the roof slope, twittering
Happily and sweetly as if the sun itself

> Extracted the song
> As the hand makes sparks from the fur of a cat.

Although he begins by denying the comparison with the bird, he then considers it in detail, delighting in its pictorial movement as if to counteract his denial. Thought and reverie, assertion and imagery pull the argument in different directions. He indulges a correspondence with nature he has already declared false. In the simile of stroking a cat, he then complicates the comparison by blending human and natural orders even more intimately. Man, cat, bird, and sun are united in an image of sparkling song. But he knows the union to be illusory, and repeats his denial:

> I could not be as the sun.
> Nor should I be content to be
> As little as the bird or as mighty as the sun.
> For the bird knows not the sun,
> And the sun regards not the bird.
> But I am almost proud to love both bird and sun,
> Though scarce this Spring could my body leap four yards.

Still dissatisfied and "almost proud," Thomas now finds a compensating contentment in his discontent. As in "Liberty," he discovers that human awareness offers life richness as well as dissatisfaction. Because the similes fail, they distinguish him from nature. But because they are so whimsical and seductive and because they illustrate the delights of language, they offer him a contentment which bird and sun cannot experience.

Although he uses metaphors, too, he seems to prefer the overt comparison of a simile because it is a rhetorical figure that announces its own contrivance. It displays an analogy, that he can use in his attempt to reunite watcher and scene. He makes several suggestive comments about the authority of such analogies and hence their validity in poetic arguments. Sometimes he speaks enthusiastically, if vaguely, about the "magic felicity of words" (*ACS*, 96), which cast a spell over the reader by transforming his vision. The prose writer "cannot change the things themselves – flower, and leaf, and sky – into melody and words, as the poet can in verse" (*RJ*, 198). For Thomas, as for Coleridge, poetic diction is a special use of language that draws things closer to words and words closer to things. Some writers such as Oscar Wilde, Walter Pater, Dante Gabriel Rossetti, and Francis Thompson create an independent, verbal realm, which is artificial, if fascinating.

But the greatest poets give language the vitality of immediate experience, healing the rift between mind and world:

> The magic of words is due to their living freely among things, and no man knows how they came together in just that order when a beautiful thing is made like "Full fathom five." ... in this unprejudiced singing voice that knows not what it sings, is some reason for us to believe that poets are not merely writing figuratively when they say, "My love is like a red, red rose," but that they are to be taken more literally than they commonly are ... What they say is not chosen to represent what they feel or think, but is itself the very substance of what had before lain dark and unapparent, is itself all that survives of feeling and thought, and cannot be expanded or reduced without dulling or falsification. (*FI*, 85-86)

Thomas suggests here that poetry is not a description of or an argument about an experience; it is the experience itself evoked through music, simile, and metaphor. Words, thoughts, and things concur perfectly in an intuition that persuades us by its power and beauty. This is the closest he comes to proposing an independent, magical unreason. It is not quite clear what he means by saying that the simile "My love is like a red, red rose" should be taken "more literally" than it commonly is. Perhaps he refers to the urgency of a simile which blends with and becomes "the very substance of" the emotion it expresses. Through poetic intensity, words are "transmuted into the very things that they describe."[17] When words cling so closely to things, they no longer seem to intervene between us and our experience, and so must in a sense be taken literally. In that case, as Kirkham explains, "Meaning is inherent in, not an interpretation of, our experience of nature. Nature and human feeling have a meaning in common...."[18] Consequently, certain similes by Shelley "are more than comparisons; they have an intenser life than life itself as it is commonly lived" (*FI*, 33). Urgent vitality is what Thomas values in poetic diction, what Marianne Moore calls gusto, what operates in poetic arguments as aggression. He insists on the compelling quality of poetry: we must be won over by a poem and so convinced of its validity. But the goal of "literal," immediate, or natural meaning is an ideal and an effect achieved through the art that conceals art. Although such meaning seems to triumph over argument, it is really the product of argument.

When in his perplexity Thomas turns to metaphor and simile, therefore, he seeks the assurance of a proof that is not illogical, but convinces him by the lyrical intensity with which it is formulated. However, such linguistic power is again dangerous. The strategy may succeed (as in "Aspens" and "Health") or offer some consolation (as in "Liberty"), but when the experience presented is a bewildering one, the argument may articulate and so confirm that bewilderment, thereby denying him self-possession. This is the case in poems where the similes prove unsatisfactory or unsatisfying. In "Rain" (*CP*, 259) the similes convey such emotional uncertainty that, despite the prevailing desolate mood, Thomas's feelings elude him. After establishing the scene and setting himself within it, he uses a simile to blend scene and observer:

> Blessed are the dead that the rain rains upon:
> But here I pray that none whom once I loved
> Is dying tonight or lying still awake
> Solitary, listening to the rain,
> Either in pain or thus in sympathy
> Helpless among the living and the dead,
> Like a cold water among broken reeds,
> Myriads of broken reeds all still and stiff
> Like me who have no love which this wild rain
> Has not dissolved ...

The analogy between water and reeds, living and dead, which seems clear at first, proves puzzling. William Cooke explains it as follows: "The image of the cold water (himself) among, yet unable to sustain, the reeds that are 'broken' (the dead and dying soldiers) reinforces his feeling of helplessness. 'Myriads' shows an unusual awareness of the slaughter that was taking place, while 'still and stiff' instantly suggests the laid-out corpses."[19] But the simile is ambiguous. Water among reeds is life-giving, and elsewhere in the poem it is associated with love, sympathy, and the purity of "washing me cleaner than I have been." On the other hand, the water is a flood, drowning life, breaking the reeds, and dissolving emotions, whether of pain, sympathy, or love. Moreover, Thomas presents himself as "Helpless among the living and the dead," as if he were in some third condition between the two. The simile is then complicated further when it prompts another comparison:

> Like me who have no love which this wild rain
> Has not dissolved except the love of death,
> If love it be towards what is perfect and
> Cannot, the tempest tells me, disappoint.

Love is now transferred to death, but the emotion is still uncertain ("if love it be"), and we feel this is no simple death-wish. The perfection of death is challenged by the hesitation of the last line whose disappointment suggests that even death offers an ambiguous release. What started, then, as a familiar pathetic fallacy has become more complicated. Thomas's meditation turns on itself, drawing images of the external world into its operation, confusing them, making them serve in its self-questioning. He finds no consolation or assurance in his feelings, as he dramatizes them through the play of images. He worries at an image until it becomes an expression of his worry.

His loss is even greater in "The Glory" (*CP*, 199), where he seeks in himself human qualities (wisdom, strength, happiness) to match the glory of the beauty of the morning. His argument falls into a series of unanswerable questions, through which he challenges himself until even his own feelings are in doubt. The more he questions, the more he obscures his goal, until he again resorts to simile: "Or must I be content with discontent / As larks and swallows are perhaps with wings?" The paradox of being content with discontent can be resolved, although it is cold comfort; but how is it analogous to the relation between bird and wing, and what is its relation to the original, glorious scene where we first met these birds? Thomas criticized Swinburne for using similes so contrived that there is a "confusion of categories and indefinite definiteness of images"; they are "carried so far that the matter of the simile is more important in the total than what it appeared to intensify" (*ACS*, 92, 90). In his own practice, however, Thomas puts the indefinite definiteness of his imagery to good use. The comparison is vivid, yet it puzzles us by its remoteness and so conveys the intensity and complexity of his state of mind. As in "Rain," he weaves into his meditation images from the scene which originally provoked it, but he does not succeed in making the scene more accessible. The simile attempts but fails to establish the correspondence between scene and observer that the poem set out to find: the "happiness ... fit to dwell / In beauty's presence." Consequently, at the end of the poem Thomas is forced to admit: "I cannot bite the day to the core." His inability to identify, let alone seize, his happiness leads to an inability to appreciate natural beauty. He is then cut off from the glory which at first seemed so apparent.

His arguments may lead to union with or alienation from the source of life, health, peace, glory. Bottomley once claimed that Thomas's poetry was able to "touch natural things 'with a large and simple emotion' " (*LGB*, 158), but Thomas knew this was false. On the contrary, his emotions become so complex that they refuse to be argued into submission. Instead they disclose a personality acquainted with its own intricacies, but unable to touch or possess itself. He indicates this problem when he offers to his wife, Helen: "myself, too, if I could find / Where it lay hidden and it proved kind" (*CP*, 299). Furthermore, he cannot always "touch natural things"; often they, too, elude his grasp. His poems begin by exploring and celebrating natural beauty, but they sometimes end by losing touch with its glory. At one limit of Thomas's argument, therefore, is a loss of vision. One of the characters in *The South Country* laments: "I am weary of seeing things, the outsides of things, for I see nothing else. It makes me wretched to think what swallows are to many children and poets and other men, while to me they are nothing but inimitable, compact dark weights tumbling I do not know how through the translucent air – nothing more, and yet I know they are something more. I apprehend their weight, buoyancy and velocity as they really are, but I have no vision." (SC, 86). This is a familiar romantic dilemma. The world divorced from the self becomes lifeless and mechanical when the poetic observer loses what Coleridge calls "My shaping spirit of Imagination," or Thomas calls "the power to see a thing as one and whole, and apart from its mechanism and anatomy" (*WP*, 130). It is characteristic of Thomas that a traditional, literary problem is also a matter of painful, personal experience. As we have seen (in the treatment of love in "These Things that Poets Said"; in the description of poppies in *The Heart of England*), he assesses his own character and articulates his depression by citing literary precedents. Like Wordsworth and Coleridge, then, he loses the "clear eye" which, in his poem to Helen, he presents as one of his talents. He sees the outside of things but not the inner reality. In his letters, too, he laments his inability to see or to appreciate what he sees. Vision is defeated by argument: "then suddenly seeing how beautiful it was, I thought I ought to enjoy it & could not think how.... It is no use walking, for I do nothing but feed my eyes when I walk, and it has at last occurred to me that that is not enough ... (*LGB*, 139); "The weather is often perfect for walking & this country provides innumerable walks ... I wish I could enjoy with something more than my senses & a sort of .00001 of my soul, the rest being either torpid or hunched up thinking long exhausted thoughts" (*LFY*, 51).

Hugh Underhill argues that Thomas imaginatively removes himself from "the actual" in order to return and reconcile himself with it, that he employs a "paradoxical means of reconciliation with life through escape." Later in his essay, Underhill notes a "curious distancing of the experiencing mind from the subject of its rumination."[20] In several poems, however, Thomas does not succeed in reducing this distance and remains at odds with his own meditation. Nor does he return to or reconcile himself with the world of palpable fact. He fails to recapture reality or to possess himself. He finds not joy but melancholy, not "home" but "Only an avenue, dark, nameless, without end" (*CP*, 21). The avenue of long exhausted thought leads not to "liberty" but, in

"The Signpost," to an inability to seize the moment of choice and the immediate reality it offers. He finds not "a season of bliss unchangeable," but only "How dreary-swift is time, with naught to travel to" (*CP*, 199). In the beginning of this line of argument is the desire to be "As happy as the earth is beautiful"; at its conclusion is the discovery, "I cannot bite the day to the core."

I do not mean to imply in the preceding discussion that Thomas is a poet who fails, or who writes only about failure. I hope I have shown, on the contrary, that his arguments and his personality - each serving the other - are far too complex to be judged in the simple terms of success or failure. Nor do his poems always leave him in despair. They end in various and varied moods, in which he may be content with discontent or discontented with contentment. But his arguments are often inconclusive and puzzling, especially when, in their "lucid uncertainty," they fail to achieve the self-possession that is their declared aim. They then provide an unstable locus of argument, understood as both a state of being (a fully integrated self) and a basis for thought (an unreasonable reverie). The poetic personality fails to locate, define, or master itself - to find its "home." In this respect Edward resembles Dylan Thomas, who is so different in other ways. Dylan also charts the waking dream of unreason, although he would like not only to bite the day to the core, but to swallow it whole. His epic appetite is the subject of the next chapter.

CHAPTER FOUR

Dylan Thomas

In a letter complaining about the composition of *Under Milk Wood*, Dylan Thomas noted that through "the complicated violence of the words" his comedy was turning into "some savage and devious metaphysical lyric" (*SL*, 364).[1] The phrase more accurately describes his poetry, which deviously and energetically argues about questions of life and death in a manner that is nevertheless lyrical. Although never a learned thinker,[2] he was fascinated by thought and by the intensity and intricacy of its operation; that is, he had a passionate mind, which wrestled with ideas and delighted in ingenious means of expressing this conflict. Like Edward Thomas, he regards the dispute of the mind with itself as an essential human characteristic and a model of poetic effort. In different ways both writers define themselves through poetic argument, but only by rooting their efforts in a problematic sense of self that must always prove its worth by contesting its fate. Both aim at self-possession, but they are often bewildered by a logic through which they intend initially to affirm and free themselves. The locus of their arguments is intimate, moral, unreasonable, and, for Dylan Thomas, highly theatrical. Where Edward is tentative but thorough, Dylan is aggressive and festive, although his enthusiasm sometimes leads him to unexpected conclusions. The word "festive" suggests joyful celebration, a tone Dylan often adopts; but festivals can also be bizarre or grotesque, and I have already suggested that the festival of reason reveals the darker implications of logic. In his poetry Thomas contests these disconcerting implications. He employs a rhetoric of celebration, insistence, and aggrandizement, by which his poems strain to become epic arguments, that turn even the loss of self into a grand adventure.

Northrop Frye points out an interesting connection between festivity, in the classical comic sense, and the irrational. The tragic myth that expresses the inevitable progress from birth to death "is the basis of the great alliance of nature and reason, the sense of nature as a rational order in which all movement is toward the increasingly predictable." The comic myth, leading from death back to rebirth, is also natural, yet it seems irrational, unpredictable, and miraculous: "We can see that death is the inevitable result of birth, but new life is not the inevitable result of death. It is hoped for, even expected, but at its core is something unpredictable and mysterious, something that belongs to the imaginative equivalents of faith, hope, and love, not to the rational virtues."[3] This sense of the unreasonable side of reason, and of the way that the human comedy is frustrated by a mortal doublecross that must be met by faith and love, suffuses the poetry of Dylan Thomas. Of all the poets studied in this book, he seems to be the most in love with unreason, that beguiling fiction of modernist theory that allows it to argue cogently yet wonderfully. His sense of the unreasonable is less sophisticated than Moore's and less thoughtful than Edward Thomas's, but it is more wonderful, festive, and defiant. Its effect is disruptive but not, he insists, anarchic. He agrees with Graves that Mr Hyde should never escape the sober influence of Dr Jekyll. Nevertheless, even as he claims that his poems are not surrealistic, amorphous, or random, they tap a primal energy that precedes and defies reason, because it derives from a larger, wilder vitality associated with sex, imagination, and death –"the force that through the green fuse drives the flower." The result is an elegantly formal poetry, which mistrusts the forms that give it shape. Thomas proposes what he calls "shapes" and "adventures" – arguments about himself and his poetic destiny – through which he tries to define himself and master his fate. But he does not always reach the conclusion he sought, not because he is illogical, but because his logic proves disruptive. It discovers darker truths.

Thomas's critics have in effect acknowledged this difficulty by making two rival claims: on the one hand that he is "the least intellectual poet of this century" because his poetry does not appeal to or depend on reason;[4] on the other hand that his work displays "rigorous intellectual organization" which provokes a subtle play of thought.[5] The contradiction is in keeping with the modernist ambition to be irrational yet cogent. Thomas, the boisterous magician and bard, seems to provide a fine example of the logic of the imagination. The first claim is not just that his "mind had no metaphysical proclivities,"[6] but that his poems rely on unreason rather than logic, because they are "not intellectual or cerebral, but so spontaneous that the poet himself might well be amazed and bewildered in the face of them."[7] They attempt to "short-cut the reason" in pursuit of "extra-rational communication."[8] The second claim stresses the vigilance of the waking dream. It may accept "the cult of irrationality," but it insists that Thomas combines "the irrational bases of poetic power with a rigorous intellectual control,"[9] which permits his metaphysical debate: "Central to his work, therefore, is a proto-philosophical, impassioned *questioning* of the the ultimates – origins and ends – of existence. The vision which results is not philosophical in the abstract sense, but concrete, imaginative, poetic."[10]

Thomas seems to sanction both views. On the one hand he warns, "The head's vacuity can breed no truth / Out of its sensible tedium" (*N*, 126). He mischievously defends his poems by telling Vernon Watkins that their form is "consistently emotional" and "illogical naturally: except by a process it's too naturally obvious to misexplain" (*VW*, 54, 56). On the other hand he proclaims himself a "painstaking, conscientious, involved and devious craftsman in words,"[11] and advises Pamela Hansford Johnson to "intellectualize more," to put her "literary intelligence to work" (*EPW*, 136, 128) so that her poetry will express a "mentally digested experience" (*SL*, 57). Inevitably, he seeks to reconcile the two views by advocating "passionate ideas" that come to life "out of the red heart through the brain" (*EPW*, 165). Thought and reverie must equally be engaged in an "antagonistic interplay of emotion and ideas" (*SL*, 14). The song must be devious and thought provoking; the metaphysic must be lyrical. In "Should Lanterns Shine" (*P*, 116), however, he discovers a problem that upsets the neat balance:

> I have been told to reason by the heart,
> But heart, like head, leads helplessly;
> I have been told to reason by the pulse,
> And, when it quickens, alter the actions' pace
> Till field and roof lie level and the same
> So fast I move defying time ...

How can he reconcile the two faculties (thought and feeling, reason and imagination), which are unruly in themselves as well as antagonistic? Even reason proves unreasonable when it leads helplessly. How can the pulse of life and intelligence, which registers the passing of time, be used to defy time in a work of art? In other words, how can he successfully argue against death, when death is the grand irrationality that confutes his arguments? For Thomas, unreason is always in some way plagued by death.

These questions are disputed in his poetry, where they provoke both theoretical and thematic difficulties, because they engage his fundamental notions about what poetry is, how it makes its statements and argues its case. Several critics insist that Thomas never solved his problem, because he never learned to "reason by the heart." He abused his reason, and wasted an "alert and sober intelligence" on verbal tricks,[12] instead of using it to create a coherent "system" or "poetic."[13] The intricate "rhetorical plan" of many poems offers the semblance of orderly thought, but no real "development or argument";[14] it is metaphorically and metaphysically irresponsible. But Thomas's poems, as well as his many comments on poetry, show that he appreciated the dilemma and was in fact trying to define a poetic system. He condemned his own emotional and oratorical excesses ("immature violence ... frequent muddleheadedness, and very much overweighted imagery that leads too often to incoherence"), precisely because he wished to be systematic and to devise a rigorous "poetical argument" that "can only be worked out in the poems" (*SL*, 161, 196). His problem arises because his head leads logically but "helplessly." In this chapter I wish to show how he devised an equivocal system with which to argue against death, a system that is challenged by its own claims about unreason, since it frustrates the poet even as it liberates him. His early writing especially shows how he came to regard poetry as a vehicle of thought, debate, and persuasion; how he sets himself within his poetic disputes or, conversely, how he sets them within the epic drama of himself; and what rhetoric he uses to shape his arguments.

Thomas believes that a poem must prove itself by engaging the reader in a strenuous emotional and intellectual adventure. John Malcolm Brinnen reports that Thomas "had picked up somewhere a notion that he liked: poems are hypothetical and theorematic. In this view the hypothesis of a poem would be the emotional experience, the instant of vision or insight, the source of radiance, the minute focal point of impulse and impression. While these make up what is commonly called inspiration, poetic logic should prove the validity of the ephemeral moments they describe. To look at a new poem, then, is to ask: How successfully does it demonstrate its hypothesis?"[15] To be valid, every poem must establish an argument through which it "moves only towards its own end." It has to prove something, though what it proves is nothing but itself: it is "its own question and answer ... the bullet and the bull's-eye" (*SL*, 196). It must strive to make itself self-evident, to demonstrate rather than to make statements. Thomas advises Pamela Hansford Johnson not just to assert in her verse that she is one with nature, but also to "prove it" through "the magic of words and images" (*SL*, 80). He sees no contradiction in uniting proof with magic - the waking dream again - because a poet must make his or her words not simply true, but "effectively true" (*VW*, 53). They must overwhelm the reader and win assent. Consequently, he is not content with ordinary logic, which seems too pedestrian, but insists on an impassioned unreason that displays "heart and mind and muscle" (*SL*, 338). Poetry is also an argument in the sense of a dispute, a "rumpus of shapes" (*P*, 4), which is muscular and brawling. Its passionate ideas require a "passionate wordiness," which comes from "a pen dipped in fire and vinegar" (*SL*, 14), writing in "the final intensity of language" (*QEM*, 99). Through the urgency of its language a poem not only wins approval, but triumphs over doubt. Hence the immature violence of his early poems which Thomas wished to control, but not to subdue. The momentary peace which is a poem comes only after a battle of words and wits, a prolonged effort which he often calls an "adventure."

The adventure of a poem is the unfolding and enforcing of its hypothesis. "All poetical impulses are toward the creation of adventure. And adventure is movement. And the end of each adventure is a new impulse to move again towards creation" (*QEM*, 99). This grand conception of poetry and its mission promises truth not solely as a logical conclusion, but as a dramatic victory of thought over the forces that would extinguish it. If poems are adventures, then they are risky and inquisitive, and in order to invigorate his arguments, Thomas tries to harness what he treats as an unreasonable, dangerous vitality. Poems flirt with creative disaster. As they advance toward their desired ends, they raise questions, explore the unknown, conduct a "brief adventure in the wilderness" (*SL*, 24). The wildness and wilderness of thought – which the poet must tap and control, but not succumb to – are located deep within the writer, because poetry is essentially introspective. Thomas's arguments, after venturing outward, circle back on himself and give rise to his characteristic themes. Although he told Trevor Hughes that he was fascinated by "each bright and naked object" in the "literal world," he is genuinely interested in things only when they contribute to the adventure of himself. He wants "to bring these wonders into myself, to prove beyond doubt to myself that the flesh that covers me is the flesh that covers the sun, that the blood in my lungs is the blood that goes up and down in a tree" (*SL*, 91, 87). Sun and tree become aspects of himself, the reverse of what occurs with Edward Thomas, who more modestly wishes to yield himself to his surroundings. If Edward suggests the sympathetic, unassuming aspect of romantic imagination, Dylan suggests the complementary egotistical sublime. He displays the proud humility that Hazlitt found in Wordsworth who, even when describing nature, "sees all things in himself ... An intense intellectual egotism swallows up everything ... The power of his mind preys upon itself. It is as if there were nothing but himself and the universe."[16] Similarly, when Thomas argues that "The force that through the green fuse drives the flower / Drives my green age" (*P*, 77), he draws the energy of the universe into himself, until he becomes the epic hero of his life.

"Like Whitman before him, he must make his poetry his own ego," explains John Bayley, because of a compulsion "to embody the experience of being himself."[17] This identification of poetry and ego means that the self is not just the hero of a story; it is the locus of the adventure and the argument: "I was aware of myself in the exact middle of a living story, and my body was my adventure and my name" (*PAD*, 18). The story is both Thomas's hazardous trial of being himself and the process of disputing that experience in poetry. It is the story told by "hero," "neophyte," "animal," and "intricate image" about their journey through life, and it is the argument that the poem conducts in order to justify that journey. The concurrence of adventure and argument means that the forms of Thomas's poems are determined by the complex way in which he conceives of the self. He rarely writes autobiographically, especially in the early poetry, perhaps because he was aware of the dangers of arrogance and sentimentality that beset the lyrical narcissist. Later he feels mature enough to be personal, but in the meantime, he disparages the "saccharine wallowings of near-schoolboys in the bowels of a castrated muse" (*SL*, 25) and the "private masturbatory preoccupation of the compulsive egoist" (*EPW*, 80). As a corrective he creates an impersonal, fabulous self that is set at a safe distance from the author to serve as hero and victim of a dangerous voyage. Like other mythical heroes, the self is born to face a great curse and a great destiny. From the instant of conception it has an unformulated potential that it strives to realize. Implicit in it is a prelogical instinct, which it shares with all life and which drives it on a quest for liberation, self-assertion and self-possession. There is little peace or repose in Thomas's poetry, even in the later brooding and nostalgic works, because of the passionate wordiness that urges the hero through his fate. In the notebook poems the impulse for liberation first appears as a vague yearning for power, love, faith, sanity, escape, or hope:

> Let me escape,
> Be free, (wind for my tree and water for my flower),
> Live self for self
> And drown the gods in me. (*N*, 77)
> Hold on whatever slips beyond the edge
> To hope, a firefly in the veins, to trust
> Of loving, to keeping close. (*N*, 167)

In the published poetry the impulse is expressed through imagery of sun, song, ascent, and later by grace, joy, glory. In "If I Were Tickled by the Rub of Love" (*P*, 94-96) a slight irritation prompts him to explore his humanity, but when at the end he proclaims "Man be my metaphor" (*P*, 96), he makes the ultimate affirmation of his adventure and of the self, despite its contradictions, as the standard of all creation. As we shall see, this is the conclusion to which many of his arguments are directed, but which not all achieve.

His effort to liberate the self and celebrate its life is continually thwarted by the problematic nature of the self's power and enterprise. Because the hero identifies himself with all creation, he is engaged in a "total cosmic adventure"[18] so vast that it seems fatal rather than free. He is swept through a predestined history by forces beyond his control. Because he cannot control even his own impulses, he must assert and free himself through duplicitous powers, which he has not mastered and which often betray him. Consequently, he seems to be the "victim of his experience,"[19] and is often defeated by his own argument, the logic of which becomes damning. The poetic testimony of unreason – which I have defined more carefully as the festival of reason – proves that life is a "mortal miracle," a "doublecross," a wound healed only by death. Very early in his career Thomas seized on the dilemma that was to provoke and hinder all his arguments: "my everlasting idea of the importance of death on the living" (*SL*, 122). From the moment of birth, the neophyte

> sucks no sweetness from the willing mouth,
> Nothing but poison from the breath,
> And, in the grief of certainty,
> Knows his love rots. (*N*, 115)

Although Thomas insists on the dynamic energy of poetry, his rendering of its birth is strangely stultifying. Poetry debates whether or not death will have dominion and questions the nature of death's sovereignty and the worth of the self that is subject to its rule. The debate is endless, marked by temporary victories and defeats, and because of its paradoxical nature, the argument rarely achieves a clear assertion or denial. The characteristic argument is one that sets out as a high adventure but then goes subtly astray, as the poem struggles, with or without success, to set itself straight. It subverts the very terms through which it defines and affirms the self, because it aims at liberation but cannot identify its freedom within the "grief of certainty" or time. It sings of love, but tastes the poison of sin and sex. The hero discovers that he is his own adversary, and through his argument he may condemn rather than redeem himself.

Thomas's challenge, as a young writer, was to express the everlasting dilemma that provoked his poetry. When he tried to give shape to his yearnings for power and freedom, he experimented with techniques that would offer perspective, direction, and momentum to them. He sought a system by which to turn them into adventures and arguments. A common theme that acknowledges the problem is his desire to reason by the heart, to display in an orderly manner the troubled feelings of adolescence:

And my thoughts flow so uneasily
There is no measured sea for them,
No place in which, wave perched on wave,
Such energy may gain
The sense it has to have. (*N*, 89)

The measured sea he lacks is a poetic, which will give coherence and energy ("wave perched on wave") to his ideas and sense to his emotions. It is a principle of order, a logic:

Tether the first thought if you will,
And take the second to yourself
Close for companion, and dissect it, too,
It stays for me
With your no toil....

The aim of his analysis is to interpret and so liberate all aspects of his being:

Have I to show myself to you
In every way I am,
Classic, erotic, and obscene,
Dead and alive,
In sleep and out of sleep,
Tracking my sensibilities,
Gratyfying [sic] my sensualities,
Taking my thoughts piece from piece? (*N*, 96–97)

The first logical order that Thomas tries and immediately rejects is narrative. It provides a sequential pattern, the "movement" of a "living story," and a strong narrating voice to give rhetorical power to his adventures. After a few attempts, often in a Yeatsian manner ("Osiris, Come to Isis," "Hassan's Journey into the World"), he abandons this method, but he retains the desire for a narrative principle. He continues to stress the need for a "progressive line, or theme, of movement in every poem. The more subjective a poem, the clearer the narrative line" it needs in order to ensure its "rhythmic, inevitably narrative movement."[20] Only in poems like "A Winter's Tale" and "Ballad of the Long-

Legged Bait" does narrative in the strict sense return to his work, but the progressive line appears in other, curtailed forms. Instead of stories we find dramatic situations, moments of insight or conflict from a narrative whose pattern they suggest: "We who [are] young are old. It is the oldest cry. / Age sours before youth's tasted in the mouth" (*N*, 169). Or they show through temporal clauses that they are parts of a more extensive plan: "Before We Sinned", "Before I Knocked," "Before we mothernaked fell," "When once the twilight locks." Other poems suggest a progressive structure that indicates the shape of the adventure: "From love's first fever to her plague," "A process in the weather of the heart / Turns damp to dry."

In these instances, it is the narrative shape, the contours of the experience, that Thomas retains. From a comment in a letter to Vernon Watkins – "I have made such a difficult shape" (*VW*, 93) – it is apparent that Thomas regarded the whole poem as a shape. Poetry is the "sound of shape" or a "rumpus of shapes," using figures of speech which are "wordy shapes." The figure a poem makes as it traces the curves of emotion and thought is its argument: "A hole in space shall keep the shape of thought, / The lines of earth, the curving of the heart, / And from this darkness spin the golden soul" (*N*, 237). These quotations suggest that the rational shapes of poetry conceal a chaotic "rumpus" or, even more mysterious, a dark "hole" that inhabits yet confounds thought. Because Thomas's argument is always about himself, because poem, ego, and adventure are identified, this interplay of the shapely and the shapeless must reflect the paradoxical nature of the self, which is cursed to live only by dying. The shape that always threatens to grow deformed is in one sense his personality, as it develops from birth to death. When he speaks of his "wizard shape," he means the magical life of a poet; when he prays, "I would be woven a religious shape," he means a holy life. Several of the "process" poems follow the shape of the hero's life from love's first fever to her plague, and the later birthday poems are stages in the same adventure. The shape is also the disposition of the self, which struggles to free itself by articulating and composing itself. And the shape is the poem's unfolding argument, as it seeks an adequate form, as Raymond Stevens shows when he describes the development of "I See the Boys of Summer": "In fact, this poem, in so far as it is successful, actually provides the shaping process of the poet's own awareness, reveals the poet's self in the task of its own self-definition, which is the principle of its own organization dramatically enacted. The organization of the poem is the organization of the poet's mind as it grows to self-realization."[21]

As we have seen, the shape of Thomas's adventure is a mythic struggle from dark to light, a voyage "into the sea of yourself like a young dog and bring out a pearl" (*SL*, 16). The pearl is an ideal self-possession. It is the "golden soul" or "merry manshape" spun from the mind's darkness. It is the victory of both the self and its adventure: the poet-creator must look upon his work and see that it is whole and splendid. Poetry aspires to be the triumph of life – which means the triumph of thought – over the forces that menace it. By arguing against death, it makes "an affirmation of the beautiful and terrible worth of the Earth" (*QEM*, 157). But as we have also seen, the terror comes from within thought, which harbours what Thomas calls a curse, sin, hole, darkness, poison, doublecross, wildness, grief, thief – all manifestations of unreason that threatens to subvert thought and to disintegrate the self. I must now prove again that these destructive forces are not irrational in the sense of being alogical, but are manifestations of logic, which for all its darkness, remains rational. To do so, I must again examine the rhetoric of the arguments.

Thomas sought to replace narrative with a system that would retain a narrative dynamic, that would trace the contours of his experience without relying on autobiography, and that would dramatize the shaping process of his own awareness. This is a large task for a young poet, but he did not deliberately set out to devise such a system; he merely followed the example of other poets. Donald Davie suggests that the desire to "articulate without asserting," to give the "morphology of the feeling, not its distinctive nature" – or, in our terms, to give the shape of the experience, not its substance – is part of the symbolist legacy to modern poetry. It is the desire to write poetry that aspires to the condition of music. He gives as characteristic techniques: "the invention of a fable or an 'unreal' landscape, or the arrangement of images, not for their own sakes, but to stand as a correlative for the experience that is thus the true subject of a poem in which it is never named."[22] This list is not prescriptive or exhaustive, but it provides three useful examples of the rhetorical shaping of Thomas's arguments.

His fondness for heroic fables reflects not so much his egotism, as his compelling need to dominate the waking dream by formulating its inchoate basis. In other words, he must tame unreason if he is to face death. Fables appear to offer him stability and certainty in the midst of adventure, but in practice they also enchant him and frustrate his arguments: "I have divided / Sense into sight and trust. / The certain is a fable" (*N*, 103–4). Fables appeal to both heart and head through their sensuous images (sight) and through the hidden significance or moral (trust), which they dramatize; but because they are fabulous, they are rarely certain and sometimes dangerous. They aid Thomas in what Walford Davies calls "mythologizing the actual,"[23] giving a vivid and noble shape to his experiences. For example, "Today, This Insect"

(*P*, 124–5), which adapts these lines, shows the poet as he transforms an ordinary insect into the "plague of fables." The inversion of terms hints, however, that, as stories proliferate, they may become destructive. The poet, as sorcerer's apprentice, releases a magic that plagues him. Nevertheless, fables offer the power and elevation that Thomas demands of poetry, contact with other literary works, and, above all, heroes to undertake the quest of self-liberation. His favourite stories are the biblical adventure from Genesis to Apocalypse, the "Christian voyage" from annunciation to resurrection, and the human pilgrimage from conception to death. Comparable to these and giving voice to them is a fable of language, advancing from "rocking alphabet" and creative Word to a "world of words" (*PS*, 85), promising a redemptive vision of the whole universe made eloquent, as it arises from and returns to silence: "In the beginning was a word I can't spell, not a reversed Dog, or a physical light, but a word as long as Glastonbury and as short as pith. Nor does it lisp like the last word, break wind like Balzac through a calligraphied window, but speaks out sharp & everlastingly with the intonations of death and doom on the magnificent syllables" (*SL*, 127). The fascination with words expressed here reflects a delight in life and a faith that language can articulate our doom and thus redeem us from it, rather than allow us to succumb blindly to it. The redemption is aesthetic in nature more than it is religious.

The virtue of these fables is that they have congruent, organic, temporal shapes. All are voyages over the "seafaring years" impelled by the "drive of time." Time is the forum and often the antagonist of the early adventures ("But time has set its maggot on their track") and sometimes seems to be the cruel god from whose disfavour the epic hero flees. But through Thomas's favourite paradox it is also the impulse of growth and liberation. It both sustains and kills us, providing the energy to live and to die. It is thief and surgeon, grief and patient gentleman. The temporal shape of the fables is both aided and plagued by the continuity provided by inheritance – the heritage of biblical sin, of Christian suffering and redemption, of human and family traits, of "All that I owe the fellows of the grave." Inheritance is the ambiguous blessing of time, since it is both an external force, the curse of "bonebound fortune" imposed on us, and an inner compulsion working within us from the moment of conception. It is a principle of comforting unity amid diversity, but also of baffling variety within unity. It gives us our peculiar, mercurial features, even as it merges us with the family of mankind from Adam to the present. It both identifies us and deprives us of individuality:

> Am I not father, too, and the ascending boy,
> The boy of woman and the wanton starer

Marking the flesh and summer in the bay?
Am I not sister, too, who is my saviour?
Am I not all of you by the directed sea ... (*P*, 112)

Inheritance is the legacy of pleasure and pain, of "all the flesh inherits." It is a legacy of growth through decay, as Thomas suggests through puns on the words wax, sheet, and grain:

All night and day I wander in these same
Wax clothes that wax upon the ageing ribs;
All night my fortune slumbers in its sheet.
Then look, my heart, upon the scarlet trove,
And look, my grain, upon the falling wheat. (*P*, 81)

Through puns and oxymorons, Thomas likes to fuse the beginning and end of a fable in a clever phrase: "the living grave," "the milk of death," "the endless beginning," "My Jack of Christ born thorny on the tree." Three fables converge in "the Christ-cross-row [alphabet] of death." This compression has the ambiguous effect of celebrating the tragic grandeur of our fate, yet of suggesting also that it is stultifying, because it repeats itself without truly progressing. The narrative impulse of growth is stymied, because the same fatal conclusion is always presupposed by the beginning. The dynamic adventure proves to be strangely static, as all its energy is dissipated. We find this dilemma in the poem, "In the Beginning":

In the beginning was the pale signature,
Three-syllabled and starry as the smile;
And after came the imprints on the water,
Stamp of the minted face upon the moon;
The blood that touched the crosstree and the grail
Touched the first cloud and left a sign. (*P*, 94)

The starry three-syllabled signature is Jehovah, Jesus Christ, zodiac, *lux fiat*, the poet's work, and all of creation. The imprints on the water are Christ's footsteps, poetry, the face of the waters at creation and at birth. The man in the moon adds another fable to the freshly coined creation, while the grail suggests the quests of Christ, Adam ("the ribbed original of love"), and of every nobleman through a universe marked with ambivalent signs and portents. The poem's biblical tone proclaims the harmony, vitality, and sexuality of creation. It demonstrates that every beginning implies a motive ("the mounting fire"), purpose ("the secret brain"), pattern ("The word flowed up"), end, and new beginning – the endless adventure of human life. Optimistically, it aims to prove that man is heroic and at home in a universe which, for all its terror, remains passionately human. But at the same time it reveals that genesis is moribund. Because the poem is plagued by its dilemma, it cannot really develop, only circle back on itself. This does not mean that it is illogical, only that its argument discovers unexpected consequences, which in one sense have been foreseen all along. Its logic depends on a compression of evocative images ("burning ciphers"), which reveal the endless correspondences between fables. The argument of the poem develops by increasing its density and range of reference, making its texture increasingly rich, but thereby confirming the doom already present in the generative imagery.

The culmination of this dual argument is "Altarwise by Owl-Light" (*P*, 116–21), the most devious of Thomas's adventures. Its ideas are debated with passion and wit, yet it remains lyrical, a sonnet-sequence whose musical imagery expresses the cosmic harmony that its hero, at war with his own impulses, continually disrupts and recomposes. The "tale's sailor" is Christ, Adam, the poet, Rip Van Winkle, Ishmael, Odysseus, and Pharoah, all intermingled through a network of cross-references and the deliberate confusion of personal pronouns. Its shape depends on the circle of its adventures that are impelled by a series of contests between rival forces: devil and angel, Abaddon and Jack Christ, winter and spring, worm and whale, evil index and Lord's prayer, furies and ladies, Cancer and Capricorn, crossbones and sawbones, time's joker and time's nerve, hollow and marrow, flood and rainbow, desert and garden. The profusion of terms expresses the richness of life and the corresponding richness of the mind, which relishes the spectacle of its own workings as it contemplates that wealth. The strength of the argument is that, despite its compressed allusiveness, it remains remarkably neat and logical. It grows in range and complexity through an expansion from the microscopic to the cosmic, from "short spark" to "long world," an elaboration that accounts for, though it may not always justify, the encyclopaedic imagery. The danger is that network will become clutter. The mind may not be content with the spectacle of its own activity, but will grow suspicious of – to use Raymond Stevens's phrase cited above – the shaping process of the poet's own awareness. When the poem mistrusts the forms that it relies on to give it shape, the glorious cycle of creation becomes a vicious circle.

Although the fables contribute patterns of imagery to the poem, they never supply a purposeful narrative development. All their episodes are present simultaneously, often compressed in a phrase: "the scarecrow word," "The gentleman lay graveward with his furies," "December's thorn screwed in a brow of holly." The dynamic, which Thomas sees as the essence of narrative, derives only from the proliferation of contrasts and correspondences between and within fables, from the sense of expansion and elaboration, and from a regular rhythm of affirmation and denial that dramatizes the poet's struggle to understand and accept his fate. Each sonnet disputes the central issue - "the importance of death on the living" and of life on the dying - seeking to affirm the validity of the dispute and the worth of the self, but inevitably casting doubt on the enterprise. The poetic self is alternately affirmed and denied, composed and dispersed, as the poet argues himself into and out of existence. If we consider the shape of the entire poem, we find its argument arranged in pairs; each sonnet examines one stage of the adventure, but reaches a different conclusion. The first and last sonnets provide a frame, by setting the limits of the fables from genesis in the Christward shelter to the harbour of the Day of Judgment. Corresponding images suggest at first, departure on the adventure, and at the end, arrival or completion. We begin in the direction of the beginning, altarwise, approaching the mystery, hatching heaven's egg; and we end atlaswise, after seeing the world and its wonders. We start with the windy salvage of creation, and finish with the ship-racked gospel of the Apocalypse. Despite the religious vocabulary, however, Thomas does not commit himself to a truly transcendent perspective. Consequently, he remains tossed by the unavailing terms (time, milk, generation, fate, thought) of his argument.

Sonnets II and III focus on cradle and garden time and dispute the death implicit in the age of innocence. Both try to climb the rungs of Jacob's ladder and Adam's rib, that is, to triumph over death through the very means of generation that ensures our destruction. This paradox is at the heart of the poem and prompts the zigzag of its argument, as the same images generate opposite conclusions, not because they defy logic, but because they depend on the attitude of the poet toward the unreasonableness of death. On the one hand, if death is "all metaphors, shape in one history," then all history is negated or "shapeless," because every moment, including the first, is doomed. The hollow agent mocks us with the last word in the first contest. On the other hand, in the second contest grave and worm are horned down, spring prevails, and Rip Van Winkle awakens because he has been baptized "breast-deep in the descending bone." This image, which is both Christian and sexual, suggests a victory not over but through generative forces, whose essential vitality is reaffirmed by recognizing how they are bound up with death. The chimes at the end celebrate the vitality of time and its "weathering changes," thus restoring a temporary shape and purpose to history.

Sonnets IV and V bring the young hero (the "shape of years") into the adventure of time, and raise similar questions to which they give different answers. Shape is again a moment's confidence, shapelessness a moment's doubt. The first, by questioning the scope and value of the voyage of life, confirms death as a destructive flood that drowns the child, who is love's reflection and God's image. The ribs of Adam prove a boneyard corset, a cemetery that offers little protection to the hump of splinters it guards. The hollow agent triumphs again as the bamboo man; but as the fake gentleman in the next sonnet, he is defeated and exposed as cheat and false prophet. The flood continues as a climbing sea, which provides another baptism in life and is identified through medusa and sirens with sin and sexuality. But it is also identified through "our lady's sea-straw" with redemption. This time the hero is rescued and rises like Jonah from the whale or Rip Van Winkle from the undertaker's van, to withstand his hazardous odyssey.

Sonnets VI and VII unite hero, lover, and poet, and shift to the fable of speech, which advances from oyster vowels and the kindling of the wick of words to the full scripture of the "Bible-leaved ... book of trees." The poems describe a quest through language, which offers either prayer or curse, remedy or plague, eloquence or silence. In both, words provide a means of liberation and celebration, the source of creative power, which he needs in order to free himself, but in which he is also trapped. Both attempt to be love songs that praise "time, milk and magic," but the first proves to be a witch's spell or evil index that makes Adam time's joker; while the second proves to be a blessing (the Lord's prayer), by once again affirming life (milk), time, and history. In the linguistic terms of these two sonnets, however, time and history depend on the temporal unfolding of narrative which, as we have seen, offers only the illusion of progress as it circles back to its beginning. "Time tracks the sound of shape on man and cloud" suggests that the song – now on a phonograph – is the poetry of man's life and the beauty of his adventure through the world. At the same time the "sound of shape" suggests how insubstantial are the words – associated with light, air, sea, and music – to which the poet has entrusted his fate.

In parallel paradoxes, sonnets VIII and IX present crucifixion and resurrection. The first is a bitter death that ensures life and victory for "Time's nerve in vinegar," Christ; the second is an elaborate ritual of immortality, a mummification that ensures only "Death from a bandage." In the first, the world's wound is tended by all glory's sawbones; in the second, as in sonnet VI, the wound never heals. These paradoxes and contradictions emphasize that the hero exists in a permanent state of conflict with fate, furies, sex, and time, because the same conditions grant him victory and defeat. However, "Altarwise By Owl-Light" is so persistent in rediscovering, as if for the first time, the wonder of its everyday magic, that its final impression is positive. Its tone is celebratory, as it returns to the fables and delights in the growing density of their interrelation. Its argument is conducted with equivocal terms and images, through assertion and denial to a final affirmation, which prevails not despite but because of the periodic defeats. At the end the call is to "let the garden diving / Soar." The "nest of mercies" is woven with the "gold straws of venom." Death is not negated but temporarily incorporated into the harmonious shape of the whole argument.

Death is not negated, because it cannot be argued away. The argument of the poem never becomes a true dialectic, because the opposing forces continually oscillate but reach no higher synthesis or resolution. For all its expansiveness, therefore, the entire sonnet sequence continually reaffirms and seeks comfort in its own limitations. Perhaps this is the reason why Thomas never completed it: the debate can always be renewed. The resurrections that it proclaims occur only *within* a life of "Time, milk and magic." The triumph of sonnet VIII is not over but through time, as measured by Christ's great heartbeat, just as in sonnets III, V and VII the victories are sung and rung to "Time's tune." This redemption of time through time is quite different from the conditional but confident transcendental hope in Moore's later poems and utterly different from the mystical pattern of motion and stillness, shape and shapelessness in Eliot's *Four Quartets*. For Thomas, the Christian fable is only one story among others. It does not provide a means of transcending the plague of time, only of raging against it, or at best, of accepting it and its heartbreak. Similarly, his triumph is not over but through generation, the baptism of the descending bone. Viewed optimistically in Sonnet VIII, time and milk (generation) are themselves magical, and the hero proves that he is heroic and lives "in the exact centre of enchantment" (*PS*, 93). His life is a marvel, because the forces that shape and limit it – history, sex, and death – are marvellous. Viewed pessimistically, the enchantment again becomes a curse, the magic an evil index.

The second rhetorical technique that Thomas uses to shape his arguments – imaginary landscape – is an aspect of his interest in fables. It, too, first appears in the notebooks, where he relies on the changing features of a scene to establish a pattern of thought and feeling. The setting is sometimes literal, sometimes metaphorical:

The hill of sea and sky is carried
High on the sounding wave,
To float, an island in its size,
And stem the waters of the sun

Which fall and fall. (*N*, 69–70)
Your voice can be the voice
Of the sea under the hard sun,
The sea speaking keenly,
Or the voice of the river
Moving in one direction,
In a pattern like a shell
Lying upon the yellow beach. (*N*, 61)

The landscape that appears in the early poetry is a generalized one, composed of earth, air, fire, and water, driven by elemental forces of weather, wind, tides, and seasons. It varies little from poem to poem. In the "process" poems the scene moves inward and becomes the human anatomy, which Thomas called "my solid and fluid world of flesh and blood" (*SL*, 47):

We see rise the secret wind behind the brain,
The sphinx of light sit on the eyes,
The code of stars translate in heaven.
A secret night descends between
The skull, the cells, the cabinned ears
Holding for ever the dead moon. (*N*, 233)

This poem looks ahead to the more familiar "Ears in the turrets hear" and indicates the profusion of symbols, codes, and secrets by which Thomas kept his literary world articulate but mysterious. The text of the earth and of the body speaks to us, but only in riddles, as it draws us into debate. In later poems, such as "Over Sir John's Hill" and "In the White Giant's Thigh," the landscape reemerges as a recognizable Welsh scene, but even then it retains some of its fabulous qualities. Thomas notes the shift in his use of landscape, when he refers to "Poem in October" (published February 1945) as "a Laugharne poem: the first place poem I've written" (*VW*, 114).

Thomas argues through landscape, just as he does through fables. The setting provides images that represent the experience that occurs within it. Poems of this sort give only the lie of the land, or present a land that lies (speaks equivocally), because, in Donald Davie's terms, they give the morphology of the experience but not its distinctive nature. They never declare what the experience in question actually is; they present a conflict of natural forces or evoke an atmosphere that is never precisely defined. The best example of a poem that argues equivocally by exploring its landscape is "We Lying by Seasand." In the notebook version (16 May 1933; *N*, 198–9) Thomas compresses his narrative into one episode of effort and failure. Very little happens to the unnamed people, whose ineffectual desires are given by the verbs of the poem: mock, deride, follow, watch, fend off. Instead, Thomas concentrates on the setting and establishes, mainly through nouns and adjectives, a contrast between the grave, yellow seasand on the one hand and the more colourful red rivers and "Navy blue bellies of the tribes" on the other. The first setting is passive and supine; the second, with its suggestion of poetry ("Alcove of words") and sailors is active and adventurous. This neat balancing of terms gives a symmetrical shape to an argument that ultimately cannot be trusted. At first, however, it sustains the "calling for colour," which is the main desire of the poem and which is also expressed through landscape, in particular through the wind, which will "blow away / The strata of the shore and leave red rock." Feeble though it may be, this is the call to active self-assertion that Thomas's poems frequently make. But the characters make no real effort ("But wishes breed not"), and their desires are thwarted by the very landscape through which they tried to assert them. The wind proves ambiguous. Instead of a breath of life, it is a "sandy smother ... of death."

The argument of "We Lying by Seasand" is subverted by the landscape, which proves ambiguous and untrustworthy, and by the lethargic rhythm, which undercuts the call to action. The logic, too, is confounded by confusing syntax ("mock who deride / Who follow"), which makes it unclear who is doing what; and by misleading connectives. In the lines, "For in this yellow grave twixt sea and sand / A calling for colour calls with the wind," the word "For" seems to announce a logical connection to advance the argument. But it does not relate the earlier mocking and deriding to the subsequent calling for colour. A similar lapse in logic occurs in the lines, "But wishes breed not, neither / Can we fend off the sandy smother." The sequence "But ... neither" seems to announce a logical relation but fails to do so. The wish for a cleansing wind is declared ineffectual, but the very next line contradicts the declaration by saying that the wind – now a sandy smother – is inevitable. Davie claims that such "pseudo-syntax," while formally correct, "cannot mime, as it offers to do, a movement of the mind"[24] and therefore cannot argue. In this case, however, the mind tries and fails to make sense of its experience. It confounds itself and, through its attempt to reason, dramatizes a state of torpor and confusion. The failure to argue coherently by interpreting the landscape expresses the lethargy of the characters, whose attempt to rouse themselves is discouraged by the very effort of doing so.

Thomas's revision of the poem (published January 1937), far from clarifying the argument, subverts it further. He expands and complicates the landscape, thereby complicating the experience it represents. The additions increase the poem's density and ambiguity, by confusing the impulses toward affirmation and dissolution. They both counter and confirm the torpor which inhibits the poem's development. For example, the line "That's grave and *gray* as grave and sea" becomes "That's grave and *gay* as grave and sea," relaxing the music of the line slightly and making wind and sea simultaneously deadly and lively. A moon is added which "should cure our ills," yet it is dry, silent, and ribbed. The "heavenly music over the sand" implies poetry, inspiration, winds of order, and beauty; or perhaps they are destructive winds, bearing the smothering sands of time. The wind will no longer "*leave* red rock," but will "*drown* red rock." This change gives another twist to the logic by contradicting the "calling for colours" and calling instead for a "one coloured calm." It obscures the colour code which, in the earlier version, made the alternatives offered by the landscape (passive-active, mocking-performing, desiring-striving, yellow-red/blue) clearer. Now there are no clear alternatives because the landscape is not symbolic in any trustworthy way.

Setting, rhythm, and the confusion of syntax, logic, and imagery all serve to portray a divided state of mind, striving but failing to come to terms with its own confusion, asserting itself yet lapsing back into lethargy and anguish. And after all, we still do not know exactly what the experience is. W.Y. Tindall detects love and poetry, T.S. Eliot, politics, Hitler, and war in this poem.[25] Tindall's interpretation cannot be disproved but seems far-fetched, because Thomas resolutely argues only through the landscape, finding in it the shapes of feeling and desire and of his poetic effort to master them.

From fable and landscape Thomas draws his third technique: the "host of images" that generate, as he explains in his most elaborate account of his methods, a "dialectical" sequence of destructive and constructive ideas, a battle, whose violence permits the "momentary peace which is a poem" (*SL*, 190). For our purposes the most telling aspect of his description is not its dialectic - which, as "Altarwise by Owl-Light" shows, may vacillate and fail to resolve itself - but its insistence on the generative power of language. He wants to account for what he calls the "life in any poem of mine." In the letter to Henry Treece, he speaks in organic terms (breed, central seed, born, and die, womb of war), in order to indicate the vitality and aggression through which poetry enforces its claims and compels belief. Poetry must be "orgastic and organic as copulation," as it forces its way "from words, from the substance of words and the rhythm of substantial words set together, not towards words" (*SL*, 151). The poet works "out of" rather than "towards" words (a distinction Thomas used frequently), because they are the source of energy, the means of his argument, and his main weapon in the war of images and ideas. Their power resides in their music and rhetoric and in the various ways they can convey meaning. Sound and rhythm may be enough to animate language: "And what a pleasure of baskets! Trugs, creels, pottles and punnets, heppers, dorsers and mounds, wiskets and whiskets. And if these are not the proper words, they should be" (*QEM*, 55). Thomas plays with words here to dazzle the reader into admiration and approval. Admitting that he has invented some of the terms is itself a tactic, a way of drawing attention to them, delighting in their sounds, and endowing them with power. They are coined for the occasion and meaningful only in context, not because they provide more precise definitions, but because they are convincing or "effectively true." Such words "acquire a surprising pleasant strangeness when boomed, minced, Keened, crooned, Dyalled, or Wolfitted. Known words grow wings ..." (*QEM*, 126).

Words are generative when they display such vitality or when they expand in significance or implication. In his early work Thomas experimented with various ways of compressing and concealing meaning, of saying "two things at once in one word, four in two and one in six" (*SL*, 152). One tactic was simply to use images of multiplication in order to insist, sometimes without further proof, on a process of growth and complication.

> In me ten paradoxes make one truth,
> Ten twining roots meet twining in the earth
> To make one root that never strangles light ... (*N*, 207)
> From the divorcing sky I learnt the double,
> The two-framed globe that spun into a score;
> A million minds gave suck to such a bud
> As forks my eye. (*P*, 79)

He also cultivated ambiguity through puns and conflated or rearranged words – manwax, tide-tongued, Bible-leaved, the man in the wind and the west moon. He stretched metaphors and similes to see how far they could extend, how far they could stretch the imagination, although some of his early efforts are clumsy compared to the far-reaching analogies of Moore or Edward Thomas:

> She is a lady of high degree,
> Proud and hard, and she wears a coat

Clinging and strident,
Like a net or a basket of berries. (*N*, 51)

He elaborated the oppositions of a paradox to explore its ramifications:

For welcoming sleep we welcome death,
And death's an end to sleep,
And sleep to death, an end to love,
Ending and sleeping,
Love sleeps and ends for it cannot last. (*N*, 136)

These are early, sometimes awkward, efforts to tap the darker side of reason by using ambiguity, comparison, analogy, and contradiction as principles of elaboration to expand the meaning condensed in imagery. Because they are *principles*, however, they show how logical and calculated are techniques which may strike the reader as unreasonable. Although Thomas loved to wrap himself in obscurity, he objected to the charge that his work was unpremeditated, thoughtless, or irrational: "every line *is* meant to be understood; the reader *is* meant to understand every poem by thinking and feeling about it, not by sucking it in through his pores, or whatever he is meant to do with surrealist writing" (*SL*, 161). His early experiments were attempts to portray "A season's fancy flown into a figure" (*N*, 197) – to express ideas and their flight through images. That figure or shape, as we have seen, is ultimately a portrait of the artist, a myth of the poetic self, living its heroic life. The progression of images charts its adventure and directs its struggle for self-understanding and assertion. Self-possession is the reward of a successful argument.

The progression of images defines the self and dramatizes its life, because, in Alistair Fowler's words, it can "mime the growth of consciousness."[26] It can display a process of thought. As in the case of fable and landscape, however, it can also hinder understanding by disclosing the ambiguities inherent in the imagery. The poem then disrupts its own argument, showing how the poet fails to master himself or his fate. "I Know this Vicious Minute's Hour" (*P*, 9), for example, is based on a series of contrasting images that track the poet's sensibilities and divided impulses in his quest for escape ("Go is my wish") and self-possession ("I want reality to hold / within my palm"). The paradox of time, suggested by the "vicious minute's hour" – an hour's anguish compressed into a minute – prompts a contest between head and heart, silver moment and vicious moment, circle and stair, love and lust. Because the heart, with its "sour motion in the blood," is the source of anguish, it is condemned for being offensive and passionate: "Too full with blood to let my love flow in." But here the paradox comes into play: the stable reality with which he seeks to oppose the unruly heart is associated with time ("Stop is unreal") and therefore with the "periodic heart" which beats out the vicious minutes of life. To renounce the heart is to renounce the life it gives. Consequently, the argument confutes itself. "I go or die," the poet concludes, showing that he remains "caught in mid-air" between the contradictions of his nature, unable to stop, yet unable to proceed confidently.

A similar argument in a different tone is found in "Upon Your Held-Out Hand" (*P*, 32–3), which also starts with a temporal paradox that provides the conflict of images to be developed through the poem: "Upon your held-out hand / Count the endless days until they end ... Learn to be merry with the merriest." At first the poet recommends a joyful reconciliation with the course of life, although he stresses the petty, tedious things ("The sideboard fruit, the ferns, the picture houses / And pack of cards") rather than the anguish of existence. By a process of association, however, the sequence of images leads him astray and undermines the advice given so easily. Hand and counting prompt images of the tired pulse, beating out the endless days; and then of counting trees as a boy, to "symbolize the maddening factors" that increase as the days pass. His advice now is "count or go mad," but the imagery shows that to count is to go mad. The two are not alternatives:

> The new asylum on the hill
> Leers down the valley like a fool
> Waiting and watching for your fingers to fail
> To keep count of the stiles
> The thousand sheep
> Leap over to my criss-cross rhythms.

The earlier advice to count the endless days in a spirit of acceptance has changed through the sequence of images into an admission that we foolishly count sheep for the sleep of death. All our efforts only madden us and confirm our mortality. The argument, in criss-cross fashion, has reversed itself.

Fables, landscapes, and images all provide the rhetorical and dramatic basis for logical, but wayward arguments whose perversity produces cryptic poems that defy not only the reader's, but also the poet's attempt to reason out his dilemma. "Grief Thief of Time" (*P*, 107–8) is our last example of a poem of this sort. It argues through competing images whose proliferation is sustained by the paradox of time, but whose argument is subverted by the inconsistency of its own premises.

Thomas revised the early version of the poem, obscured its clear statements, and made its images ambiguous, in order to render a complex vision of the interdependence of grief, love, life, and death. He made the key words interchangeable. Time, traditionally the subtle thief of youth, is identified with both life and the ageing that leads to death. Grief is the thief that robs us of time, life, and love. Yet grief is time, because the passage of time is a process of grieving (as in "A Grief Ago"). And grief is love with its attendant pain, because lovers lie "loving with the thief," just as in a later poem they will lie "abed / With all their griefs in their arms" (*P*, 197). Love is the force that defies time ("blew time to his knees") and sustains life; but it is also, as agent of generation and grief, an ally of time and death. Implicit in the poem is the old sexual pun on the verb, to die; hence "the bone of youth" and the "stallion grave." The argument, therefore, is conducted with equivocal terms so that all assertions suggest their opposites, adversaries prove to be allies, affirmations prove to be denials.

The first stanza elaborates the image of the sea, which provides the seascape for another fabulous adventure. Its heroes are predecessors of Captain Cat in *Under Milk Wood*: they recall the high-tide of passion from their "seafaring years ... in a time of stories." Robbed of vitality, the old forget the pain, the "lean time," and the shame ("albatross") of their grief, and remember only the lusty adventures ("salt-eyed stumble bedwards where she lies"), which seem to defy time. But the images of their memory are untrustworthy, revealing that there is no escape from time or grief. The adventurous sea is tomb as well as womb ("moon-drawn grave"); the tide measures the flight of time as well as the height of passion; the "salt-eyed" sailors stumble from tears of grief as well as excitement. Even crueller is the paradox that the remembered woman "timelessly lies loving with the thief" who, we realize, is both grief and time. She lies timelessly loving with time, suggesting that we must embrace our fate even when it proves vicious. But in the fable she lies with the sailor-hero: he himself is the thief, both victim and perpetrator of the crime of life. The identity of thief and hero is confirmed in the next stanza, where the old men are called "Jack my fathers," a name which corresponds to the "knave of pain" or grief from the first stanza.

The second stanza elaborates the image of the thief, as the poet addresses the old men, speaking with a confidence that the poem does not support, offering advice rendered equivocal by its ambiguous terms. He advises them to let the thief escape because his loot is deadly, sinful, and ghoulish: "These stolen bubbles have the bites of snakes / And the undead eye-teeth." He tells them not to indulge the "third eye" of memory, now reduced to a "eunuch crack," not to recall the rainbow of sexual union, and not to chase and so prolong grief throughout one's life "down the weeks' / Dayed peaks." In short, he counsels them to accept their losses and their lives. But paradoxically, to release grief ("free the twin-boxed grief") is to cry or grieve for bed and coffin, the one lost, the other approaching. There is no escape from grief or from time, because the hero has already been identified with his enemy. In the final judgment of the poem, the criminal is condemned to contemplate images of his own condition. He is punished with his own crime: "All shall remain and on the graveward gulf / Shape with my fathers' thieves."

How far this conclusion is from a direct affirmation of life or from transcendence of the vicious circle of life and death, is apparent by comparing an earlier version of the last lines:

> When the knave of death arrives,
> Yield the lost flesh to him and give your ghost;
> All shall remain, and on the cloudy coast
> Walk the blithe host
> Of god and ghost with you, their newborn son. (*N*, 245)

Instead of a blithe resurrection of the spirit, the later version presents a recapitulation of the paradoxes that prompted the poem. "All shall remain"; yet all shall be stolen. The "graveward gulf," like the "moon-drawn grave," is the abyss of life, both womb and tomb. The fathers both steal and are stolen by time and grief in the phrase "my fathers' thieves." The newborn son from the notebook is still present, not as an angel, but as a future thief. The figure taking "shape" (being born and dying) in the last line is the poet himself, since he has acknowledged himself offspring of the old men ("Jack my fathers"), the son of love, grief and time. He inherits their crime and their adventure and – as in "Altarwise by Owl-Light" – finds himself entrenched in the human condition of time and generation. But the poem does not offer the same affirmation from within that condition. Instead – as in "Upon Your Held-Out Hand" – it attempts to offer consoling advice that is called into question by the very images in which it is expressed. The poem concludes with the self, the point at which all Thomas's arguments begin, but with a self which has not been liberated, because it is defined in terms of its own dissolution.

Given Thomas's mistrustful self-consciousness, his reliance on unstable premises, equivocal images, and techniques that complicate and contradict, it is not surprising that his poems grow more and more devious until they argue themselves into ambiguity. They begin in celebration, but quickly engage in a strange festivity of the mind. In subsequent work he tries to simplify his poetry, though in ways that do not rob it of its aggressive adventurousness. In his best work, however, the savagery is finely crafted, because it expresses his effort to understand and free himself, or at least to affirm a self he has failed to understand. He must always poetically prove his own worth. This is true not only in his bewildering poems, but also in those where his case seems beyond dispute. In "After the Funeral" and in "A Refusal to Mourn the Death by Fire, of a Child in London" the poet is overcome with grief, yet he cannot convey his feelings until he has debated them and questioned his power to express them. He mourns only by first refusing to mourn, so that he can examine the terms of his grief. Only by confronting himself can he purge his writing of sentimentality, honour the dead, and construct for them "this monumental / Argument of the hewn voice" (*P*, 137).

CHAPTER FIVE

T.S. Eliot

Throughout this book I have used the ungainly term "unreason" to suggest and to challenge a number of questionable assumptions of modernist theory. In different ways for different poets and critics, unreason is whatever necessitates and permits the unreasonable aggression of poetic argument. It is the special means by which, in Octavio Paz's phrase, poetry liberates thought; or it is the contradictory ability of thought to think the unthinkable and say the unsayable; or it is the fundamental life of the mind prior to rational organization, whether understood as intuition, experience, subjectivity, or the inner self; or it is the primary impetus of thought, an elusive energy that, like the Kantian *Ding an sich* or the Freudian subconscious, can never be known directly but must be assumed as a precondition of thought. In any case the awkward negative form implies that unreason can only be imagined in opposition to what it is not, as part of the mind's effort to compensate for an insufficiency in reason and language. In every case unreason represents the beginning of thought by providing a locus for argument, an imagined stage from which poetry can launch its operation; and it represents the frontier of thought by projecting a path that the argument, following its own peculiar logic, can trace but never fully complete, control, or foresee.

The last two descriptions of unreason as the avenue of experience or of energy apply especially to T.S. Eliot, who gives one of the most intricate and painful accounts of the trajectory of argument from imagined beginning to imagined end. In the beginning is a fundamental energy, will, or immediate experience that sets the mind in motion and directs it toward truth. It is the point of conception, where the mind originates, but also corrupts its thoughts in pursuit of an ultimate understanding, which for Eliot is the goal of criticism and philosophy. In the end is transcendence, the elusive vanishing point of comprehension and comprehensiveness, where thought finally succeeds in mastering itself by surmounting its limitations. But in a paradox that becomes a religious mystery, the point of mastery is also the point of self-abandonment. At the end of argument Eliot discovers a new ignorance that is made possible by the triumph of poetry over criticism and of religion over philosophy. To adapt his own words, transcendence "represents an attempt to extend the confines of human consciousness and to report things unknown, to express the inexpressible" (*OPP*, 193)[1] It is a sublime idea, an enigma that is generated by thought, but one that thought cannot think. Consequently, he must show how imaginative arguments confound, transgress, and ultimately redeem the logic that they rely on, but cannot trust.

We have already encountered the paradox of transcendence as the limitless limit of argument in Moore's poetry, and we shall see it again in Stevens's work. Eliot's treatment is the most mystical, but its mysticism is earned through critical speculation, and I shall therefore begin this chapter by considering his notion of criticism, its goals and limitations. The trajectory of his arguments leads from a formative mystery (conception) to a reformative mystery (redemption). It arises from a prelogical need and then searches for the moment of daring surrender, when the poet can leap from logic to faith and advance "Into another intensity / For a further union, a deeper communion" (*CP*, 204). Where criticism ends, poetry begins; where poetry ends, faith begins. In order to follow this path, I intend to study first the contest between critical and poetic thought and secondly the notion of transcendence as the paradoxical victory and defeat of poetic argument. To illustrate the second point, I shall examine "Ash Wednesday," because it circles around the redemptive moment, driven by contrary forces of impulsion and revulsion.

Eliot the poet and Eliot the critic are often at odds, and I wish to consider the oddity of their relation. I am not concerned with the question of whether or not he practises poetically what he preaches critically, but with the strained, theoretical relation between practising and preaching. I am interested in the relation between philosophic and poetic arguments and, more specifically, in the restrictions of critical thought as opposed to the boundless aspirations of poetic thought. "Literary criticism is an activity which must constantly define its own boundaries," he advises in an essay on another poet/critic, Goethe; "also, it must constantly be going beyond them" (*OPP*, 250). What are the boundaries of criticism, and what begins where it leaves off? Throughout his career he studied the affiliation between poet and critic – the poet as poet, the poet as critic, and the critic as critic; the man who suffers, the mind which creates, and the reader who contemplates. Ideally, these functions should enhance each other, and Eliot often calls for peaceful cooperation among them. Ultimately, however, he divorces poet from critic in order to protect poetry within its own formal, inviolable sphere, which is comparable to the waking dream. He imagines a golden "pre-critical" age when poetry was "the expression of the mind of a whole people" and criticism was unnecessary because subsumed by poetry (*UPC*, 21–2). Unfortunately, we have fallen from this unified state into philosophy and its discontents. We now require criticism as a necessary evil, a supplementary discipline that illuminates poetry but also perversely threatens to overwhelm it by supplanting poetic with critical arguments. Hence the need to protect poetry from the violence of criticism. Michel Foucault claims that philology as exegesis, as intrusive deciphering or demystifying, as the paralysing "analysis of what is said in the depths of discourse, has become the modern form of criticism.... The truth of discourse is caught in the trap of philology."[2] Accordingly, even as he promotes good criticism, Eliot tries to keep poetic truth one step ahead of philology, just out of reach of the criticism that pursues it.

After his religious conversion Eliot increasingly thought of criticism as a necessary impertinence and an impertinent necessity. Earlier in his career, however, he and Pound called for intelligent criticism to reassess the past and to foster an atmosphere conducive to good writing. Pound calls criticism the gun-sight of composition and treats both as "two feet of one biped,"[3] while Eliot advocates "the ceaseless employment of criticism by men engaged in creative work."[4] One should nourish the other. Fresh from his philosophicial studies at Harvard, Eliot argues further that, because criticism is a natural disposition of thought "as inevitable as breathing," we should be none the worse "for criticizing our own minds in their work of criticism" (*SE*, 13–14). His early essays counter the undisciplined impressionism of contemporary commentators by proposing a criticism of criticism and a theory of theory. Although his remarks are fragmentary and their coherence has been questioned,[5] they nevertheless consistently invite us to investigate the principles that establish criticism as a philosophical study and distinguish it from its object, literature, which in contrast depends on its own "creative" thought. Criticism, he explains later, is "that department of thought which either seeks to find out what poetry is, what its use is, what desires it satisfies, why it is written and read, or recited; or which, making some conscious or unconscious assumption that we do know these things, assesses actual poetry ... there are these two theoretical limits of criticism: at one of which we attempt to answer the questions 'what is poetry?' and at the other 'is this a good poem?' " (*UPC*, 16). Criticism depends on analysis and appreciation in order to elucidate the laws of art and improve taste, but its arguments by their very nature arrive at limits, which we must recognize and respect.

This prescription seems tidy, but Eliot's attempt to define limits immediately provokes a series of problems inherent in the principles that he invokes. Although criticism is "as inevitable as breathing," it proves difficult to do it well, and he diagnoses widespread literary asthma. Although he wishes to establish criticism as a rational study with secure laws and objectives, criticism proves oddly inadequate to its task, because the very effort by which he defines it as a science and distinguishes it from poetry, forces him to limit its power. Criticism is analysis and appreciation, but it pursues something prouder and loftier, something that rational discourse merely promises. Ultimately it aims at intellectual mastery, which is the presumed ability of the mind to rule experience by understanding it. However, the grandiose desire to dominate reality through thought becomes a painfully absurd yearning in "Gerontion," where the speaker wonders: "After such knowledge, what forgiveness?" Some redemptive promise, sacrifice, or mystery must lie beyond the grasp of understanding, but the poem offers no assurance that it can be attained. Despite his classical stance, therefore, Eliot continues the romantic tradition of poetic unreason, whereby the "pure contemplation" of poetry not only does not require "a labour of the intelligence" (*SW*, 14), but thrives in opposition to discursive understanding. He protects poetic suggestiveness and indeterminacy at the expense of critical certainty. Consequently, he both recommends good criticism and makes it impossible.

Because Eliot is both poet and critic, the problematic relation between the two disciplines with their different modes of argument becomes particularly dramatic. In order to enforce the opposition, he warns that poets are not in a privileged position to explain what good poetry is, since their domain is creative, not critical; their talent is expression, not theory. He offers a compliment when he says that Swinburne "is one man in his poetry and a different man in his criticism; to this extent and in this respect only, that he is satisfying a different impulse; he is criticizing, expounding, arranging" (*SW*, 5), not creating. He is competent in both areas precisely because he is able to keep them distinct. For the same reason poets often cannot even explain their own work: "There are two reasons why the writer of poetry must not be thought to have any great advantage. One is that a discussion of poetry such as this takes us far outside the limits within which a poet may speak with authority; the other is that the poet does many things upon instinct, for which he can give no better account than anyone else" (*UPC*, 129–30). The regulatory limits proposed and patrolled by critical authority must be respected, if one is to protect oneself from the limitlessness of the instincts, out of which poetry arises. Instincts – or more generally, the subjective experience surveyed only by unreason – are unfathomable and, as we shall see, dangerous.

As an avowed classicist, Eliot refutes romantic notions of spontaneous intuition and defends the intelligence of the poet, who is not in the throes of a fine frenzy but is as alert and thoughtful as any critic. He praises Pound for his intelligence and learning and for insisting on "the immensity of the amount of *conscious* labor to be performed by the poet." However, as various critics have argued,[6] Eliot tacitly reinstates the romantic principles that he scorns. He maintains the binary division of faculties and their operations (understanding/intuition, reason/unreason, logic/poetics), when he contrasts "The critical mind operating in poetry" and "the critical mind operating *upon* poetry" (*UPC*, 30). The intellectual effort that goes into the writing of poetry precedes the analysis of the reader and is different in kind, although it is as strenuous and as much a product of thought. The differentiation of critical activities operating within and upon poetry reflects a larger opposition of human faculties. Criticism, like any philosophical discourse, is the product of reason, whereas poetry is a product of the "logic of the imagination." Earlier I quoted the famous passage in the preface to *Anabase*, where Eliot proposes two independent modes of thought, a "logic of concepts," which is rational, discursive, sequential, and abstract, and a "logic of the imagination," which is "unreasonable," imagistic, instantaneous, and concrete. Although the latter is playful and intuitive, it requires as much "fundamental brainwork" as the former, but a different kind of "brainwork," achieving different ends. While this binary opposition seems clear and firm, it is not consistent, as I argued in Chapter 1, because the principles of rhythm, juxtaposition, dislocation, and association, by which Eliot defines the logic of the imagination, all prove to be quite logical in the ordinary sense. However, it is characteristic of his thinking to be first firm, then flexible; to separate the kinds of argument, for example, and then to allow them interplay. He recognizes the need for systematic thought, but he is wary of the neatly balanced structures in which thought delights. In this case he wishes to maintain a working distinction between creative and critical arguments. He expresses his "double impulse," as William Righter calls it, "to point to the special nature and apartness of poetry, and to regard one's other uses of language as ancillary. And the result is not to distinguish alternative forms of the imagination, but to focus on one's own creative process as the ground on which one sees the extending out of subsidiary and wholly dependent comment."[7] Commentary follows in the shadow of the poetry that it seeks to illuminate.

Creation is the ground of commentary, but from Eliot's point of view the ground proves to be shaky, since it arises from what he treats variously as instinct, will, and immediate experience, all of which stubbornly defy discursive analysis. The nature of and need for poetic arguments, which can do justice to this mysterious ground of thought, become clearer if we pursue the problematic relationship between creation and criticism. René Wellek objects that the criticism operating within poetry, as Eliot describes it, is not really criticism at all, but "merely a metaphor for the labor of composing" that indicates "the share of intellect in the creative process."[8] Eliot ignores this equivocation in order to endorse the formalist opposition between poetry, which is an autotelic activity, and criticism, which has an ulterior purpose: "criticism, by definition, is *about* something other than itself. Hence you cannot fuse creation with criticism as you can fuse criticism with creation" (*SE*, 30–1). The poet can be critical in his own special way, but the critic cannot, or should not, transgress the boundaries of his discipline to become poetic. Citing this passage, Geoffrey Hartman observes that Eliot hints at but then "draws back from what seems to him an ultimate and dangerous sophistication."[9] He does not want to grant criticism too much independent, subversive power, because it then threatens to displace poetry with its own creative energy. Eliot fights for the integrity and priority of poetry by insisting on the subservience of criticism.

Hartman claims that Eliot's distinguishing between kinds of criticism is specious, not only because all arguments are the same in kind, but, more importantly, because all are unreasonable in the sense that they depend on deconstructive logic. Criticism is not supplementary to poetry or inferior in its mode of thought, because it is an "intellectual poem" in its own right: "literary commentary may cross the line and become as demanding as literature: it is an unpredictable or unstable genre that cannot be subordinated, a priori, to its referential or commentating function ... a reversal must be possible whereby this 'secondary' piece of writing turns out to be 'primary.' "[10] As I argued in the first chapter, deconstruction rejects the opposition between poetic and logical argument by insisting that all arguments depend on the "illogic" of "rhetoricity," *aporia*, or poetic unreason. I, too, have argued throughout this book that poetic arguments are not different in kind – but for a different reason. I contend that all are equally rational, because poetic rhetoric is equally logical, if sometimes more dramatic, festive, or flamboyant than the rhetoric displayed in other arguments. It is important to keep this prevailing rationality in mind when we examine how Eliot pushes logic to its limit and finds it unavailing. He, of course, maintains the intermediary modernist position, the implications of which we must now examine. His differentiation between critical faculties operating within and upon poetry reflects a larger opposition of human faculties and expresses a philosophical and ultimately religious attitude toward the mind and toward the reality that it seeks to dominate through thought.

The two kinds of criticism (operating within/upon poetry) reflect a distinction between modes of thought (logical/poetical), which in turn arise from a philosophical disjunction between language and immediate experience, a disjunction that Eliot learned from F.H. Bradley. For Bradley, immediate experience is the simple, undifferentiated unity of reality ("that"), the fusion of being and knowing that precedes the fragmenting analysis of thought ("what"). In a sense it is the unified, poetic awareness that precedes and forever eludes criticism: "There is but one Reality, and its being consists in experience. In this one whole all appearances come together, and in coming together they in various degrees lose their distinctive natures. The essence of reality lies in the union and agreement of existence and content, and, on the other side, appearance consists in the discrepancy between these two aspects. And reality in the end belongs to nothing but the single Real." Unfortunately, but inevitably, any act of judgment, understanding, or speech fractures the unity of the Real, leaving us with an articulated but specious appearance: "For take anything, no matter what it is, which is less than the Absolute, and the inner discrepancy at once proclaims that what you have taken is appearance. The alleged reality divides itself and falls apart into two jarring factors." Philosophy by its very nature seeks truth by misrepresenting it and can therefore take us only to the point where we discover the limitations of thought and recognize the need to transcend them. It discovers that: "The internal being of everything finite depends on that which is beyond it" (*AR*, 455–6).[11]

This summary of Bradley's metaphysics is familiar to students of Eliot's philosophical background, but its implications for poetry as argument are not. Eliot was well acquainted with the pattern of alienation implicit in Bradley's work, a pattern that extends from Rousseau to Heidegger and that divorces the mind from reality by the very intellectual effort used to master it. This predicament gives poetry its philosophical task. Though verbal, it arises from a primary cognition that precedes language and then strives for a meaning that exceeds it. These two limits, from which criticism is barred, mark the beginning and end of poetic argument. Its goal, as we saw in the discussion of poetic language and silence, is to reappropriate the reality it has forfeited. Presence and value, being and meaning have been torn apart into jarring factors and must now be reunited. In this context "meaning" must be understood as fullness and integrity of experience rather than as significance; that is, it is conceived of as an accord between mind and world, rather than as the product of a signifying linguistic system. This conception of meaning distinguishes Eliot's modernism from Hartman's postmodernism, and it explains why Eliot finds the origins and ends of a poem ineffable and beyond the purview of any critic, even of the author. Something essential stubbornly escapes all our efforts to analyse or assess it. Eliot's respect for this wordless ground of poetic meaning forces him to impede the philosophical criticism that he has recommended. In an odd way it is the critic, not the poet, who is lost in language, because the former is bound to and blinded by words. He is confined by his discursive medium, while the poet more successfully uses words to transcend their limitations. Only the poet can use words to free himself from their constraint.

For Eliot, the locus of poetic argument lies in a complex yet unified immediate experience, and it is manifest as an instinct, "obscure impulse," "burden," or "demon" (*OPP*, 107), which the poet must exorcize through speech. It lies in a "fusion of feelings so numerous, and ultimately so obscure in their origins, that even if there be communication of them, the poet must hardly be aware of what he is communicating." It lies in "depths of feeling into which we cannot peer," not only because they are so remote, but because they are inchoate and are falsified when formulated in words. They are "the deeper, unnamed [and unnamable] feelings which form the substratum of our being" and which take on a new verbal form in poetry" (*UPC*, 138, 148, 155). At the other extreme, with regard to its reception, meaning depends on the poem's effect in the experience of the reader, and the "experience of poetry, like any other experience, is only partially translatable into words" (*UPC*, 17). In the greatest poetry, especially, there is "something which must remain unaccountable" (*OPP*, 124), not only because it is so obscure but once again, because by its very nature it is ineffable: "It is commonplace to observe that the meaning of a poem may wholly escape paraphrase. It is not quite so commonplace to observe that the meaning of a poem may be something larger than its author's conscious purpose, and something remote from its origins.... If, as we are aware, only a part of the meaning can be conveyed by paraphrase, that is because the poet is occupied with frontiers of consciousness beyond which words fail, though meanings still exist.... the poem means more, not less than ordinary speech can communicate" (*SP*, 110–11). If the consciousness encoded in poetry can move beyond the reach of words, then no criticism can do justice to it. The authority of the critic must falter before an experience – including his own experience as reader – that defies his powers of thought and speech. The poet as critic therefore suffers a curious alienation. He cannot interpret his most intimate experiences, because no critical discourse, since it is discursive, can fully do the job it sets itself. Confined to ordinary speech, it cannot elucidate a poem completely, judge it, or explain its laws. It is a flawed supplement to poetry, and flawed precisely by its supplementarity.

Thus Eliot sets out to establish criticism as an objective, authoritative discipline, but concludes by questioning its competence and its authority. The dilemma whereby criticism is distinguished from the autotelic poetry it studies by having an ulterior purpose which it cannot fulfil, troubles him, but only in a special way. It prompts him to look to the superior powers of poetic argument and of faith, which promise a value or meaning beyond the competence of rational discourse. I believe he would consider this perplexing condition not so much mystical as philosophical in nature, that is, in accordance with the sceptical philosophy he learned from Bradley, who shows how reason, rigorously applied, must eventually reveal its darker side. It must discover its own frontiers and defeat itself by concluding in paradox: "Truth cannot in the end become consistent and ultimately true" (*ETR*, 430). The problem for Eliot is how to get beyond "the end," by using paradox not as a sign of defeat, but as a means of proceeding further. As Gerontion's question shows, if only through its despair, there must be something beyond truth in this self-confuting philosophical sense.

Eliot seems to endorse Bacon's aphorism in "Of Atheism:" "It is true that a little philosophy inclineth men's mind to atheism, but depth in philosophy bringeth men's minds about to religion."[12] The puzzling relations between poetry and criticism, creation and comprehension, direct him to a higher ground of meaning. The restless pursuit of truth through necessary but inadequate means (intellect, language) testifies to man's fallen state. It is a "raid on the inarticulate / With shabby equipment always deteriorating" (*CP*, 203), but pointing through its very inadequacy to a transcendental truth. Thus the divorce between language and experience becomes the plight of corrupt humanity, and what started as an aesthetic problem, a dispute between poet and critic, becomes a religious ordeal. Through critical thought Eliot formulates a productive dissatisfaction with logic that is the product of logic, and that directs him to religion. He remarked in 1924, shortly before his religious conversion, that accepting Bradley's theory of judgment leads to "resignation or despair – the bewildered despair of wondering why you ever wanted anything, or what it was that you wanted, since this philosophy seems to give you everything that you ask and yet render it not worth wanting."[13] These words express nicely the baffled despair of *Ash-Wednesday*, where the argument turns in circles, seeking escape from the trap of its own ambitions. They also indicate Eliot's discontent with philosophical argument in general: its conclusions offer no sustenance. His problem is how to transcend the unsatisfying, self-confuting limits of rational argument, and his poems characteristically hover over the precarious moment of hope and despair when transcendence is first imagined. This unstable point is "The awful daring of a moment's surrender" (*CP*, 78).

The moment of daring surrender represents the culmination of both a logical and a moral paradox. The logical difficulty is to discover how reason can use its resources to surpass itself. The moral difficulty arises from the nature of unreason as Eliot formulates it. As we have seen, poetic unreason is the response of the imagination to a philosophical assumption. If reality consists of immediate experience that is unavailable to reason, then truth must be conceived by an intuitive "wisdom ... communicated on a deeper level than that of logical propositions" (*OPP*, 264). But unreason is also a matter of instinct: it is the violent, dangerous, inchoate inner life that the poet draws on and appeals to, but mistrusts. In his early poems, especially, Eliot associates instinct with bestial indulgence of appetite (Sweeney), with low life and the working class, with the decay of European culture, and with women: "The same eternal and consuming itch / Can make a martyr, or a plain simple bitch" (*WL*, 41). How then can the poet draw on unreason for holy rather than profane purposes, without succumbing to its baser, wilful nature?

In fact Bradley had already suggested a path through this dilemma in an early work, *Ethical Studies* (1876), which Eliot reread and reviewed in 1927, just when he was conducting his debate with humanism and making his own logical and spiritual leap of faith. Bradley contends that morality proposes an ideal conduct that flawed, inconsistent reality can never satisfy. This contradiction then reveals the necessity of a religious point of view. Religion proposes as its object the "ideal self" of morality, but now "considered as realized and real. The ideal self, which in morality is to be, is here the real ideal which truly is" (*ES*, 153). Morality offers hope, desire, speculation, argument; religion offers truth. More specifically, "In the very essence of the religious consciousness we find the relation of our *will* to the real ideal self. We find ourselves, as this or that will, against the object as the real ideal will...." (*ES*, 154). God is "the good will" or will made perfect. Religion is the commerce between human and divine wills, a mysterious relation that baffles and triumphs over ordinary understanding by reconciling all that is limited, fallible and vicious in human will with God's perfection.

Bradley's account of the imperfections of philosophy, which must be redeemed by divine will and love, offers Eliot a way of solving his intellectual and moral dilemma by distinguishing between the motives of unreason. At its basest, unreason is the wilful "inner voice" of instinct and appetite, which he rejects with abhorrence: "The possessors of the inner voice ride ten in a compartment to a football match at Swansea, listening to the inner voice, which breathes the eternal message of vanity, fear, and lust" (*SE*, 27). At the level of thought, unreason is still a kind of appetite, but it is now an intellectual grasping, a will to argue in order to subdue through thought. Carried too far, it becomes a voracious intellectual pride. At the spiritual level, however, it is a redemptive mystery. Like Eliot, Bradley is not concerned to dispel the mystery, as he shows in a later essay, because he uses its inconsistency as a strategy in his own argument: "We have the perfect real will, and we have my will, and the practical relation of these wills is what we mean by religion. And yet, if perfection is actually realized, what becomes of my will which is over against the complete Good Will? While on the other hand, if there is no such Will, what becomes of God? ... Is there any need for our attempt to avoid self-contradiction? Has religion really got to be consistent theoretically? ... The religious consciousness must represent to itself the Good Will in its relation to mine. It must express both our difference and our unity" (*ETR*, 429, 430, 432). Contradiction is inevitable, given the state of fallen man, alienated from a perfection he can conceive of only in terms of his own imperfections purifed. Salvation comes from this very contradiction, which is the paradox of transcendence whose essential mystery gives human life its meaning. Salvation comes from "our difference and our unity." It comes from recognizing the utter separation between man and God, and from overcoming that gulf through the grace of God. In the final words of *Ethical Studies*, it is "that 'immortal Love,' which builds itself forever on contradiction, but in which the contradiction is eternally resolved" (*ES*, 174).

What I have discussed coldly and abstractly is, of course, a painful emotional and spiritual ordeal in Eliot's poetry. To muster the terms of my own analysis: his arguments are highly dramatic in a drama that depends on an intricate and anguished rhetorical play, a play that remains logical but continually contests its own logical form. His poems brood over the gulf between experience and meaning, reason and faith. In dramatic terms this gulf is expressed as the plight of being trapped "in between," in that awkward middle ground that is his favourite territory between life and death, memory and desire, profit and loss, either and neither (*CP*, 135). In the early poetry his characters are inert, diffident, impotent, and lost "Among velleities and carefully caught regrets" (*CP*, 18). Prufrock, Burbank, Gerontion, and the young man in "Portrait of a Lady" are trapped between indecisions and revisions. They are overwhelmed by their own questions and do not dare to seek conclusions. The place "in between" is the barren psychological ground where they can neither assert nor deny their desires. It is the moral dilemma that makes them guilty of both action and inaction. It is the ontological puzzle that paralyses the Hollow Men in the shadow that falls between conception and creation, potency and existence. In the later, religious poetry, it is the historical interregnum where the Magi and Simeon are caught between the old dispensation and the new; or the place of disaffection in "Burnt Norton," where there is neither before nor after, light nor dark, motion nor permanence, "plenitude nor vacancy," where we are "Caught in the form of limitation / Between un-being and being" (*CP*, 192, 195).

To these characters, any effort to argue themselves out of the trap or to resolve their problem by defining its conditions, seems doomed. Therefore the limbo "in between" also represents an argumentative listlessness or intellectual tedium which is expressed so effectively in the opening lines of *Ash-Wednesday*. Attempting to understand their plight either leads these characters to further confusion (Prufrock's "tedious argument," Gerontion's "cunning passages, contrived corridors"); or it confirms their entrapment ("each in his prison / Thinking of the key, each confirms a prison," *CP*, 79). Arguing seems useless, because it is an ineffectual stirring of memory and desire or, worse, because it is a vain intellectual pride that may actually be a hindrance to salvation. Consequently, Eliot resolves neither to assert nor restrain the mind, but to abandon it to something larger:

> I said to my soul, be still, and wait without hope
> For hope would be hope for the wrong thing; wait without love
> For love would be love of the wrong thing; there is yet faith
> But the faith and the love and the hope are all in the waiting. (*CP*, 200)

Waiting in the right spirit is an attending, a special act of attention, which is at once active and passive: "We must be still and still moving / Into another intensity" (*CP*, 203–4). Waiting intently is an argumentative strategy that claims not to argue and thereby prepares the conditions for transcendence. Because *Ash-Wednesday* so clearly illustrates the strategy and its logical evocation of unreason, I now wish to examine it at length.

Ash-Wednesday is a poem of bewilderment. At once active and passive, it restlessly probes its own listlessness in order to define and to overcome the conditions that bewilder it. Through his probing, Eliot encounters the logical and moral puzzles outlined above, but solves them through an argument that twists into a sequence of return, ascent, and intercession. This rhetorical pattern of rising by circling, of succeeding by confessing one's failure, transcends his dilemma by transcribing it in religious terms. More importantly from our point of view, the pattern also expresses a process of interpretation; that is, it displays a will to argue – to make sense of sinful experience and, through knowledge, to master it and expiate the past. This effort is promising, but it necessarily fails, since human will is corrupt and human knowledge flawed. Nevertheless, it ultimately permits a strategic reversal through asceticism, whereby failure turns to victory, or at least, the promise of victory.

The argument begins at the point of revulsion, when weariness, disgust, and despair make the poet turn trom his past, where he has wavered "in between" competing desires: "torn on the horn between season and season, time and time, between / Hour and hour, word and word, power and power" (*CP*, 102). In this "dreamcrossed twilight between birth and dying" (*CP*, 104), he can neither act nor suffer. Now he desires not to desire and is torn by three competing impulses, which he must resolve. First and weakest is the longing for the energy, beauty, and sensuality of the physical world. This is Dylan Thomas's desire to live fully within the contradictions of generation, a misguided hope that seems at first extinguished, but returns enticingly at the end as a persistent temptation of human nature. Second, and opposing the first, is the stoical impulse by which Eliot turns away from the world to the desert of self-denial, vacancy, oblivion, and death. Third is the desire to ascend to plenitude and transcendence, a journey which he does not complete, but which he implies by alluding to Dante, who in the final cantos of the *Purgatorio* mounts through fire and water to the Earthly Paradise, where he meets first Matilda and then Beatrice. Return and ascent combine in the image of the winding, purgatorial staircase. By turning, Eliot also rises (part III) until he envisages the Lady, who intercedes for him in "the Garden / Where all love ends" (*CP*, 98). Together, return and ascent suggest a spiritual path for overcoming the logical and moral impasses of his argument. The first impasse I have called the "will to argue": it is the baffling, interpretive process by which logic strives to exceed its own limits in order to envisage what cannot be known but must be true. The second impasse I shall call "the argument of will": it is the dramatic struggle by which will renounces itself in order to lose itself in the divine will.[14] In order to succeed on its quest, the mind must be simultaneously daring and submissive. It must argue, while appearing to refrain from argument.

In one respect the argument of *Ash-Wednesday* suggests the daring poetic "adventures" launched by Dylan Thomas in his attempt to master life by arguing against death. Both are projects of redemption conducted by a restless or listless but always flawed understanding. They are quite different in scope, of course, since Eliot strives to transcend the secular conditions ("The vanished power of the usual reign," *CP*, 95) that Thomas embraces so fervently. Nevertheless, both poets treat time as the painful medium or "grief" that simultaneously permits and confounds their quests. They must prove themselves in the course of time, but they are corrupted by its sinfulness. The penitential point of revulsion at the beginning of *Ash-Wednesday* marks the twist in time, when Eliot faces and offers to forget the reproach of the past. Ultimately, he hopes for timeless salvation; in the meantime he does not even dare to hope, and seeks oblivion because it dissolves the afflictions of time: "Let these words answer / For what is done, not to be done again" (*CP*, 96). He tries to stifle the self-consciousness of a mind always arguing with itself ("that I may forget / These matters that with myself I too much discuss"), and so to escape from an irremediable past ("what is actual is actual only for one time"). By not hoping to turn again, he tries to achieve the daring surrender that is both active and passive. However, as F. Peter Dzwonkoski, Jr. observes, subduing time through self-denial is really a victory of the mind, not a chastening of it: "The speaker of *Ash-Wednesday* wills passivity as a means of conquering time by laying himself open to the purifying darkness of God." Through a self-deprecating and apparently self-nullifying argument, he achieves "the willed perception that all time is eternally present."[15] In other words, the will to argue appears to be renounced, but only by being concealed within the drama of will.

The logical impasse that confuses argument, ignorance, will, time, and transcendence is clarified by Friedrich Nietzsche. I readily admit that Nietzsche and Eliot make strange bedfellows, but their similar though divergent attitudes toward argument and what lies beyond the reach of thought show how logic, rigorously applied, proposes a hope or appetite for transcendence. Both men contrast reason with poetic prophecy. Both regard logic as a necessary but flawed instrument, valuable up to a point but serving ends beyond that point. They disagree profoundly, however, about the drama of will that directs logic and about the will to argue that impels and evaluates the ambitions of thought. Eliot criticizes Nietzsche as "one of those authors whose philosophy evaporates when detached from its literary qualities,"[16] an interesting comment, since Eliot's own argument requires literary qualities to surmount what he sees as the shortcomings of philosophy.

Nietzsche agreed that time is the one constraint that perplexes and imprisons us. Turning back terrifies us, because it reveals that no effort of thought can change or redeem what we have already done: "Willing liberates: but what is it that fastens in fetters even the liberator? 'It was': that is what the will's teeth-gnashing and most lonely affliction is called. Powerless against that which has been done, the will is an angry spectator of all things past. The will cannot will backwards; that it cannot break time and time's desire – that is the will's most lonely affliction (*Z*, 161).[17] Nietzsche rebukes moralists like Eliot, who in their anger take revenge on the will for its inability to conquer time. They foolishly regard it as a jailer instead of a liberator and punish it through asceticism. They propose an opposition between will and knowledge, falsely believing that self-denial grants self-knowledge, which in turn atones for the past: " 'Except the will at last redeem itself and willing become not-willing –': but you, my brothers, know this fable-song of madness!" (Z,162). This song is sung by the "ascetic priest" who is a sadist who creates sin and guilt in order to punish himself, to triumph through his agony, and so to rise to an inspired knowledge of "Truth." This is the ascending path of *Ash-Wednesday* and of mystical experience in general. Nietzsche attacks asceticism, therefore, not only because it denies life, but because it lurks in all philosophy, promoting the supreme delusion: the belief that renunciation can lead to transcendent truth. The "absolute will to truth" – the compulsion within metaphysics, the seed of all argument – is faith in an absolute truth, a philosophical ground always secure because it is "truth ... premised as Being, as God, as supreme sanction" (*GM*, 289). It is the will to argue, the unreason that empowers our rational arguments.

According to Nietzsche's analysis, therefore, Eliot can never rid himself of the will to argue, because he carries it with him, undetected, as an absolute will to truth. He sublimates his own need and desire into a pure, divine will that subsumes the corrupt, personal will. This is the same pattern of thought recommended by Bradley, but Nietzsche judges the sublimation it offers to be not mystical, but rhetorical in nature, in the sense that it is permitted and envisaged solely by language. All such absolutes (will, God, essence, being, self, thing-in-itself) are metaphysical fictions or rhetorical flourishes. There is a theological mythology concealed in language, but "we must not forget that all this signifies no more than semeiotics and – nothing real" (*WP*, 118). It is interesting to note that Eliot had reached a similar, sceptical conclusion in his dissertation on Bradley, when he said: "As it is metaphysics which has produced the self so it is epistemology, we may say, which has produced knowledge" (*KE*, 146). Our systems of thought and speech give us those basic concepts with which we build our philosophy. Our arguments create the truths they seek. After his disillusion with philosophy and his religious conversion, however, he accepts theological absolutes as necessary and redeeming mysteries. He offers himself to a purifying darkness that Nietzsche regards as only a figure of speech. However, his earlier scepticism is still evident as a turbulence within faith or, in *Ash-Wednesday*, at the threshold of faith.

To return to the beginning of Eliot's argument: at first a restless passivity dominates the poem. The speaker abandons the "one veritable transitory power" (*CP*, 95) of instinct, will, or thought - all ways of expressing the energy that impels his argument - which dwindles and becomes "small and dry" as a grasshopper. When he no longer hopes to hope or strives to strive or wishes to think, he retreats behind the indefinable impulse of thought in search of a place where he can sit still and wait attentively. This intermediary realm of "higher aimlessness"[18] will relieve him of the torments of love unsatisfied (Prufrock) and of love satisfied (Sweeney). It is the active/passive, expectant/resigned attitude that Eliot calls "the Christian humility ... of the concentrated mind seeking God"[19] - concentrated, in that it is reduced and confined, but determined in that it is "devoted, concentrated in purpose" (*CP*, 97). The mind must remain active, even when it renounces and rejoices, "having to construct something / Upon which to rejoice" (*CP*, 95). Its self-sacrifice helps to prepare the ground of faith.

After the renunciation and dissolution of the body (II), Eliot encounters the mystery of transcendence expressed through two figures: the winding staircase (III) and the Lady acting as intermediary (II, IV). They are the spiritual and rhetorical means of surmounting the frailty (V) and the lingering attractions (VI) of the world. In the first figure Eliot's ascent of "steps of the mind" (*CP*, 99) is a progress through self-denial that remains an argument in the Nietzschean sense of an act of interpretation: "The Will to Power *interprets* ... it defines, it determines gradations, differences of power.... Continual *interpretation* is the first principle of the organic process" (*WP*, 124-25). Eliot's emotional, intellectual, and spiritual ascent is always an argument; it is an attempt to explain, surmount, and expiate past experience, and to rise through gradations of power. His original epigraph to Part II clarifies his task: "The Hand of the Lord Was Upon Me: - *e vo significando*." The final words (from Dante *Purgatorio*, 24:52-4) explain how, when inspired by love, he attends and then sets forth or interprets what love dictates within him ("quando / Amor me spira, noto, e a quel modo / ch' e' ditta dentro vo significando"). Dante is directed from within by his love and from without by his Lady. Eliot, too, proceeds through interpretation. He rises through a process of "signifying," until he reaches the point where he is baffled and can go no further on his own, but requires external assistance. Unlike Nietzsche, for whom the will to truth is always commanding, Eliot undertakes interpretation through a rhetoric of denial - abandoning, fading, renouncing, submitting. Denial is the power of will turned against itself; it is the aggressiveness of argument disputing itself. Denial appears as the three stairs to be climbed in part III, and in the allegories of desert and drought, and of the leopards that consume everything but the marrow of his being. It appears as the word which is lost, spent, unheard, and unspoken; as a failure of speech which, through biblical allusion, yields to a more authoritative text ("but speak the word only"); and it appears as the fragmentary prayers of supplication and unworthiness.

Transcendence is a sublime idea, a mystery that is generated by thought, but that thought cannot think and faith must embrace fervently. It is "the impossible union / Of spheres of existence" (*CP*, 231), human and divine. Eliot says of Lancelot Andrewes's sermons that we follow the movement of thought until "we find his examination of words terminating in the ecstasy of assent" (*SE*, 347). Eliot's own argument rises painfully to the point where such assent might be possible, but argument alone will not suffice. Just as criticism and philosophy eventually push against the frontiers of thought, so poetry reaches its hinterland, where reason yields to an ecstatic unreason. Even poetic argument is too weak and corrupt to redeem itself or to command its own salvation. Fallen man requires divine grace. In his study of Eliot's drama of consciousness, Charles Altieri explains the shortcomings of a mind limited to its own power of interpretation. In *The Waste Land*, for example, Eliot shows "the limits of reflective consciousness not informed by the grace of Incarnation." The poem demonstrates that "events are interpretable but unaffected by interpretation." Our ability to find patterns of significance ("e vo significando") in the world and in history in no way ensures that these meanings are true or final. Unless they are sanctioned by something beyond the figments of consciousness and the illusions of language, they remain shadowy fictions of our own invention. The "path of consciousness reflecting on itself leads us nowhere."[20]

For this reason *Ash-Wednesday* renounces the power of argument, which can present only "empty forms" to the "blind eye" (*CP*, 104) of deceitful dreams. Nevertheless, the poem which turns from language, thought, and desire is itself a lyrical meditation, a prayer expressing Eliot's yearning to rise through negation to the ecstasy of assent. At the top of the stairs he finds the triumphant end of interpretation in paradox:

> End of the endless
> Journey to no end
> Conclusion of all that
> Is inconclusible
> Speech without word and
> Word of no speech (*CP*, 98)

He uses these logical contradictions to gesture toward a mystical truth beyond secular knowledge, a truth made visible only by the darkness of thought. Such truth defies our ability to express it and is therefore unreasonable in our sense of the word, but it is not irrational. Rather, it is the mysterious fruition of reason and, as Eliot says of the concept of destiny, "it is a mystery not contrary to reason, for it implies that the world and the course of human history have meaning" (*OPP*, 144). "Meaning" has a special sense here, since it is a meaning that must be felt and trusted, but cannot be defined adequately. It is the highest form of unreason, lodged in the province of religious experience ("the ecstasy of assent"), not of language. Even though it must be expressed in terms of language, it is not itself linguistic and therefore must be imagined through the paradox of language that falls silent: "Lord, I am not worthy / but speak the word only" (*CP*, 99). The word as *logos* is the ideally fulfilled reference of language; it is what words mean to say, but never quite manage to say fully.

For Eliot, meaning, presence, and value are discovered through experience, not through linguistic signification, and we can see now why he mistrusts the exegetical trap noted by Foucault and the critical creativity recommended by Hartman. They endanger his argument in *Ash-Wednesday* by prolonging indefinitely the circle of its despair. For Nietzsche and Hartman, an ultimate, enigmatic truth like Eliot's is unattainable, because interpretation is insatiable and endless. The will to truth is always will for greater significance, generating interpretations of interpretations. Criticism overwhelms and displaces the poetry it studies, because it projects a perpetual process that permits no final truth: "Thus 'truth' is not something which is present and which has to be found and discovered; it is something *which has to be created* and which *gives* its name *to a process*, or, better still, to the Will to overpower, which in itself has no purpose: to introduce truth is a *processus in infinitum* ..." (*WP*, 60). Eliot cannot accept the revolving of thought as an infinite, purposeless process, continually creating but creating nothing absolute. He refuses to "Prophesy to the wind, to the wind only" (*CP*, 97) and prays for a completion of thought in a sovereign truth: "Redeem / The unread vision in the higher dream" (*CP*, 100).

Thus Eliot's pilgrim soul discovers what Moore's parade of elephants has already shown, that in poetic arguments, mysteries expound mysteries. I have spent some time examining the obscure origins and impulses that provide a locus for these arguments, but we can also compare the poets by watching how their arguments end or aspire to end. With Eliot, we see most clearly how the trajectory of thought foresees a conclusion that will respond to its beginning; and how, like the asymptote in geometry, its argument projects a goal that it continually approaches and promises but never quite achieves, because it can only envision the goal in terms of the corrupt conditions of thought that it hopes to supersede. In terms of modernist theory, the goal is comprehension and reappropriation or, as Moore calls them, wholeness and wholesomeness. It is the victory of mind when it masters the reality that has baffled it, just as it is the self-justification of language when it escapes the trap of philology by overcoming the rift between word and thing. In festive terms, the goal of poetic argument is the comic sublimation of reason through an argument that resolves the dark perplexities cast up by the process of arguing. Frye explains that festive comedies awaken us within a dream only when they succeed in cutting their Gordian knots (the involutions of logic). The comic argument is truly dialectical, because through its synthesis or metamorphosis, "the renewing power of the final action lifts us into a higher world,"[21] as it strives to do in *Ash-Wednesday* and *Four Quartets*. For Moore and for Edward Thomas, transcendence is conditional, always held in check by practical reservations, proprieties and doubts. For Dylan Thomas, transcendence is thwarted by a vacillation of terms, rather than permitted by an effective notion of sublimation. For Stevens, as we shall see in the final chapter, the vacillation – the push and pull of argument – is still more complex. But Eliot's goal is the most splendid, because it claims to be the glorious argument of argument; not just the successful completion of a given line of thought, but the dialectic of thought itself, the sublimation of thought in a higher unreason – "The unread vision in the higher dream." It is a triumph *of* reason and *through* reason that aspires also to be a triumph *over* reason.

All this is promised, of course, not achieved, and we are left with the problem of accounting for the operation of Eliot's complex notion of unreason. His sublime argument provides a mystical solution to the logical and moral entanglements of human experience. Enigma is solved by mystery; paradox is answered by paradox. The agent of defeat becomes the vehicle of victory, just as later in "Little Gidding" time will be redeemed by time, and history will become a pattern of timeless moments. What was a vicious circle of unavailing thought, and the bewildering will to argue becomes a means of liberation rather than entrapment. But what kind of argument, or system of persuasion and approval, can outwit itself by embracing its contradictions so fervently? To persist in contradiction is to express a need, wish or desire. Fervent persistence testifies to heroic desire. In a lower key, Moore reaches the same conclusion in "The Pangolin" and "To a Giraffe," where she proves our psychological need for and our spiritual faith in transcendent grace; she discovers the conditions of our hope. This conclusion does not make her or Eliot's arguments irrational in the sense of being supra-rational, aber-rational, or contra-rational, although it does make them unreasonable in the sense that I have been using the word.

As we have seen, an argument that lays such stress on unreason depends heavily on the dramatic appeal of its rhetoric and on the persuasiveness of its figures. It relies, says Frye in his essay on comedy, on the "metamorphosis" (a term he borrows from Stevens) that rhetoric employs and inspires. In *Ash-Wednesday*, Eliot concludes his argument by transcribing it in the key of his hope. Just as flawed human will must be absorbed by divine will, so the corrupt powers of logic and rhetoric must be absorbed by the *logos*. Since he is obliged to argue his case with the imperfect materials at hand, he must express the promised goal *as* logic and rhetoric – as the rigorous progress of thought and the "metamorphosis" that it promises. To bridge the immense gap between human logic and divine truth requires yet another rhetorical figure, an intermediary who belongs to both realms. The Lady represents the neo-Platonic ideal of transcendence, which Eliot describes as "the reaching out towards something which cannot be had *in*, but which may be had partly *through* personal relations" (*SE*, 428). This description recalls the accounts of thought and language, which must exercise themselves in order to exceed themselves. Similarly, this spiritual "something," this perfection, must also be expressed as personal relations, that is, as love and understanding. Therefore the Lady reaffirms all that Eliot has so painfully denied, proposing a redemptive reversal that the poem anticipates but does not quite achieve. It ends confronting the gulf still to be overcome: "Suffer me not to be separated" (*CP*, 105).

Altieri treats this reversal as a rhetorical doubling which opens up an "inner" or "negative space" where the mind can free itself from self-consciousness through prayer.[22] J. Hillis Miller treats it as a "turning inside-out of the mind, a reversal which recognizes that time, nature, other people and God are external to the self" and are not figments of the imagination or mere interpretations.[23] In both cases, the Lady permits Eliot to escape from the confines of the self. In our terms the Lady allows a transcendence by passing through the limits proposed in the paradoxical litany, but only by transcribing the poetic argument in what is assumed to be a superior manner. When Eliot prays to her, she in turn contemplates (II) and prays (V) for him. Her actions are the same as his. Through a figure who is both human and divine ("Blessed sister, holy mother"), he reinstates the argument at a higher level, where it becomes a redemptive mystery. What exactly is the divine mystery? The question is presumptuous. "The Christian only gives the mystery a name when he speaks of grace," explains Helen Gardner.[24] Inexplicable in itself and subject to all the contradictions of transcendence, the divine will nevertheless makes human destiny meaningful. Eliot learned from Bradley that faith demands a creative tension between knowledge and ignorance. In the tension of *Ash-Wednesday* we feel the difficulty with which the mind rises through its own interpretations, until it is defeated and yields to an awesome power that renders meaningful its own failure to understand. When the Lady talks "In ignorance and in knowledge of eternal dolour" (*CP*, 100), the conditions of her faith correspond at a higher level to Eliot's. Like him she meditates and prays, but her actions are considered efficacious, not a puzzle or an unavailing process of interpretation. Accordingly, she reverses Eliot's imagery – restoring the desert, refreshing the fountain, redeeming the past. Her paradoxical position, now conceived of as a position of strength, is celebrated in the litany in part II: "Lady of silences / Calm and distressed / Torn and most whole...." (*CP*, 97). In each case the failures of human argument (distress, torn, exhausted) are absorbed by the peace of divine grace (calm, whole, reposeful). She is "spirit of the river, spirit of the sea," because she represents the effortless interpenetration ("The desert in the garden the garden in the desert") of human and divine wills.

Eliot has not yet attained this effortless condition, and, given his conception of poetic argument as an unreasonable process of thought that redeems itself only by reformulating its paradoxes at a transcendent level, he can never fully attain it. Poetry lies beyond the reach of criticism, just as truth lies beyond the reach of philosophy. But poetry, too, reaches an outer limit that mirrors the inner limit of its origin. "The poetry does not matter" (*CP*, 198), he says in "East Coker," because it is only a means to an end, which it can predict, promise, and long for, but not reach. As David Ward explains, Eliot believes in a "poetry whose subject is what is beyond poetry": "the half-known experience, and the emotion that would go with it are, we are made to understand, *outside* the poetry; the poetry is located in one way or another in time or in space, the experience which motivates it, or towards which the poetry points in different ways and at different moments, is protected from the contamination of time and space."[25] Accordingly, the dominant impression of *Ash-Wednesday* is not of calm, but of a passionate intellect arguing with itself. Through his dispute, however, he also gives a sense of the peace that might follow when all passions and all arguments are spent. Therefore, with this higher vision imagined if not achieved, the poem concludes by invoking Dante's great promise: "Our peace in His will."

CHAPTER SIX

Wallace Stevens

Because Wallace Stevens is one of the most argumentative of modern poets, he allows us to recapitulate our terms of discussion by reviewing the logical, rhetorical, and dramatic resources of poetic argument. His arguments move between the poles of immanence and transcendence, correlative limits of thought, which, he suggests, can only be imagined by means of unreason. In a sense they move between the inward and outward extremes proposed by Edward Thomas and T.S. Eliot and scrupulously surveyed by Marianne Moore, but Stevens addresses those limits rather differently. On the one hand, he, too, believes that poetry requires unreason: it provides a special understanding of the world by enabling us to "think / Without the labor of thought" (*CP*, 248).[1] On the other, he shows that it can achieve this effortless knowledge only by resisting and engaging the intellect. Poetry aims at a simplicity that is difficult to attain. It is a freshness of vision and a "perfection of thought" (*CP*, 358), achieved only when the mind disputes and perfects itself. Although he always denied he was a philosopher and called himself "at best, an erratic and inconsequential thinker" (*L*, 186), he was a thoughtful poet who read philosophy and was fascinated by the relationship between it and poetry. Throughout his career he studied the interdependence of philosophic knowledge and poetic perception, of argument and vision. When certitude and desire agree perfectly, "The thought makes the world sweeter" (*SP*, 215). When uncertainty or despair finds its perfect expression, the vision gained is not sweet, but it is still thrilling, and poetry remains "the thesis scrivened in delight" (*CP*, 326).

Like all advocates of the reasoned unreasonableness of poetry, Stevens enjoys the urgency, the cogency, but also the unruliness of imaginative thought. He presents poetry at its most festive. The air of celebration ("Tum-ti-tum, / Ti-tum-tum-tum! / The turkey-cock's tail / Spreads to the sun," *CP*, 20) is manifest and needs no proof. But poetic argument as a festival of reason involves something more, as I noted in Chapter One, when I introduced the problematic of reason. The festive spirit is rational, not irrational, but, like Puck in *A Midsummer Night's Dream*, it is also a mischievous goblin, always threatening to frolic out of control. Dylan Thomas's poetry shows how the festivities prove dangerous, even anarchic, how they combine celebration with subversion. In Stevens's famous phrase, poetry is a "rage for order." The rage is *within* the order, within the rational forms, which its arguments muster and direct to a transcendent end - "sublimated wisdom," Moore calls it - an end that will unify the preceding discourse. Poetic argument aspires to be an imaginative reconciliation of perception and conception, of sensation and significance. It is an integration of thought or "composing of senses" (*CP*, 168). The mind organizes, pacifies, and expresses itself as it conducts, entertains, and satisfies thought. But thought is also unruly, so delighted in tumult that the very energy with which it pursues its goal can shatter its orderly progress. Accordingly, in the discussion that follows, we shall often find a festive interplay of argument and counterargument. For Stevens, poetry is a noble project of understanding in which the "pensive man" (*CP*, 216) must argue with himself ("One would continue to contend with one's ideas," *CP*, 198); with his readers, whom he challenges and persuades; and with the world itself, as he wages "the fundamental and endless struggle with fact" (*PEM*, 206) that is the fate of consciousness.

Following the general pattern of the preceding chapters, I intend to study the origins, means, and ends of Stevens's poetic arguments. He, too, examines where poetic thought starts, or how it arises; he develops intricate logical and lyrical strategies; and he proposes goals that poetry aims at, reaches, or fails to reach. Before analysing these three stages, however, I wish to consider a complication arising from his treatment of unreason, which he regards as the unruly energy of poetic arguments.

Stevens's poems are highly aggressive in Quintilian's sense of forceful, disputacious, and provocative. They offer arguments within arguments that often prove circular or inconclusive. As I have contended several times in the course of this book, such arguments can only be *logically* circular, ambiguous, paradoxical, or inconclusive. Nevertheless their logic must still account for a nonrational provocation that declares itself in what Stevens presents as an interplay of reason and unreason. A useful example occurs in "Extracts from Addresses to the Academy of Fine Ideas":

Of systematic thinking ... Ercole,
O, skin and spine and hair of you, Ercole,
Of what do you lie thinking in your cavern?
To think it is to think the way to death ...

That other one wanted to think his way to life,
Sure that the ultimate poem was the mind,
Or of the mind, or of the mind in these
Elysia, these days, half earth, half mind;
Half sun, half thinking of the sun; half sky,
Half desire for indifference about the sky. (*CP*, 256–7)

The academician speaking here condemns moribund rationalism by attributing it, with ironic inappropriateness, to a brutish Hercules who is more physical than intellectual. The speaker endorses another, heroic argument that truly informs the mind; that is, it shapes, takes possession of the mind, and fuses it with the world. To think one's way to life is the aim of poetry: "the end of the poet is fulfillment, since the poet finds a sanction for life in poetry that satisfies the imagination" (*NA*, 43). It satisfies and teases the reason, too, as the first confident assertion ("Sure ...") is eroded by the qualifications and alternatives that follow. The reader detects a second line of thought that questions the explanation given by the pompous speaker who seems so unsure of his calculations. Therefore the ultimate poem is not one mind secure in its ideas, but a competition of minds, a debate which the reader must referee. He must judge not only the primary argument, but also the half-thinking, ignorance, and indifference which contribute to a larger rhetoric of "musing." The poem of the mind is a self-questioning argument that satisfies itself through its questions, which temporarily grant it the composure of an Elysian state. It is the working of the imagination as it shapes and dignifies the quest for knowledge:

the mind
Turns to its own figurations and declares,
"This image, this love, I compose myself
Of these. In these come forth outwardly." (*CP*, 226)

Several critics have studied Stevens's ambiguous style of argument, which produces "a poem of pure provisionality" and depends on "a rhetoric of intermittances, of false starts and misleading clues, of centerless labyrinths, hollow resonances, eloquent silence, visionary blankness."[2] One convenient way to justify and discipline these ambiguities is to assimilate them in a larger dramatic unity. This is the approach of New Criticism which regards every poem as a little play, displaying or acting out its ideas, rather than asserting them as propositions. Statements are more important for their dramatic propriety than for their truth or consistency. Thus Eugene Nassar calls Stevens "an anti-rationalist who played with ideas, with the experience of thinking,"[3] who committed himself to the play more than the ideas. However, deconstructive criticism rejects dramatic propriety and unity as principles able to subdue the unruliness of Stevens's self-confuting arguments. Whereas New Criticism posits an overriding logic (the drama), deconstruction posits an underlying rhetoric which, it claims, is illogical. In Paul de Man's view, "Rhetoric radically suspends logic and opens up vertiginous possibilities of referential aberration."[4] Quintilian's aggression now becomes a corrosive scepticism that forces poetry to argue – that is, to propose axioms and progressive patterns leading to conclusions – but forbids it to abide by those axioms, patterns, or conclusions. Poetry becomes an endless and originless argument that is the dispute of language with itself. For example, in J. Hillis Miller's account of "The Rock," the key terms (rock, ground, cure) grow ambiguous as the meditation "swirls and weaves its web" over a "treacherous abyss of doubled and redoubled meanings."[5] We can no longer distinguish two opposed lines of thought in debate, because one of them (the web: Robert Graves's Dr Jekyll) is orderly, logical, and grammatical while the other (the abyss: Mr Hyde) is subversive, uncanny, and rhetorical. The relationship between the two cannot be dialectical, because deconstruction disclaims any logical synthesis comparable to dramatic propriety. It refuses to take refuge in a higher unity – the leap of faith made by Eliot in "Ash-Wednesday." Nevertheless the referential aberration is not a mindless wandering; it is still a project of understanding even if it refutes itself. In this view, poetic argument is now the "detour" of an "errant semantics" moving via metaphor between sense and nonsense, continually proposing and contesting truth: "Signification, by its capacity for metaphorical displacement, will be in what we might think of as a state of readiness, lying between the non-sense which precedes language (for it has sense) and the truth of that language which tells it how it is ... Metaphor is the moment of possible sense as the possibility of non-truth. It is the moment of detour in which truth can still be lost."[6]

When Stevens praises the "anti-logician" who thinks "With a logic of transforming certitudes" (*OP*, 66), he seems to endorse the deconstructive detour. Like Roger Caillois, whose devious arguments he describes in a letter, he tries "to evade direct thinking by lapsing into a metaphor or a parable and, in this way, he proves things, not by expressing reasons but by intimations to be derived from analogies" (*L*, 494). Like

Eliot, he is concerned with what Susanne Langer calls the beginning and the end of logic – the uncertainty of its intuitive basis and the indeterminacy of its transcendent goals. But unlike De Man and Miller and, in different way, unlike the religious Eliot, his treatment of poetic unreason gives greater prominence to the logic required even in the midst of indeterminacy or apparent irrationality. Two essays by Joseph Riddel will help to clarify Stevens's position.

In an essay of 1971 Riddel examines the point of departure, or locus of argument, in Stevens's poetry. It is "the point from which the self begins," emerges from "nothingness," and embarks on an endless project of renewing its humanity and its world. I detected a similar project in Dylan Thomas's work. The as yet undefined imaginative self is characterized only by an "energy of being" that propels it urgently onward "from a beginning toward some end that is not defined but nonetheless premised." Although this pattern recurs in each poem and is the very act of the mind, the self that initiates the pattern is not a stable entity, essence, ego, or origin. It is simply the "point of remotest interiority" where nothingness and identity meet, where "mystery informs fact." In the phenomenological/existential terms of this essay, the self must accept and proceed from its own vacancy: "The imagination is reborn in the moment of its annihilation, a 'Will' to be that arises at the ultimate point of nothingness."[7] In his essay of 1980 Riddel recasts his discussion in deconstructive tems, but traces the same pattern. The course of a poem is no longer an existential drama, but an ungovernable play of language in a textual field that cannot define itself. It begins in writing and rewriting rather than in the self, which accordingly becomes a product of the text: "The self no longer governs language, but is governed by it." Desires and impulses, formerly the indefinable motivations of the self, now become a play of metaphor without correction. And at the deepest interior of the text we find a referential abyss or *aporia* corresponding to the nothingness of the self.[8]

In both essays Riddel stresses the problematical point of departure and the violent energy pushing first the self and then language on a quest for meaning that is subverted by the "aber-rational" character of that energy. This pattern also corresponds to the argumentative one with its premises, inferential patterns, and ambiguous conclusions. The first essay, however, by giving priority to the self, is closer to Stevens's own practice. Admittedly, for Stevens, too, the mind is an inaccessible mystery, which he expresses through the familiar images of madness, sleep, and dreaming. Poetry again becomes a waking dream. Nevertheless, the mind is something whose primary force and primitive being precede language and reason, even though they are manifest only through rhetoric and logic. The advantage of positing a nonverbal, nonrational and ultimately unknowable mental energy is that it provides for – even if it cannot fully account for – the desire which makes the mind so aggressive as it rages against chaos. Poetry is aggressive, not just because it gives free play to language, but also because it responds to an urgent need that demands but refuses satisfaction. An important advantage of this model is that it emphasizes the role of logic as a prevailing discipline essential to any argument. Thought begins with something "elemental" rather than instrumental, with an involuntary, nonrational energy that provokes the dynamics of thought (*OP*, 228–9). The subsequent motions of thought, however, are instrumental and logical, as are the arguments of poetry.

To return to unreason as the locus of argument: the major premise in all Stevens's work is simply the need to argue, a need which he treats as a defining feature of the self. If "the mind is the Arena of life" (*L*, 144), then life is the contest of consciousness with itself and with the conditions of its being. "We live in the mind" (*NA*, 140), but we reside there so uneasily that we constantly question and test ourselves. When he proclaims, "Let the place of the solitaires / Be a place of perpetual undulation.... And, most, of the motion of thought / And its restless iteration" (*CP*, 60), his exhortation is redundant. He urges on what is already urgent, because the mind is always a place of undulation. Man is "fierce / In his body, fiercer in his mind, merciless / To accomplish the truth of his intelligence" (*CP*, 321). The adjectives and verbs which Stevens uses to describe the motion of thought in its pursuit of truth tend to be aggressive. It is furious, insatiable, powerful, dissatisfied, terrible, destructive, wild; it hums, revolves, snarls, simmers, swarms, skitters, devastates, and even assassinates.

Such inner ferment ensures that our first link with reality – sensation or immediate experience – is an aspect of thought and consequently of argument. Stevens often celebrates the rich and apparently thoughtless life of the senses, which, like Edward Thomas, he associates with health, light, air, freedom, and the body. Man must "mate his life with life / That is the sensual, pearly spouse" (*CP*, 222). Only then can he attain "a passion merely to be / For the gaudium of being" (*OP*, 71). But the phrase "gaudium of being" suggests delight, sport, rejoicing, ornamentation, and praise. Sensation may be unreasonable in that it is logically prior to thought, but it engages thought as soon as it is remarked and relished. In Stevens's poetry sensation requires appreciation, which is why vision immediately becomes interpretation. Seeing is a "will to see" (*CP*, 451) that becomes a will to argue. It is reflective and self-reflexive rather than passive: "It is desire, set deep in the eye, / Behind all actual seeing, in the actual scene" (*CP*, 467). As a result, the "reality of the eye" becomes "an artifice, / Nothing much, a flitter that reflects itself" (*CP*, 448). This pattern of vision and argument appears in "Bouquet of Roses in Sunlight" (*CP*, 430–1), where the flowers in their first crude effect seem to overpower the viewer. They are "too actual" and "Make any imaginings of them lesser things." But the argument then reverses cause and effect: "And yet this effect is a consequence of the way / We feel and, therefore, is not real, except / In our sense of it, our sense of the fertilest red." Sense and sensation are interdependent because it is the mind that intensifies and savours the vividness of perception.

The fertile growth of thought therefore originates in a violent need that precedes and feeds on sensation. It is impelled by an urging variously identified as appetite, will, desire, inspiration, freedom, unconsciousness, "merely poetic energy" (*OP*, 219), or simply the unknown. Consciousness is a vast impatience, and in his deepest self man "Knows desire without an object of desire, / All mind and violence and nothing felt. / He knows he has nothing more to think about, / Like the wind that lashes everything at once" (*CP*, 358). In the midst of the storm of thought he has nothing to think about because its violence lurks behind or before all thought. Citing Coleridge (via I.A. Richards), Stevens calls it "the will, as a principle of the mind's being, striving to realize itself in knowing itself" (*NA*, 10). This is will in what Eliot considers its basest, most instinctive, and most untrustworthy sense; and for Stevens, too, will is unknowable and uncontrollable, because it is not itself rational, although the thinking that it prompts, is. It is not subject to control, but is the mysterious source of our control, that is, the origin of our systematic power. As such, it is "The gathering of the imbecile" that provokes "The desire for speech and meaning gallantly fulfilled" (*OP*, 95). Like Eliot, Stevens treats will as the dangerous starting point of argument. It is the primitive force behind our orderly or disorderly structures of thought.

In a comparable discussion of structuralism, Edward Said observes that, although principles of order make thought intelligible, structure itself, as the precondition of order, is nonrational:"Structure hides behind the actuality of our existence because it is the nature of structure to refuse to reveal its presence directly; only language can solicit structure out of the back-ground in which it hovers. Structure is nonrational: it is not thought thinking about anything, but thought itself as the merest possibility of activity. It can offer no rationale for its presence, once discovered, other than its primitive *thereness*."[9] In Stevens's poetry this primitive, indefinable presence takes various forms, such as the subman in "Owl's Clover," the "hermitage" at the "centre of the unintelligible" (*CP*, 495), and the master seated "in space and motionless and yet / Of motion the ever-brightening origin" (*CP*, 414). It is located at the paradoxical juncture of reason and unreason, logic and need. It is the vital, aggressiveness of poetic argument: "The centre of transformations that / Transform for transformation's self. / In a glitter that is a life, a gold / That is a being, a will, a fate" (*CP*, 363).

In the first manuscript of "A Collect of Philosophy," Stevens comments on the automatism by which a poem seems to write itself effortlessly. The "intentions" and the "will" of the imagination, which he also calls "the source of poetic urgings," are realized instantaneously. The poet is inspired. The philosopher, too, sometimes finds that "the intentions of the reason" and "the reason's will" are accomplished by similar "miraculous accelerations." All thought, therefore, is urged on by an unreasonable power, which poet and philosopher require but cannot specify or control. It is the origin to which the most rigorous poems return, "to catch from that / Irrational moment its unreasoning" (*CP*, 398). Although Said's carefully chosen term, nonrational (not a matter of reason) does not mean irrational (counter to reason), irrational is the term Stevens prefers, following the romantic preference for the waking dream. He is intrigued by the paradox that irrationality should impel the exercise of reason, not only in poetry and philosophy, but even in our everyday sense of the world: "Everything proves what we want to prove under the beckonings of à [sic] priori. What difference is there between the imagination realizing its intentions and the reason finding a reason for what is irrational?"[10] The nonrational reason behind the apparent reason is Said's "primitive *thereness*." It makes all thought imaginative because its origins and ends, its desires and intentions, remain mysterious. A poetic gloss on Stevens's question occurs in "Desire & the Object" (*OP*, 85):

> I had not invented my own thoughts,
> When I was sleeping, nor by day,
> So that thinking was a madness, and is:
>
> It was to be as mad as everyone was,
> And is.

Stevens sought the premise or starting point of all poetic arguments. It is the origin of desire where thought and feeling arise from madness. It is the point of transition where desire impinges on logic. Thomas Hardy had proposed a similar intersection of faculties as "a principle for which there is no exact name, lying at the indifference point between rationality and irrationality."[11] For Stevens the point is not indifferent but violent, the moment of incitement and excitement.

Another poetic examination of the locus of argument, where desire and logic meet, occurs in "The Bed of Old John Zeller" (*CP*, 326–7). This poem tries to argue itself out of perplexity, but is baffled by its own ancestry, that is, by its nonrational origin. At the beginning the poet is dissatisfied with reason, because it is a "structure of ideas," whose "ghostly sequences / Of the mind, result only in disaster." He does not want to be like Ercole, who thinks his way to death and whose arguments ("sequences of the mind") are ghostly because, no matter how rigorous, they remain incapable of providing certain knowledge. Despite his disavowal of reason, the poet's own tactics and terms ("It follows") are logical as he offers another hypothesis. It might be possible to escape into "another structure / Of ideas," that is, into the "luminous" sequences of the imagination. But he cannot affirm an independent logic of the imagination to set against reason, even though he admits it is the customary romantic ploy "to say as usual that there must be / Other ghostly sequences ... thought of among spheres in the old peak of night." Instead, his wish for such a glorious structure reveals the logic of desire – "the habit of wishing." This is the hidden impulse provoking reason and imagination, both ghostly and insistent. It is an inner turmoil that in a daring simile appears as John Zeller, tossing and turning within his grandson's heart. The grandfather cannot sleep in the disorderly heart/bed because he is himself the principle of restless desire, prompting all the ghostly sequences of thought that keep him awake. The unappeasable principle of desire also appears in "The Men that are Falling" as "an intenser instinct" (*CP*, 188), and in "A Duck for Dinner" as "that old assassin, heart's desire" (*OP*, 66). In "The Bed of Old John Zeller" the diction ("ting-tang tossing") and the convoluted syntax convey a fitfulness that upsets the poet's calculations. Ironically, his final desire is to evade desire, in order "to accept the structure / Of things as the structure of ideas." He wants to see a world uncoerced by thought. Such comfortable realism was perhaps the faith that John Zeller once enjoyed (as indicated in *NA*, 100 and *L*, 469). But all structures, including realistic ones, have a restless ancestor: they are informed by a nonrational impulse which cannot be evaded. The poet actually complicates his desires by wishing them away. When he imagines a stable past, his nostalgia also issues from "the old peak of night."

"The Bed of Old John Zeller" reveals that poetry is "a passion of thinking" (*L*, 513), in which thought contends with its own unease. Grandfather Zeller is "the unknown always behind and beyond the known, giving it the appearance, at best, of chiaroscuro" (*OP*, 228) even on the clearest of days. Early in his career Stevens endorsed the romantic distrust of reason and favoured poetic unreason, which roams "Beyond thought's regulation" (*OP*, 54). The "sterile rationalist" (*OP*, 67) is often a figure of fun, appearing as the logician, doctor, scientist, or metaphysician who studiously seeks truth but is bewildered by love, beauty, and the oracular presence of reality. As critics have noted, however, Stevens later brought poetic thinking more clearly under the sway of logic. Frank Doggett suggests that he had two theories of the imagination: in one aspect it was unconscious, involuntary, spontaneous; in a second it was conscious, deliberate, purposeful. Doggett then warns: "Stevens's lifelong interest in the unconscious and the fortuitous as sources of inceptions, especially those of poems, in no sense obviates his dependence on the work of the intelligence in the making of poems. When his subject enters the center of consciousness, then the poet is the maker; he meditates the idea and shaping of his poem as carefully as a philosopher the logic of his thought."[12]

Doggett locates the transition where inspiration joins reason. Stevens has several names for this process whereby a nonrational spark ignites an argument. He calls it: "a miracle of logic" (*NA*, 154), "an incandescence of the intelligence" (*NA*, 60) and "radiant reason" (*CP*, 124). This fusion means, not just that the poet is a clever craftsman, but that the shaping of his poem – the rhetorical strategy employed – is also logical. Poetry "composes" the violent life of the mind, which may be nonrational in its impulses but is rational in its forms and arguments, no matter how contentious they may be. Stevens sums up this condition in his famous phrase: "Blessed rage for order ... The maker's rage to order words of the sea" (*CP*, 130). The rage is the nonrational violence that forces the mind to make rationality prevail in a chaotic world (the sea). It is a Dionysian impulse that makes us Apollonian connoisseurs of chaos. Although the organizing intention is "the reason in a storm" (*CP*, 169), it has a storm within itself. Although it is the "intelligence" in the "monster" (*CP*, 175), there is a monster within its intelligence. The raging of our inner sea impels us to calm the outer waters and achieve a momentary peace that is "For a moment final, in the way / The thinking of art seems final" (*CP*, 168).

The thinking of art and its appropriate rhetorical forms are the next phase of Stevens's arguments. It is important to recall, however, that such thinking must be provisional, because it can never be satisfied by the finality it proposes. It consists of a "tumult of integrations" (*CP*, 518), because there will always be something incalculable or erratic even in the most rigorous motions of thought. In his poetry these fortuitous redirections of thought appear as hazard, improvisation, variation, the sleight-of-hand man, and "an intellect / Of windings round and dodges to and fro" (*CP*, 429). Nevertheless, Stevens recognizes that in one of its moods the mind of its own accord prefers recognizable patterns. "Thought tends to collect in pools" (*OP*, 170), although we cannot fully account for the tendency or say why it collects in one particular pool at a certain time. He often speaks of the motions, shapes, manner, and habits of the mind; of the transit, drift, and flow of ideas; of the "parade / Of motions in the mind and heart" (*CP*, 439). When examining the inferential patterns of poetry, he is not concerned to catalogue with Kantian precision the transcendental forms of understanding. He is content to observe and illustrate tendencies of thought, the most important of which is already apparent in his contrast of reason and unreason. It is the disposition of thought to deviate in opposite directions. The thinking of art tends toward abstraction and concretion, affirmation and denial, synthesis and analysis, resemblance and difference, reduction and expansion, affluence and poverty, and so on. In a letter to Hi Simons he describes this process of interdependent contraries and indicates the pleasure that comes from giving them full play: "When I was a boy I used to think that things progressed by contraries, that there was a law of contrasts. But this was building the world out of blocks. Afterwards I came to think more of the energizing that comes from mere interplay, interaction. Thus, the various faculties of the mind co-exist and interact, and there is as much delight in this mere co-existence as a man and a woman find in each other's company. This is rather a crude illustration, but it makes the point. Cross-reflections, modifications, counter-balances, complements, giving and taking are illimitable. They make things inter-dependent, and their inter-dependence sustains them and gives pleasure" (*L*, 368).

This account of the mind in action, propelled by the pleasure of its own conflicting energies, may find confirmation in the vitalist philosophies of Bergson or Santayana, but it does not require any specific philosophical commitment. Stevens offers it not as a rigid "law of contrasts," but as a general disposition of thought. Part IV of "It Must Change" (*CP*, 392) illustrates the ease with which the mind resorts to correlative terms, but it also shows the difficulty of maintaining the opposition according to a strict dialectical law. The poem appears to argue by deduction, since it states a general principle ("Two things of opposite natures seem to depend / On one another") and then cites examples: man/woman, day/night, winter/spring, north/south, sun/rain, imagined/real. Meanwhile an inductive counterargument illustrates the logic of desire – the "energizing that comes from mere interplay." It generalizes from specific experiences, just as rhetorically it proceeds through the paired images and drama of their "passion" as they embrace and partake of each other. It begins not with theory, but with sensation – "the particulars of rapture."

First comes sensory enjoyment of the world ("the greenest body"), which is associated with the pleasures of love and poetry. Although sensation precedes thought, it can never remain pure or independent, because it immediately engages thought. Although it is "A passion that we feel, not understand," we can only appreciate it by embracing and following it. In a precise but circular argument, Stevens disposes his terms of reference. He begins with *pleasure* and then finds the basis of pleasure in *change*. As he says elsewhere: "the essence of change is that it gives pleasure" (*L*, 430). He then finds the basis of change in *dependence*: opposites "seem to depend / On one another ... This is the origin of change." Dependence suggests at first the mere connection or sequence of things, one following another, but it also suggests a connection of need or *requirement*, one necessarily following from another. It is here that sensation yields to logic, but the logic is festive. Thought then moves in a circle, and the argument ultimately is circular. Its terms - sensation, change, pleasure, dependence, need - are interchangeable, each confirming the other, no one term claiming absolute priority. Change arises from dependence which arises from pleasure and sensation, which in turn arise from change. The poem is caught up in the transformation it describes, a pattern whose logic gives it the force of destiny, a pattern reinforced by the cyclical imagery of time, season, direction, and family. The merging of terms, of subject and object, of imagination and reality also appears in the transposition: "Music falls on the silence like a sense, / A passion." Music is no longer the sensation received passionately by the senses. It becomes the sense that receives it.

As this example shows, the arguments in Stevens's poetry both follow and interrogate the natural directions of thought. The most common are those which vacillate between abstraction and concretion as they oppose and implicate each other. In each case the mind uses its own momentum to project an end to thought. It moves toward a permanence that would grace the process of arguing by cancelling the movement of its seeking. The mind is always in motion, yet it desires finality. Through abstraction it seeks the permanence of ideas that are timelessly unaffected by physical change. Through concretion it seeks the permanence of things that seem, if only temporarily, complete, absolute, and perfect. The ideas are fictions such as the hero, major man, thinker of the first idea and, ultimately, God. In this case, "The momentum of the mind is all toward abstraction" (*OP*, 179), which it achieves by comparing and synthesizing the particulars of experience. "One either amalgamates distinctions" in this way through synthesis, "or, for true exactness, spreads them out." The latter case, through analysis, reverts to concrete facts. Stevens then comments: "The more one spreads them out, the more one amalgamates them."[13] The two operations are really interdependent. The ideal or general "mass of meaning" grows from and returns to "a singular romance" (*CP*, 256).

The momentum toward abstraction appears most clearly in "The Sail of Ulysses," where the introspective voyager celebrates the expansion of thought, as it rises by observing resemblances until it attains a sublime vision. It proceeds from "the particular thought" to "Plantagenet abstractions"; from "the difficult inch" to "the vast arches of space"; from "credible thought" to "incredible sytems." Generalizing on this pattern, the poet affirms "a law / That bends the particulars to the abstract," until he is checked by the warning phrase "a relative sublime." He then admits that abstraction is a grand temptation we must sometimes resist: "This is not the poet's ease of mind. / It is the fate that dwells in truth. / We obey the coaxings of our end" (*OP*, 103). The "coaxings of our end" suggest nicely the enticing power of argument to project a wonderful destination that will bless our intellectual efforts. As we are urged toward an all-encompassing abstraction, however, we are also drawn fatally away from sensation, pleasure, and fact, the humble ground on which we live. Therefore, the poet must oppose his grand fate with a countercurrent in which "everything moves in the direction of reality" (*OP*, 165). Stevens might have said of Ulysses what he said of H.G. Wells: "When he passes from the international to the interstellar, we hug the purely local."[14] We encourage a momentum of the mind toward concretion.

In part Stevens endorses the epic argument of a Ulysses or a Faust. He admires the ideal of German romanticism: a transcendental poetry which would poeticize philosophy and philosophize poetry. In such "supreme poetry," he writes in "A Collect of Philosophy," the truth would be so radiant that "the particulars of reality would be shadows among the poem's disclosures" (*OP*, 187). But he immediately admits that this lofty ideal has become outmoded and grandiose, and that the modern poet must resist the coaxing of abstraction. "I would sacrifice a great deal to be a Saint Augustine but modernity is so Chicagoan, so plain, so unmeditative," (*L*, 32), he lamented in 1899. Later, when Chicago became Oxidia, he realized that an even more difficult meditation is necessary to appreciate the plainness of reality. In another letter he writes of the "ordinary, everyday search of the romantic mind," not for the sublime but simply for "the discovery of a value that really suffices" (*L*, 345–6). In such poetry the mind directs itself toward the concrete, sufficient, local, particular and vulgar. It considers not the hero, but "the naked man in a state of fact" (*CP*, 263). Against the "German quality of cosmic abstractness" it sets the "piquancy" of "the specific, concrete thing one is keen for" (*L*, 210). To reach this end requires a logic of reduction, abatement, and deflation, "a flow of thought through disillusion and the stinting of any grandiloquence until a minimum or a poverty of being is asserted as value."[15] For example, in "On the Road Home" (*CP*, 203–4), by renouncing abstraction, the poet finds the world more vivid and palpable. In "The Latest Freed Man" (*CP*, 204–5) he rejects doctrine and finds himself at the "centre of reality" with "everything bulging and blazing and big in itself." In "Woman Looking at Flowers" (*CP*, 246–7) reality becomes piquant:

> the central essential red
> Escaped its large abstractions, became,
> First, summer, then a lesser time,
> Then the sides of peaches, of dusky pears.

The arguments that conduct the mind toward abstraction and concretion or demonstrate the confusion of the two, depend on appropriate rhetorical strategies. Critics often refer to Stevens's "alogical" analysis, his paradoxical defiance of logic, or in the case of deconstruction, his "aber-rational" sabotage of logic.[16] As I have indicated, however, for Stevens the nonrational element enters at an earlier stage. Although it lurks in the "unknown" that is "part of the dynamics of the known" (*OP*, 228), it does not operate in rhetorical strategies, which must remain logical because their principles and operations (analogy, resemblance, substitution, predication, inversion, and conventional association) are all logical. If rhetoric leads us on a detour from literal truth, it nevertheless leads us by rational means. If it misdirects us through subversive tropes of reversal such as irony, paradox, or oxymoron, then this reversal – itself a logical procedure – depends on the logical relations of part and whole, cause and effect, before and after, internal and external, etc. Only by recognizing these categories and appreciating how they have been deliberately upset, can we follow the directions and indirections of his arguments.

In *On Extended Wings*, Helen Vendler analyses an impressive array of rhetorical strategies by which Stevens achieves his "sensible ecstasy," yet another way of expressing the waking dream. She considers verb tenses, parts of speech, and grammatical forms; combinations of hypotheses, antitheses, appositives, tautologies, and puzzles; chains of logic, repetition, opposition, and denial. Although she, too, refers to the "quasi-rational progress" of "pseudo-logical statements" in a "sophistic logic," her careful documentation shows, on the contrary, how strenuous is Stevens's logic and confirms that he remains logical, even when his arguments grow circular, paradoxical, or, in our own term, festive. In "Description without Place," for example, his aim "is to preserve the appearance of logic while the incessant vagaries of repetition confuse logical distinctions, the whole being enclosed in a kind of baby talk in which the complicated and abstract philosophical vocabulary usual to such arguments is deliberately replaced by its simplest and most primitive vocabulary." Nowhere here do the confusion and unusual diction defy or exceed logic; they merely complicate it. The *rhetorical* techniques (repetition, variation, substitution) still depend on *logical* principles (identity, analogy, association) even to gain their perverse effects.

Of the patterns that Vendler studies, I wish to consider only a few larger ones, the most important of which expresses the momentum that pushes the mind toward abstraction, a process that depends on synecdoche.[17] According to this pattern, particulars of experience evoke a larger whole of which they are parts. Individual facts become representative and exemplary. This argument is inductive, expansive, and inconclusive, since there is no limit to the generality of truth. The most general truth is reality. Also inductive are the allegories, parables, and fables, which suggest a governing theory or moral, and the longer poems, which are composed of notes and fragments. Marie Borroff believes that these fragments contribute to a vast edifice – "the whole of harmonium," the totality of the imagination, the supreme fiction – which is never complete.[18] Synecdoche promises that each part belongs to something greater, and mere size stirs the imagination (*NA*, 150). It is characteristic of thought and language to push themselves to ever higher levels of abstraction. Even if we begin with a passion for particulars and a "romance of the precise" (*CP*, 353), the precise will suggest the typical, the part will suggest the whole. Poetry is essentially romantic, as Stevens often observed, because it makes the most ordinary object or event seem enchanting: "the most casual things take on transcendence" (*L*, 277). In this case, transcendence is the ambition and goal of abstract thinking, not as part of a redemptive religious ordeal, as it is for Eliot, but as a logical consequence of the dynamic of its argument, as it is for Moore.

Therefore, Stevens has not forgotten the ideal of a supreme philosophic poetry, although he remains wary of it, because the logic of his own work constantly offers it as an enticing hypothesis. By its very nature, poetry is the "growth of the mind / Of the world, the heroic effort to live expressed / As victory" (*CP*, 446). As J. Hillis Miller notes, at the point of greatest precision in Stevens's work, "The images swell up to become cosmic and universal."[19] Man expands into hero, society into utopia, the world into paradise. Through a rhetoric of aggrandizement (synecdoche, hyperbole, insistence, repetition, swelling metaphors, and paradoxes), thought strains to exceed itself and to apprehend the inconceivable. It reaches "The human end in the spirit's greatest reach, / The extreme of the known in the presence of the extreme / Of the unknown" (*CP*, 508). For Ulysses, Canon Aspirin, Hoon, Chocorua, and other aspiring characters, the sublimity of thought must be divined rather than known. It is:

> A life beyond this present knowing,
> A life lighter than this present splendor,
> Brighter, perfected and distant away,
> Not to be reached but to be known,
> Not by an attainment of the will
> But something illogically received,
> A divination ... (*OP*, 101)

Rhetorically, only the image of apotheosis can do justice to this clairvoyance: "If the idea of God is the ultimate poetic idea, then the idea of the ascent into heaven is only a little below it" (*OP*, 193). The ultimate metamorphosis of the imagination is deification. Poetry becomes "An infinite incantation of our selves" (*CP*, 145), where man and the language of his glory become indistinguishable, where logic yields to the higher unreason of divination. But for Stevens, logic does not yield; instead it raises more conditions, as it does for Moore. He seems to have reached the same transcendent moment that Eliot anticipates at the end of "Ash-Wednesday" or "Little Gidding," but heaven means something different from what it is for Eliot, something more down-to-earth. At its summit the sublime argument reaches a point of abstraction where thought either obscures itself or reverts to the "celestial ennui" (*CP*, 381) of stale imagery, because, as we ascend, we either lose our bearings amid the thickening illusions of metaphor (*NA*, 81) or fall back on a pantheon of obsolete fictions. In either case the experience of transcendence provokes anxiety, irony, and even despair. In a secular age there is an unresolvable conflict between desire and belief. Our reach exceeds our grasp, but we cannot believe in a heaven to offer recompense. We live in "a world without heaven to follow" (*CP*, 127), but yearn for a transcendence that we mistrust. Only poetry can "take the place / Of empty heaven" (*CP*, 167), but we cannot credit its exuberance, its careless escapism, and its penchant for the romantic, in the pejorative sense. Although it coaxes us with a "foyer of the spirit," lying "at the end of thought," such a refuge strikes us as the crude delusion of "ignorant men incapable / Of the least, minor, vital metaphor" (*CP*, 305).

The disillusion of "Crude Foyer" justifies Harold Bloom's warning that the "language of desire, possession and power seems to defeat Stevens whenever it becomes too unrestrained in him. ... Stevens could not live with the Sublime, as a poet, and he could not live without it and still be a poet." Bloom is the critic who charts most elaborately Stevens's inductive flights into the "beyond," by tracing his rhetorical progress into the apotheosis of "metaleptic transumption." More than any other commentator, Bloom enjoys what I have called the festive drama of rhetoric. He combines the two functions in an "agon," whereby language and the psyche dispute in the "psychopoetics" of an epic argument.[20] However, despite his insistence on the necessary error and radical indeterminacy of such arguments ("The poem is a lie about itself"[21]), he is not tempted into the irrationalism that I have attributed to both modernist and postmodernist theory. He refuses to confuse "rhetorical substitution with magic" and instead analyses poetry as "a kind of labor that has its own latent principles, principles that can be uncovered and then taught systematically."[22] He insists, in short, on the prevailing rationality of poetic argument. His critical insistence recalls Stevens's poetic refusal to permit logic to yield to unreason. What he requires at the summit of abstraction is not magic, but a reassertion of reason. What he needs is not an abdication of thought, but an even more rigorous argument.

Returning to "Crude Foyer," we find that the poem itself is far from crude and that its bleak "critique of paradise" is redeemed by its own implicit counterargument. Its despair at the self-deluding powers of human consciousness ("Thought is false happiness") is qualified by the central and centralizing image of the poem - the foyer, home, or hearth, which offers a starkly invigorating view of man's bleak condition. The poem supplies what it claims to lack: a vital metaphor. The unconvincing "landscape of the mind" is countered by the landscape of earth; heaven, in so far as we can imagine it, is "here" rather than "there." In other words, we can combat despair by sharing the vantage of characters like Professor Eucalyptus, who opposes the "instinct for heaven" with an equally powerful "instinct for earth" (*CP*, 476). We can reverse the momentum of thought and return to the particular and the concrete.

Stevens associates abstraction with the embellishments and evasions of rhetoric. Conversely, concretion appears to require pruning rhetoric, rejecting metaphor, and returning to the literal base ("the the") of reality. However, just as the absence of imagination must be imagined, so the refusal of rhetoric must be offered in a calculated rhetorical strategy. The perfectly literal depends on a rhetoric of denial - "Pure rhetoric of a language without words" (*CP*, 374). As this definition suggests, the arguments by which the mind conducts itself toward concretion depend on tropes of reversal such as irony, paradox, and oxymoron, and on various uses of metaphor. In one strategy Stevens makes a show of restraining metaphor by declaring it false, misleading, mere gibberish. It is "fictive covering," garment, disguise, or artifice. He denies it validity in order to encourage us to conceive "Things beyond resemblance" (*CP*, 516) or analogy. These are objects, factual and sufficient in themselves, like the two pears which "resemble nothing else" (*CP*, 196), only each other. "This is the figure and not / An evading metaphor" (*CP*, 199) he declares in "Add This to Rhetoric," but the figure remains inevitably a figure of speech. Only through a metaphor that murders metaphor can poetry make possible the "divination" of literal reality.

In a second strategy Stevens uses metaphors of reduction, analysis, contraction, or decreation in order to imagine "The world reduced to one thing."[23] This singular, univocal reality is often represented by a haphazard natural sound such as the wind, stray leaves, the scrawny cry of a bird, or autumnal and wintry noises. The world diminishes to "the half colors of quarter-things" (*CP*, 288), to the impoverished "Natives of a dwindled sphere" (*CP*, 504), to "a lifeless world, / Contracted like a withered stick" (*CP*, 513). In each case the minds of poet and reader are constrained by an asceticism of thought, which leaves them "naked of any illusion, in poverty, / In the exactest poverty" (*CP*, 258). Once again, a contrast with Eliot is instructive, since asceticism for Stevens is not the "askesis" of mystical discipline, but a philosophic reserve, a Cartesian resolve to doubt everything in order to discover what resists all doubt. As in the case of abstraction, however, the insight gained tends to fade just when it grows sharpest. The precision of disillusionment ultimately confounds itself because metaphors of denial and disbelief are so corrosive. They begin by calling into question everything but the immediately palpable. In "Landscape with Boat," for example, the eye contemplates only what is directly before it, but then doubts even that:

Nabob
Of bones, he rejected, he denied, to arrive
At the neutral centre, the ominous element,
The single-colored, colorless, primitive.
It was not as if the truth lay where he thought,
Like a phantom, in an uncreated night. (*CP*, 241 - 2)

The central primitive is invisible and lies beyond concretion. It is "a thing supposed / In a place supposed." Reduction to the first idea forces us back into abstraction, confounding our disciplined argument. The same reversal appears in "The Motive for Metaphor" (*CP*, 288), where the metaphors confuse abstract and concrete terms and mislead us about the direction of thought. Hammer, steel, and sharp flash insist on physicality, until they fade into the "A B C of being." The last line builds in power, until it evaporates in a pure abstraction: "The vital, arrogant, fatal, dominant X." Similarly the elemental Irish cliffs of Moher rise "Above the real" into the phantom realm of "likeness" (*CP*, 502) or analogy.

By following the momentum toward abstraction and concretion, the mind seeks but fails to find the limits of the ideal and the material. It discovers instead that the two are interdependent aspects of each other, or that they are overlapping categories of thought. Since the mind is also examining itself and the conditions of its operation, these are also arguments about the nature of humanity in its two aspects of spirit and body. It is not surprising, therefore, that another important rhetorical device is personification. Through it we ascribe human attributes to the world, until "earth becomes, / By being so much of the things we are, / Gross effigy and similacrum" (*CP*, 87). Personification is not just a technique, but an instinct of thought, and a festive one at that, since it enables us to celebrate the human form and to find it in all things. Narcissistic man sees the world as a "tangent of himself" and makes it a "human residence" (*PEM*, 296), because personification arises from a need that precedes thought and then directs it toward the human:

> The self
> Detects the sound of a voice that doubles its own,
> In the images of desire, the forms that speak,
> The ideas that come to it with a sense of speech.
> The old men, the philosophers, are haunted by that
> Maternal voice, the explanation at night. (*OP*, 82)

In this passage from "The Woman That Had More Babies Than That" the self looks outward for its double, but the maternal forms of nature which it discovers are really reflections of its own desire. Ideas and images "come to it" from a prerational source, which then directs reason (philosophers) by means of speech. Reality is humanized, not simply in its physical forms, but also in the way in which it is made to conform to the basic human structures of thought and language. In "Evening without Angels" (*CP*, 137) the "Encircling" wind "speaks always without speech" and the light "Encrusts us making visible / The motions of the mind and giving form / To moodiest nothings." Reality not only looks but lives like us. Even its emptiness has a Shakespearean mood. In both poems the argument by personification is an encircling one that begins in and returns to the human. It starts with an instinct of thought which turns into a rhetorical drama when, as Lisa Steinman explains, the mind proposes figures of its own activity: "By a characteristic play of thought and language, then, his figures of speech become human figures who are made of speech and who speak, thus suggesting the way in which man creates himself through language."[24] The maternal voice, wind, and light are human figures made out of speech, speaking to man, who comforts himself by imagining a comfortable world for himself. Even if the world seems hostile - a lion, monster, or enemy - it remains familiar and comprehensible.

In the circle of humanity man speaks to nature as to an equal by granting it a human voice. Stevens realizes, however, that to appreciate the world as it is, we must resist our tendency to think through personification. This is again the darker side of the festival that arises whenever thought interrogates and resists its own tendencies. Accordingly, we must restrain our rhetoric in order for thought to grow "less and less human" (*CP*, 327) and for it to move closer to the "inhuman depths" (*CP*, 191) of reality. But this line of argument, too, depends on rhetoric. To deny personification requires that it first be established and then abjured. Like abstraction and concretion, the human and the inhuman must oppose yet implicate each other. The argument must use the pathetic fallacy in order to expose it as fallacious and thereby illustrate the contradictory nature of reality, which we can conceive of only in terms we know to be wrong. In "The Idea of Order at Key West":

> She sang beyond the genius of the sea.
> The water never formed to mind or voice,
> Like a body wholly body, fluttering
> Its empty sleeves; and yet its mimic motion
> Made constant cry, caused constantly a cry,
> That was not ours although we understood,
> Inhuman, of the veritable ocean. (*CP*, 128)

The inhuman sea has no genius, mind, or voice, yet absence of these is conveyed by personification (sleeves, mimic, cry) and by the paradox of something which is "wholly body" yet cannot fill its "empty sleeves." A deliberate effort is needed to resist personification, but it is unavailing. Perversely, the characteristics of the sea and of bare reality in all Stevens's poems are actually human qualities: tragic, mournful, grim, ghostly, hostile, a mind of winter.

In "The Man with the Blue Guitar, XVI," we find the same self-defeating argument:

> The earth is not earth but a stone,
> Not the mother that held men as they fell
>
> But stone, but like a stone, no: not

> The mother, but an oppressor, but like
>
> An oppressor that grudges them their death,
> As it grudges the living that they live. (*CP*, 173)

The poet awkwardly disputes his own powers of thought and speech, lapsing into and out of the realm of the human through simile, which periodically corrects his instinct for personification. His first denial is weakened and then implicitly reversed by the shift from inanimate stone to grudge-bearing oppressor. The personification rejected in the second line is restored in the fourth, because to ascribe any character to reality is to acknowlege humanity as the model of all character.

The poetic attempt to exclude the human – which ultimately means to abolish consciousness – leads to its unexpected resurrection. Even if it is only in the malicious eye of a crow (*CP*, 294) or in the theatrical motion of the sea (*CP*, 129), there remains some rhetorical hint that the mind can never, short of death, empty itself entirely. Poems which attempt to nullify their own arguments inevitably disprove themselves, as the speaker in "Le Monocle de Mon Oncle" finds when he playfully yearns to become a "thinking stone," but through his yearning remains tossed in the "sea of spuming thought" (*CP*, 13). Similarly, "Like Decorations in a Nigger Cemetery, XVI" wonders "If thinking could be blown away / Yet this remain the dwelling-place / Of those with a sense for simple space" (*CP*, 153). The simple dwelling-place is the grave, whose tombstone resembles the Uncle's thinking stone. But thought cannot be obliterated, because it persists, figuratively, as the blowing of the wind, just as earlier it was the tossing of the sea. The argument of this short poem is unexpectedly complex. It offers an impossible hypothesis from which it draws no conclusion. It expresses two wishes which are never clearly related, because the logical connective ("Yet") is puzzling. Thinking cannot be blown away; nevertheless the grave will remain the simplest of places. The first is impossible, the second inevitable. The poem offers a fitful play of thought that considers its own obliteration but reaches a dead end.

In "A Clear Day and No Memories" (*OP*, 113) we find another attempt to exclude the human through a strategy of denial: "No soldiers in the scenery, / No thoughts of people now dead." Ironically, the insistent negation reminds us of all that is excluded from consciousness. The memories of youth, which the title declares void, turn out to be surprisingly precise, recalling the blue dresses and the gestures of fifty years ago. Time weighs heavily, even as we are confined to the present moment. The second stanza presents the mind as it tries to disqualify itself by considering the proposition: "Today the mind is not part of the weather."

> Today the air is clear of everything.
> It has no knowledge except of nothingness
> And it flows over us without meanings,
> As if none of us had ever been here before
> And are not here now: in this shallow spectacle,
> This invisible activity, this sense.

This poem seeks a vision of bare reality, possible only when the mind ceases its pestering and imagines its absence. Despite the declared elimination of thought, however, the weather is promptly personified as if it were a mind. As the scene is drained of the human, humanity is ascribed to the scene. Through a double negative, the air has knowledge, although it is knowledge only of nothing. Like the snow man, it is personified and then granted inhuman or subhuman ability. At the end the air is part of a "spectacle," which implies the onlookers previously excluded, and in which it participates not as an object sensed, but as "sense" itself. As in "It Must Change, IV," sense and sensation are reversed, while sense also suggests the elusive meaning denied earlier. In sum, the poem presents a mind that strains to ignore itself by arguing itself out of existence, with the perverse conclusion that it is reinstated by the strength and intricacy of its denials.

This example shows how the denial of metaphor, humanity, imagination, or consciousness actually implies the presence of a meditating, imagining, arguing mind. As Kenneth Burke (citing Bergson) notes, only man can conceive of negation, which is an act of consciousness not a state of affairs. There is no negation in nature "where everything simply is what it is and as it is." Only man is able to refuse, deny or negate things by imagining or commanding their absence. More precisely, the "negative is a function peculiar to symbol systems, quite as the square root of minus-one is an implication of a certain mathematical symbol system."[25] Negation is possible only as a proposition ("No soldiers in the scenery"), that is, as part of an argument. In Stevens's late poetry of reduction and exclusion, negation is never an end in itself but part of a project to imagine what lies at the base of humanity: "It is as if / We have come to an end of the imagination, / Inanimate in an inert savoir" (*CP*, 502). "Inert savoir," like thinking stone, is the mind at its most humble, at the opposite extreme from the inspired divination proclaimed in the poetry of abstraction and transcendence. When Stevens says, "After the final no there comes a yes" (*CP*, 247) or "The cancellings, / The negations are never final" (*CP*, 414), he is not asserting a pious hope, but indicating that consciousness by its very nature proceeds through doubt, including doubt in itself. By accepting failure, the poet succeeds in imagining what lies beyond failure: the plain sense of things and the reality of death. Thus, when Mrs Alfred Uruguay says no to everything, her denial calls forth the figure of capable imagination which she encounters.

I conclude with "Mrs. Alfred Uruguay (*CP*, 248 – 50) because it sums up succinctly the shape, the energy, and the complication of all Stevens's poetic arguments, and because her inconclusive midnight adventure recapitulates the main concerns of this study. In effect, it answers our original questions: how does modern poetry claim to argue, how does it actually argue, and what does it argue about?

Mrs Uruguay and the noble rider whom she passes join a cast of paired characters who have entered and exited from these pages: Dr Jekyll and Mr Hyde, Malvolio in his sober and antic dispositions, the wakeful dreamer and sleeping thinker, Moore's real toad in its imaginary garden. Riding on her donkey, Mrs Uruguay seems to play the role of Sancho Panza, as she conducts a mock epic quest that leads her past her counterpart, a ragged Don Quixote, who is the "figure of capable imagination." As a poetic argument, her ride is a trajectory of thought or, more correctly, one arc in a doubled process of wondering and asking: of what is thought capable? Her ride is the career of imagination, passing through the world in an effort to attain a vision of bare truth, a poetic insight that will reappropriate reality ("While she approached the real, upon her mountain") and grant self-possession ("in order to get at myself"). It is a project in understanding and redemption that will bring the world, the mind and language into accord by fusing into unity the powers of seeing, knowing, and saying.

Her ride also indicates the basic form and power that are the axioms of any argument and any poem. In dramatic terms the form of her argument is a plot with a beginning, middle, and end. It is impelled by a dynamic principle, which is felt as a need, necessity, or faith, which in turn serves to define a source and to project an end. In rhetorical terms the impulsive energy is the aggression of language, recorded in the shifting colours, tones, and sounds orchestrated through the poem. For Mrs Uruguay, the originating impulse appears in the opening question, "So what?" Although it expresses the indifference of her companions, it also shows her wonder, her need to know, and her spirit of adventure. It corresponds to the urgency of the rider who is "all will." This will is nonrational, not because it defies reason, but because it precedes reason, which it then enlists in its campaign of understanding. In logical terms an argument is an inferential pattern, which begins in premises and leads through a sequence of logical shifts to a more or less satisfactory conclusion. It moves between the ground and the goal of thought, between the beginning and the end of logic. It also tries to imagine what lies beyond either extreme. Therefore, its goal is always transcendent in the sense that it is a sovereign truth that promises to dominate, unify, and sanction the preceding argument. Truth is the unified vision of the whole that Mrs Uruguay hopes to find beyond the "degenerate forms" of the "falsifying bell."

Comically, our hero does not fully appreciate the waywardness of her mission. To achieve her unified vision she must climb not into the clarity of daylight, but into the obscurity of a "lofty darkness." The reversal of light and dark imagery is part of a system of such reversals illustrating how the apparently single plot of her argument, which should lead directly from major premise to final conclusion, is strangely doubled in the modernist aesthetic, because of the incompatible demands made of unreason – her donkey. Modern poets are torn between the competing desires to renounce and to reclaim reason. They treat the transcendent goal of thought as radically transgressive, because it must be reached through an argument which in their view subverts its logical and discursive conditions. They claim to employ the antilogic of the waking dream ("Time swished on the village clocks and dreams were alive"), by which thought manages to outwit itself. They claim to attain the nondiscursive discourse of poetic silence, by which words dissolve themselves and touch reality immediately. To achieve this paradoxical victory is Mrs Uruguay's mission; consequently she finds her argument beset by ironies and ambiguities, to which she is blind. Like "Ash-Wednesday," her poem is a song of ascents that rises only through denial, and her wayward progress is played out in the argument and counterargument of the poem's two figures. The other figure, the rider, is part of a complex rhetorical strategy which she does not control or appreciate. As Bloom observes, he is "a noble synecdoche personified"[26] – a logical projection of the imaginative truth she considers false. The bell of her falsehood rings out his truth. Although he seems to be her dialectical counterpart, the balance is upset by inconsistencies that surprise the reader and make the argument seem unstable. For example, she is a literalist and reductionist, yet she wears elegant velvet and ascends into the heights. He is a fanciful expansionist who emerges in tatters out of reality. Her rage for elegance arises from the "brown blues" of the unconscious and from the very imagination she abjures, while her goal is not only concrete (the mountain top) but abstract (mere being), not only inhuman (the real) but human (herself). While she rises, he descends to the real village, now washed by dreams, and to sharp "pickets rocks," like real toads in an imagined land.

Although he was intent on the sun, he becomes a victor of the imagination, when he creates the elegance to which he was earlier blind.

This blending of opposed terms makes the counterpointed argument unreasonable, mischievous, and festive, but not irrational. Although Mrs Uruguay whispers her foolishness to the donkey, her efforts remain sane and calculated, as she advances through a rhetorical strategy of negation and substitution that depends on a continual exchange: sun/moon, sleep/waking, elegance/nakedness, acent/descent, wisdom/foolishness, victor/martyr. However odd or unexpected they may seem, these exchanges remain logical in their categories and in their system of opposition, substitution, and conflation. Mrs Uruguay seeks the "ultimate" victory of the mind through an "integration" of thought that is "capable" or availing. But the poem achieves instead a vision that is provisional and unstable and requires a process of readjustment, a constant balancing and interweaving of opposites. It reaches this conclusion not through Mrs Uruguay, but through the perspective of the speaker, who surveys the intersecting courses of both figures and sees that together they give form and urgency to the adventure.

Stevens wrote in one of his letters: "There is no reason why any poet should not have the status of the philosopher, nor why his poetry should not give up to the keenest minds and the most searching spirits something of what philosophy gives up and, in addition, the peculiar things that only poetry can give" (*L*, 292). Mrs Uruguay's midnight ride illustrates this logical yet sublime achievement. Its sublimity is proposed and promised by logic: it is the fruit of argument. Yet, as an ideal of fulfilment, sublimity exceeds the full grasp of reason: it is unreasonable. Stevens expresses this paradoxical force of poetic argument in another letter, when he says: "The knowledge of poetry is a part of philosophy, and a part of science; the import of poetry is the import of the spirit" (*L*, 378). He expresses it in the ironic figure of Mrs Uruguay, who is a comical Descartes, rising through the denial of all that is not clear and distinct; seeking the truth of the world by isolating the combined "cogito" and "dubito," the essential faith and doubt of her being;[27] discovering by this means not only reality, but the "ultimate elegance" of the imagination. She is a searching spirit whose mind is a poem and whose poem is a mind forever arguing with and about itself. Her argument is a bewildering yet calculated interweaving of two lines of thought that converge even though they seem divergent. It is a "calculated chaos" (*CP*, 307) because its premises and conclusions are incalculable, but the course between them is a triumph of reason.

Notes

CHAPTER ONE:

1 Francis Bacon, *The Advancement of Learning*, 177.
2 *The Poems of Dylan Thomas*, 137.
3 Dylan Thomas, *Early Prose Writings*, 155–6.
4 Marianne Moore, *Predilections*, 3.
5 *Quintilian's Institutes of Oratory*, I, 336.
6 Aristotle, *Rhetoric* III, 1411b–1412a, 189–92. Aristotle's "energy" and its critical history are discussed by Gerald L. Bruns in *Modern Poetry and the Idea of Language*, ch. 2.
7 For the Longinian tradition of expressive or passionate poetic language, see M.H. Abrams, *The Mirror and the Lamp: Romantic Theory and the Critical Tradition*, 72–8.
8 Harold Bloom, "The Breaking of Form," *Deconstruction and Criticism*, 14.
9 Matthew Arnold, *On the Classical Tradition*, 1.
10 W.B. Yeats, *Mythologies*, 331.
11 Northrop Frye, "Approaching the Lyric," *Lyric Poetry: Beyond New Criticism*, ed. Chaviva Hosek and Patricia Parker, 33. Criticism of the compressed, unified effects of lyric is a recurring theme in this collection.
12 *The Collected Poems of Wallace Stevens*, 351.
13 Octavio Paz, *The Bow and the Lyre*, 97. Further references are given in parentheses.
14 Stéphane Mallarmé, *Oeuvres Complètes*, 368. The translations of Mallarmé are my own; other translations are indicated in the notes.
15 Stéphane Mallarmé, *Oeuvres Complètes*, 368.
16 Paul Valéry, *The Art of Poetry*, 150. Further references are given in parentheses.
17 Stéphane Mallarmé, *Oeuvres Complètes*, 364, 368.

18 Paul Valéry, *The Art of Poetry*, 81. Further references are given in parentheses.
19 *Paul Valéry: An Anthology*, 112.
20 Friedrich Schlegel quoted by Ernst Cassirer, *An Essay on Man*, 161.
21 Friedrich von Schiller, *Naive and Sentimental Poetry*, 98.
22 A.E. Housman, *The Name and Nature of Poetry*, 38.
23 W.B. Yeats, *The Celtic Twilight*, 35; Yeats deleted this passage from *Mythologies*.
24 Benedetto Croce, *Æsthetic*, 14.
25 Stéphane Mallarmé, *Oeuvres Complètes*, 33.
26 *The Letters of W.B. Yeats*, 570.
27 Michael G. Cooke, *The Romantic Will*, 10–11.
28 Samuel Taylor Coleridge, *Biographia Literaria*, 179.
29 H. Stuart Hughes, *Consciousness and Society*, 17, 430.
30 *The Letters of John Keats*, I, 185.
31 *The Collected Works and Letters of Charles Lamb*, 167.
32 Henry David Thoreau, *A Week on the Concord and Merrimack Rivers*, 316.
33 Stéphane Mallarmé, *Correspondance*, 116.
34 Paul Valéry, *The Art of Poetry*, 315, 11, 20.
35 Marianne Moore, *Collected Poems*, 41.
36 Bonnie Costello, *Marianne Moore: Imaginary Possessions*, 23.
37 Susanne Langer, *Feeling and Form*, 377–8.
38 Ibid.
39 Ernst Cassirer, *An Essay on Man*, 143. Further references are given in parentheses.
40 Ernst Cassirer, *The Philosophy of Symbolic Forms*, vol 2, *Mythical Thought*, 60–1. For a criticism of Cassirer's account of reason, see Gerald Graff, *Poetic Statement and Critical Dogma*, 66–70.
41 Babette Deutsch, *Poetry in Our Time*, 87.
42 F.H. Bradley, "Our Knowledge of Immediate Experience," 40.
43 Robert Langbaum, *The Poetry of Experience*, 28–9.
44 Eleanor Farjeon, *Edward Thomas: the Last Four Years*, 51.
45 T.E. Hulme, *Further Speculations*, 77.
46 T.E. Hulme, *Speculations*, 116.
47 Andrew Welsh, *Roots of Lyric: Primitive Poetry and Modern Poetics*, 69. Further references are given in parentheses.
48 Ezra Pound, *Gaudier-Brzeska: A Memoir*, 89.
49 John T. Gage, *In the Arresting Eye: The Rhetoric of Imagism*, 76. Further references are given in parentheses.
50 Archibald MacLeish, *Poetry and Experience*, 40.
51 Owen Barfield, *Poetic Diction*, 108, 138–9.
52 "Literature of Knowledge and Power," *Thomas De Quincey's Works*, vol. 10.

53 Susan Sontag, *Styles of Radical Will*, 80–1.
54 Stéphane Mallarmé, *Oeuvres Complètes*, 378.
55 Archibald MacLeish, *Poetry and Experience*, 62; "Ars Poetica," *New and Collected Poems, 1917–1976*, 106
56 Robert Graves, "The Yet Unsayable," *Poems Selected By Himself*, 178
57 Norman N. Holland, *The I*, 88.
58 Gerald L. Bruns, *Modern Poetry and the Idea of Language*, 190–2.
59 Ferdinand de Saussure, *Course in General Linguistics*, 120–2.
60 Jacques Derrida, *Of Grammatology*, 141–2.
61 Frank Lentricchia, *After the New Criticism*, 116–17; Ferdinand de Saussure, *Course in General Linguistics*, 14–15.
62 Rosmarie Waldrop, *Against Language?*, ch. 1.
63 Hugh Kenner, *The Pound Era*, 54ff.
64 *Personae: The Collected Shorter Poems of Ezra Pound*, 112.
65 *The Complete Poems and Selected Letters and Prose of Hart Crane*, 15.
66 George Steiner, *Language and Silence*, 60ff.
67 Hugo von Hofmannsthal, *Selected Prose*, 134–5. I have also used the following studies of the poetics of silence: R.P. Blackmur, "The Language of Silence," *Language: An Enquiry into its Meaning and Function*, ed. R.N. Anshen; Roland Barthes, *Writing Degree Zero*; Susan Sontag, "The Aesthetics of Silence," *Styles of Radical Will*; Ihab Hassan, *The Literature of Silence*; Jerzy Peterkiewicz, *The Other Side of Silence*; Renato Poggioli, *The Theory of the Avant-Garde*; Karsten Harries, "Metaphor and Transcendence."
68 Wallace Stevens, *The Necessary Angel: Essays on Reality and the Imagination*, 118.
69 Northrop Frye, *Fables of Identity*, 238–9; *Anatomy of Criticism*, 83.
70 George Steiner, *On Difficulty and Other Essays*, 138, 141.
71 Samuel Taylor Coleridge, *Biographia Literaria*, ch. 18.
72 Donald Davie, *Purity of Diction in English Verse*, 113.
73 Stéphane Mallarmé, *Oeuvres Complètes*, 68, 1488; *Correspondance*, 137.
74 Francis Steegmuller, "*La Feuille Blanche*: a Valéry rarity," 1169.
75 Owen Barfield, *Poetic Diction*, 87–8. Further references are given in parentheses.
76 *The Prose Works of William Wordsworth*, 2, 84.
77 *Collected Letters of Samuel Taylor Coleridge*, 1, 625–6
78 Samuel Taylor Coleridge, *Inquiring Spirit: A New Presentation of Coleridge*, 101.
79 T.S. Eliot, *The Sacred Wood*, 149–50.
80 Ezra Pound, *Literary Essays of Ezra Pound*, 5, 9.
81 Ezra Pound, *Gaudier-Brzeska: A Memoir*, 114, 86.
82 Ibid., 88.
83 Jean Moreas's symbolist manifesto in *Les Premières armes du Symbolisme*,

ed. Michael Parkenham, 32. Wallace Stevens, *Opus Posthumous*, 164.

84 T.E. Hulme, *Further Speculations*, 10, 78; *Speculations*, 137.

85 Ernest Fenellosa and Ezra Pound, "The Chinese Written Character as a Medium for Poetry," 202–3.

86 Andrew Welsh, *Roots of Lyric*, 118, 121.

87 Ernest Fenellosa and Ezra Pound, "The Chinese Written Character as a Medium for Poetry," 202–3.

88 Paul Ricoeur, "The Metaphorical Process as Cognition, Imagination, and Feeling," *On Metaphor*, 145. Further references are given in parentheses.

89 Paul Ricoeur, *The Rule of Metaphor*, 80. Further references are given in parentheses.

90 Paul Ricoeur, "The Metaphorical Process as Cognition, Imagination, and Feeling," 144.

91 Roland Barthes, *Writing Degree Zero*, 83.

92 *The Prose Works of William Wordsworth*, 2, 85.

93 *The Collected Works of Samuel Taylor Coleridge*, 6, 29.

94 *The Complete Poems and Selected Letters and Prose of Hart Crane*, 235, 221.

95 T.S. Eliot, "Preface," *Anabasis*, 9–10. Lewis Freed discusses the meaning of logic in this passage in *T.S. Eliot: The Critic as Poet*, 189–92.

96 T.S. Eliot, "Preface," *Anabasis*, 9–10.

97 For Jarry's 'Pataphysics, see Roger Shattuck, *The Banquet Years*, 239ff. and Ihab Hassan, *The Dismemberment of Orpheus*, 48ff.

98 Arthur Rimbaud, *Collected Poems*, 10.

99 Wylie Sypher, *The Loss of the Self in Modern Literature and Art*, 99, 101, 103. Like Sypher, Norman Rabkin appeals to the radical scepticism of modern science to explain the paradox of aesthetic vision in *Shakespeare and the Common Understanding*. He discusses J. Robert Oppenheimer's notion of "complementarity" (22–3). Gerald Graff gives a detailed defence of reason in poetry in *Poetic Statement and Critical Dogma*, especially in chapters 4 and 5, where he touches on the subject of argument and concludes, as I do: "There is no logic of the imagination, no purely psychological coherence outside a mediating framework of logic" (134).

100 Ludwig Wittgenstein, *Tractatus Logico-Philosophicus*, 11, 47, 71.

101 Robert Graves, *Poetic Unreason and Other Studies*, 137, 86, 119.

102 Robert Graves, *Goodbye to All That*, 283. The term "supra-logical" recurs in Graves's criticism.

103 Robert Graves, *On Poetry: Collected Talks and Essays*, 430.

104 Robert Graves and Laura Riding, *A Survey of Modernist Poetry*, 163.

105 Robert Graves, *The Common Asphodel*, 327ff.

106 Robert Graves, *On Poetry*, 506.

107 Ibid., 413.

108 I have drawn phrases from Paul de Man's "Shelley Disfigured" and J. Hillis Miller's "The Critic as Host," both in Bloom et al., *Deconstruction*

and Criticism, and from Miller's essay, "Stevens' Rock and Criticism as Cure," 338.

109 J. Hillis Miller, "Stevens' Rock and Criticism as Cure," 331, 7.

110 J. Hillis Miller, "The Critic as Host," 229.

111 "The Man on the Dump," *The Collected Poems of Wallace Stevens*, 203.

112 J. Hillis Miller, "Stevens' Rock and Criticism as Cure," 19, 20, 29.

113 Paul de Man, *Allegories of Reading*, 10, 16, 131. See also de Man's study of the conflict between epistemology and rhetoric, truth and trope, in "Anthropomorphism and Trope in Lyric," *The Rhetoric of Romanticism*.

114 Barbara Johnson, *The Critical Difference*, xi, xii, 110.

115 Jacques Derrida, "White Mythology," 41.

116 Geoffrey H. Hartman, *Criticism in the Wilderness: The Study of Literature Today*, 202.

117 Wallace Stevens, *Opus Posthumous*, 184.

118 David Daiches, *The Place of Meaning in Poetry*, 52.

119 *Selected Prose of T.S. Eliot*, 64. Lawrence Durrell, *Key to Modern Poetry*, 31.

120 Geoffrey H. Hartman, *Criticism in the Wilderness*, 196.

121 *Literary Essays of Ezra Pound*, 25.

122 Cleanth Brooks, *The Well Wrought Urn*, 256, 207, 211. This account of poetic thought as drama has been criticized widely, notably by Gerald Graff in *Poetic Statement and Critical Dogma*, and by Fredric Jameson in *The Prison-House of Language*.

123 Francis Bacon, *The Advancement of Learning*, 178.

124 Lionel Trilling, *The Liberal Imagination*, 290.

125 Carol Johnson, *Reason's Double Agents*, 14ff.

126 Aristotle, *Rhetoric*, 1354–5.

127 Howard Nemerov, *Figures of Thought*, 103.

128 "To an Old Philosopher in Rome," *The Collected Poems of Wallace Stevens*, 50.

CHAPTER TWO

1 Marianne Moore, texts and abbreviations: *The Complete Poems of Marianne Moore*: *CP*; *Collected Poems*: *ClP*; *Predilections*: P; *A Marianne Moore Reader*: *MMR*; reviews and editorials from *The Dial*: *D*.

2 See especially Bonnie Costello, *Marianne Moore: Imaginary Possessions*, 23.

3 Randall Jarrell, *Poetry and the Age*, 182.

4 Lisa M. Steinman, "Modern America, Modernism, and Marianne Moore," 222.

5 Denis Donoghue, "The Proper Plenitude of Facts," 165.

6 A. Kingsley Weatherhead, *The Edge of the Image: Marianne Moore, William Carlos Williams and Some Other Poets*, 62.

7 From "Poetry" in the second edition of *Observations*, quoted by Helen

Vendler in *Part of Nature, Part of Us: Modern American Poets*, 61.

8 Kenneth Burke, *A Grammar of Motives*, 486–8. Hugh Kenner, *A Homemade World: The American Modernist Writers*, 111. R.P. Blackmur, *Form and Value in Modern Poetry*, 240. Charles Tomlinson, "Introduction: Marianne Moore and her Critics," *Marianne Moore: A Collection of Critical Essays*, ed. Charles Tomlinson, 3.

9 A point made by William Carlos Williams in "Marianne Moore," *Marianne Moore: A Collection of Critical Essays*, ed. Charles Tomlinson, 57–8.

10 "On Gusto," *The Complete Works of William Hazlitt*, 4, 77–80.

11 Quoted by Lisa M. Steinman, "Modern America, Modernism, and Marianne Moore," 221. Steinman shows how Moore would qualify this statement, but accepts its ranking of minor and major truths.

12 Quoted by Walter Kaufmann, *Nietzsche: Philosopher, Psychologist, Antichrist*, 204.

13 Bonnie Costello, *Marianne Moore: Imaginary Possessions*, 28, 29.

14 Quoted by Laurence Stapleton in *Marianne Moore: The Poet's Advance*, 18.

15 W.H. Auden, *The Dyer's Hand and Other Essays*, 304. John Crowe Ransom, "On Being Modern with Distinction," 102.

16 Bonnie Costello, "Marianne Moore and Elizabeth Bishop: Friendship and Influence," 137. Donald Hall, *Marianne Moore: The Cage and the Animal*, 68.

17 Andrew J. Kappel, "Introduction: The Achievement of Marianne Moore," xiv, xvi, xvii.

18 Donald Hall, *Marianne Moore: The Cage and the Animal*, 99–100.

19 Ralph Rees, "The Reality of the Imagination in the Poetry of Marianne Moore," 231, 232.

20 Michael Edwards, "Marianne Moore: 'Transcendence, Conditional,'" 110–26.

21 Quoted by Palinurus (Cyril Connolly) in *The Unquiet Grave*, 128.

22 Elizabeth Phillips, *Marianne Moore*, 143–5.

CHAPTER THREE

1 Wylie Sypher, *The Loss of the Self in Modern Literature and Art*. Edward Said discusses the theme as it reappears in postmodern studies in *Beginnings: Intention and Method*, 292ff.

2 Michael Kirkham, *The Imagination of Edward Thomas*, 205.

3 Paul de Man, *Blindness and Insight*, 39. Kirkham makes a similar point in a different way: "The poetry goes furthest in showing us not the real man but, what others could not know, the potential man, or rather, the real man of partial vision, victim of his temperament, absorbed into the potential man who has poised possession of his full experience" (144)

4 M.H. Abrams, "Style and Structure in the Greater Romantic Lyric." W.J.

Keith, *The Poetry of Nature*. See also Keith's *The Rural Tradition* and Rayner Unwin's *The Rural Muse: Studies in the Peasant Poetry of England.*

5 Edward Thomas, editions and abbreviations. *The Collected Poems of Edward Thomas*: *CP*; *Letters of Edward Thomas to Gordon Bottomley*: *LGB*; Eleanor Farjeon, *Edward Thomas: the Last Four Years*: *LFY*; *Wales*: *W*; *The Heart of England*: *HE*; *Richard Jefferies*: *RJ*; *The South Country*: *SC*; *Feminine Influence on the Poets*: *FI*; *Light and Twilight*: *LT*; *Maurice Maeterlinck*: *MM*; *Algernon Charles Swinburne, A Critical Study*: *ACS*; *Walter Pater, A Critical Study*: *WP*; *A Literary Pilgrim in England*: *LPE*.

6 F.R. Leavis, *New Bearings in English Poetry* , 61. For the relation between Thomas and the Georgians, who continued the tradition of nature poetry and with whom Thomas was associated, see Edna Longley, *Edward Thomas: Poems and Last Poems*, appendix B.

7 See W.J. Keith, *The Poetry of Nature*, 151, 154, 162.

8 Samuel Hynes, *Edwardian Occasions*, 96.

9 Michael Kirkham, *The Imagination of Edward Thomas*, 191. For his discussion of analogical thought, see chapter 9, "The Semantics of Form."

10 D.W. Harding, "A Note on Nostalgia," 19. Michael Kirkham, *The Imagination of Edward Thomas*, 59, 63, 64.

11 Andrew Motion, *The Poetry of Edward Thomas*, 51, 56.

12 Edna Longley, *Edward Thomas: Poems and Last Poems*, 303.

13 Stan Smith, *Edward Thomas*, ch.1.

14 H. Coombes, *Edward Thomas: A Critical Study*, 198.

15 John F. Danby discusses "a characteristic Thomas feeling for the universe as a structure of opposites" in "Edward Thomas," 308–17.

16 W.J. Keith, *The Poetry of Nature*, 143. Stan Smith, *Edward Thomas*, 44–5.

17 From a review of Alfred Noyes quoted by R. George Thomas, "Edward Thomas, Poet and Critic," 126.

18 Michael Kirkham, *The Imagination of Edward Thomas*, 73.

19 William Cooke, *Edward Thomas: A Critical Biography*, 181.

20 Hugh Underhill, "The 'Poetical Character' of Edward Thomas," 242, 251.

CHAPTER FOUR

1 Dylan Thomas, editions and abbreviations: *The Poems of Dylan Thomas*: *P*; *The Notebooks of Dylan Thomas*: *N*; *Quite Early One Morning*: *QEM*; *A Prospect of the Sea*: *PS*; *Early Prose Writings*: *EPW*; *Portrait of the Artist as a Young Dog*: *PAD*; *Selected Letters of Dylan Thomas*: *SL*; *Letters to Vernon Watkins*: *VW*.

2 Friends and biographers agree that, while he had a perceptive mind, Thomas was no philosopher. For example, Daniel Jones observes in *My Friend Dylan Thomas*, 55: "The light of Dylan's interest and attention was narrowly focused on a single area, and everything around this was

shrouded in darkness. All systematic studies based on observation, calculation or conjecture were abandoned to this outer darkness."

3 Northrop Frye, *A Natural Perspective: The Development of Shakespearean Comedy and Romance*, 119, 122.
4 Henry Treece, *Dylan Thomas: Dog Among the Fairies*, 34.
5 Elder Olson, *The Poetry of Dylan Thomas*, 36.
6 Stuart Holroyd, "Dylan Thomas and the Religion of the Instinctive Life," 146.
7 Francis Scarfe, *Auden and After*, 112.
8 Martin Dodsworth, "The Concept of Mind in the Poetry of Dylan Thomas," 119–20.
9 Geoffrey Moore, "Dylan Thomas," 265.
10 D.S. Savage, "The Poetry of Dylan Thomas," 142.
11 "Poetic Manifesto" quoted by Constantine Fitzgibbon, *The Life of Dylan Thomas*, 338.
12 Robert Graves, *The Crowning Privilege*, 133.
13 Karl Shapiro, "Dylan Thomas," 274.
14 John Fuller, "The Cancered Aunt on her Insanitary Farm," *Dylan Thomas*, ed. Walford Davies, 201. David Holbrook is Thomas's severest critic in this respect, especially in *Llareggub Revisited: Dylan Thomas and the State of Modern Poetry*, and *Dylan Thomas and The Code of Night*.
15 John Malcolm Brinnen, *Dylan Thomas in America*, 126.
16 "Observations on Mr. Wordsworth's Poem The Excursion," *The Compete Works of William Hazlitt*, 4, 112–13.
17 John Bayley, "Chains and the Poet," *Dylan Thomas*, ed. Walford Davies, 59, 62.
18 J. Hillis Miller, *Poets of Reality*, 190.
19 D.S. Savage, "The Poetry of Dylan Thomas," 144.
20 "Reply to an Inquiry," quoted by Constantine Fitzgibbon, *The Life of Dylan Thomas*, 151.
21 Raymond Stephens, "Self and World: The Earlier Poems," 29–30.
22 Donald Davie, *Articulate Energy*, 86.
23 Walford Davies, "The Wanton Starer," *Dylan Thomas*, ed. Walford Davies, 139.
24 Donald Davie, *Articulate Energy*, 126.
25 William York Tindall, *A Reader's Guide to Dylan Thomas*, 153.
26 Alistair Fowler, "Adder's Tongue on Maiden Hair: Early Stages in Reading 'Fern Hill,'" in Davies, 233.

CHAPTER FIVE

1 T.S. Eliot, editions and abbreviations: *Selected Essays*: *SE*; *On Poetry and*

Poets: *OPP*; *Collected Poems, 1909–1962*: *CP*; *The Use of Poetry and the Use of Criticism*: *UPC*; *Knowledge and Experience in the Philosophy of F.H. Bradley*: *KE*; *The Sacred Wood*: *SW*; *The Waste Land: Facsimile and Transcript*: *WL*; *Selected Prose of T.S. Eliot*: *SP*.

2 Michel Foucault, *The Order of Things*, 298, 297.

3 *Literary Essays of Ezra Pound*, 75.

4 *The Egoist* v (5 May 1918), quoted by John Press in *A Map of Modern English Verse*, 82.

5 See, for example, René Wellek, "The Criticism of T.S. Eliot"; John D. Margolis, *T.S. Eliot's Intellectual Development, 1922–1939*; William Righter, "The Philosophical Critic," *The Literary Criticism of T.S. Eliot*, ed. David Newton-de Molina; Edward Lobb, *T.S. Eliot and the Romantic Critical Tradition*.

6 "Ezra Pound," *Ezra Pound: A Collection of Critical Essays*, ed. Walter Sutton, 24. For Eliot's inconsistency in this matter, see Frank Kermode, *Romantic Image* and Edward Lobb, *T.S. Eliot and the Romantic Critical Tradition*.

7 William Righter, "The Philosophical Critic," 114.

8 René Wellek, *Discriminations*, 258.

9 Geoffrey H. Hartman, *Criticism in the Wilderness*, 190.

10 Ibid., 196, 201.

11 F.H. Bradley, editions and abbreviations: *Appearance and Reality*: *AR*; *Collected Essays, II*: *CE*; *Essays on Truth and Reality*: *ETR*; *Ethical Studies*: *ES*.

12 *Bacon's Essays*, 40.

13 Quoted by Lewis Freed, *T.S. Eliot: The Critic as Philosopher*, 55.

14 My discussion of *Ash-Wednesday* is based on an earlier version of this chapter, in which I consider the problem of will in Eliot's poetry. See "T.S. Eliot and the Problem of Will," 373–94.

15 F. Peter Dzwonkoski, Jr.," 'The Hollow Men' and *Ash-Wednesday*: Two Dark Nights," 26, 34.

16 Quoted by John D. Margolis, *T.S. Eliot's Intellectual Development, 1922–1939*, 14.

17 Friedrich Nietzsche, editions and abbreviations: *Thus Spake Zarathustra*: *Z*; *The Genealogy of Morals*: *GM*; *The Will to Power*: *WP*; *Twilight of the Idols*: *TI*.

18 Balachandra Rajan, *The Overwhelming Question*, 57.

19 Quoted by John D. Margolis, *T.S. Eliot's Intellectual Development, 1922–1939*, 139.

20 Charles Altieri, "Steps of the Mind in T.S. Eliot's Poetry," 198.

21 Northrop Frye, *A Natural Perspective: The Development of Shakespearean Comedy and Romance*, 129, 130, 133.

22 Charles Altieri, "Steps of the Mind in T.S. Eliot's Poetry," 201ff.

23 J. Hillis Miller, *Poets of Reality*, 180.

24 Helen Gardner, *The Art of T.S. Eliot*, 104.

25 David Ward, *T.S. Eliot: Between Two Worlds*, 226, 225.

CHAPTER SIX

1 Wallace Stevens, texts and abbreviations: *The Collected Poems of Wallace Stevens*: *CP*; *Opus Posthumous*: *OP*; *Letters of Wallace Stevens*: *L*; *Souvenirs and Prophecies: The Young Wallace Stevens*: *SP*; *The Necessary Angel*: *NA*; *The Palm at the End of the Mind*: *PEM*.

2 George Bornstein, "Provisional Romanticism in 'Notes Toward a Supreme Fiction'," 21. Isabel G. MacCaffrey, "The Ways of Truth in 'Le Monocle de Mon Oncle'," *Wallace Stevens: A Celebration*, ed. Frank Doggett and Robert Buttel, 200. For other discussions of Stevens's self-questioning or multiple arguments, see Frank Kermode, *Wallace Stevens*; Eugene Paul Nassar, *Wallace Stevens: An Anatomy of Figuration*; Helen Hennessy Vendler, *On Extended Wings*, and "The Qualified Assertions of Wallace Stevens," *The Act of the Mind*, ed. R.H. Pearce and J. Hillis Miller.

3 Eugene Paul Nassar, *Wallace Stevens: An Anatomy of Figuration*, 20.

4 Paul de Man, *Allegories of Reading*, 10.

5 J. Hillis Miller, "Stevens' Rock and Criticism as Cure," 7.

6 Jacques Derrida, "White Mythology," 41–2.

7 Joseph N. Riddel, "Stevens on Imagination – The Point of Departure," 55, 59, 60, 62, 70

8 Joseph N. Riddel, "Metaphoric Staging: Stevens' Beginning Again of the 'End of the Book,'" *Wallace Stevens: A Celebration*, ed. Frank Doggett and Robert Buttel, 311. Riddel defends his deconstructive reading in "The Climate of Our Poems." In opposition, Marjorie Perloff argues in *The Poetics of Indeterminacy: Rimbaud to Cage* that Stevens's poetry is not in the Derridean mode because he writes about absence and decentering but does not really use indeterminate poetic forms (21–2).

9 Edward W. Said, *Beginnings: Intention and Method*, 327.

10 Wallace Stevens, "Three Manuscript Endings for 'A Collect of Philosophy,'" *Wallace Stevens: A Celebration*, ed. Frank Doggett and Robert Buttel, 51, 52.

11 Florence Emily Hardy, *The Life of Thomas Hardy, 1840–1928*, 309.

12 Frank Doggett, *Wallace Stevens: The Making of the Poem*, 22. For other discussions of the irrational and its relation to reason, see Frank Doggett, *Stevens' Poetry of Thought*; Joseph N. Riddel, *The Clairvoyant Eye*; Louis L. Martz, "Wallace Stevens: The World as Meditation," *Wallace Stevens*, ed. Marie Borroff; Irvin Ehrenpreis, "Strange Relations: Stevens' Nonsense," *Wallace Stevens: A Celebration* ed. Frank Doggett and Robert Buttel.

13 Wallace Stevens, "Three Manuscript Endings for 'A Collect of Philosophy,'" *Wallace Stevens: A Celebration*, ed. Frank Doggett and Robert Buttel, 53.

14 Wallace Stevens, "Insurance and Social Change," 37.
15 Frank Doggett and Dorothy Emerson, "About Stevens' Comments on Several Poems," *The Motive for Metaphor: Essays on Modern Poetry*, ed. Francis C. Blessington and Guy Rotella, 27.
16 Roy Harvey Pearce, "Wallace Stevens: The Life of the Imagination," *Wallace Stevens*, ed. Marie Borroff, 118. Helen Vendler, "The Qualified Assertions of Wallace Stevens," *The Act of the Mind*, ed. R.H. Pearce and J. Hillis Miller, 175.
17 Helen Vendler, *On Extended Wings*, 162–3, 212, 219. For other discussions of synecdoche in Stevens's arguments, see Michel Benamou, *Wallace Stevens and the Symbolist Imagination*; Marie Borroff, "Wallace Stevens: The World and the Poet," *Wallace Stevens*, ed. Marie Borroff; Frank Doggett, *Stevens' Poetry of Thought* and *Wallace Stevens: The Making of the Poem*. In *Wallace Stevens: The Poems of Our Climate*, Harold Bloom considers synecdoche as part of a much more elaborate pattern of rhetorical arguments, a pattern whose rationality he discusses at length.
18 Marie Borroff, *Language and the Poet*, 74–8.
19 J. Hillis Miller, *Poets of Reality*, 231.
20 Harold Bloom, *Wallace Stevens: The Poems of Our Climate*, 139–40.
21 Harold Bloom, *Kabbalah and Criticism*, 112.
22 Harold Bloom, *Poetry and Repression*, 25.
23 A. Walton Litz, "Particles of Order: The Unpublished Adagia," 74.
24 Lisa Steinman, "Figures and Figuration in Stevens' Long Poems," 10.
25 Kenneth Burke, *Language as Symbolic Action*, 9.
26 Harold Bloom, *Wallace Stevens: The Poems of Our Climate*, 161.
27 A point made by Milton J. Bates in *Wallace Stevens: A Mythology of Self*, 206.

Bibliography

Abrams, M.H. *The Mirror and the Lamp: Romantic Theory and the Critical Tradition*. 1953; reprint New York: Norton 1958.

– "Style and Structure in the Greater Romantic Lyric." In *From Sensibility to Romanticism*. Ed. Frederick W. Hilles and Harold Bloom. New York: Oxford University Press 1965.

Altieri, Charles. "Steps of the Mind in T.S. Eliot's Poetry." *Bucknell Review*, 22:2 (1976): 180–207.

Anshen, R.N., ed. *Language: An Enquiry into its Meaning and Function*. New York: Harper and Brothers 1957.

Aristotle, *Rhetoric*. Trans. W. Rhys Roberts. New York: Modern Library 1954.

Arnold, Matthew. *On the Classical Tradition*. Ed. R.H. Super. Ann Arbor: University of Michigan Press 1960.

Auden, W.H. *The Dyer's Hand and Other Essays*. New York: Vintage 1968.

Bacon, Francis. *The Advancement of Learning*. Ed. W.A. Wright. Oxford: Clarendon 1957.

– *Bacon's Essays*. Ed. F.G. Selby. London: Macmillan 1904.

Bates, Milton J. *Wallace Stevens: A Mythology of Self*. Berkeley and Los Angeles: University of California Press 1985.

Barfield, Owen. *Poetic Diction*. London: Faber and Faber 1928.

Barthes, Roland. *Writing Degree Zero*. Trans. Annette Lavers and Colin Smith. London: Jonathan Cape 1967.

Bayley, John. "Chains and the Poet." *Dylan Thomas: New Critical Essays*. Ed. Walford Davies. London: Dent 1972: 56–72.

Benamou, MIchel. *Wallace Stevens and the Symbolist Imagination*. Princeton: Princeton University Press 1972.

Blackmur, R.P. *Form and Value in Modern Poetry*. Garden City, NY: Doubleday 1957.

– "The Language of Silence." In *Language: An Enquiry into its Meaning and Function*. Ed. R.N. Ashen. New York: Harper 1957.

Blessington, Francis C. and Guy Rotella. eds. *The Motive for Metaphor: Essays on Modern Poetry*. Boston: Northeastern University Press 1983.

Bloom, Harold, et. al. *Deconstruction and Criticism*. New York: Seabury Press 1979.

– *Kabbalah and Criticism*. New York: Seabury Press 1975.

– *Poetry and Repression*. New Haven and London: Yale University Press 1976.

– *Wallace Stevens: The Poems of Our Climate*. Ithaca and London: Cornell University Press 1976.

Bornstein, George. "Provisional Romanticism in 'Notes Toward a Supreme Fiction'." *The Wallace Stevens Journal* 1 (Spring 1977): 17–24.

Borroff, Marie. *Language and the Poet*. Chicago and London: Chicago University Press 1979.

– ed. *Wallace Stevens: A Collection of Critical Essays*. Englewood Cliffs, NJ: Prentice-Hall 1963.

Bradley, F.H. *Appearance and Reality*. London: Swan Sonnenschein 1902.

– *Collected Essays, II*. 1935; reprint Freeport, NY: Books for Libraries Press 1968.

– *Essays on Truth and Reality*. Oxford: Clarendon 1914.

– *Ethical Studies*. 1876; reprint New York: Liberal Arts Press 1951.

– "Our Knowledge of Immediate Experience." *Mind* 18 (Jan. 1909): 40–64.

Brinnen, John Malcolm, ed. *A Casebook on Dylan Thomas*. New York: Thomas Crowell 1960.

– *Dylan Thomas in America*. Boston and Toronto: Little, Brown 1955.

Brooke-Rose, Christine. *A Grammar of Metaphor*. London: Secker and Warburg 1958.

Brooks, Cleanth. *The Well Wrought Urn*. New York: Harcourt, Brace and World 1947.

Bruns, Gerald L. *Modern Poetry and the Idea of Language*. New Haven and London: Yale University Press 1974.

Burke, Kenneth. *A Grammar of Motives*. Berkeley and Los Angeles: University of California Press 1969.

– *Language as Symbolic Action*. Berkeley and Los Angeles: University of California Press 1968.

Cassirer, Ernst. *An Essay on Man*. New Haven: Yale University Press 1944.

– *The Philosophy of Symbolic Forms*, vol 2, *Mythical Thought*. Trans. Ralph Manheim. New Haven: Yale University Press 1955.

Coleridge, Samuel Taylor. *Biographia Literaria*. Ed. George Watson. London: Dent 1965.

– *Collected Letters of Samuel Taylor Coleridge*. Ed. E.L. Griggs. Oxford: Clarendon Press 1956.

– *The Collected Works of Samuel Taylor Coleridge*. Ed. R.J. White. London: Routledge and Kegan Paul, Princeton: Princeton University Press 1972.

- *Inquiring Spirit: A New Presentation of Coleridge*. Ed. Kathleen Coburn. London: Routledge and Kegan Paul 1951.
Connolly, Cyril. See Palinurus.
Cooke, Michael G. *The Romantic Will*. New Haven and London: Yale University Press 1976.
Cooke, William. *Edward Thomas: A Critical Biography*. London: Faber and Faber 1970.
Coombes, H. *Edward Thomas: A Critical Study*. New York: Barnes and Noble 1973.
Costello, Bonnie. "Marianne Moore and Elizabeth Bishop: Friendship and Influence." *Twentieth Century Literature*, 30 (Summer/Fall 1984): 130–49.
- *Marianne Moore: Imaginary Possessions*. Cambridge, MA and London: Harvard University Press 1981.
Crane, Hart. *The Complete Poems and Selected Letters and Prose of Hart*. Ed. Brom Weber. Garden City, NY: Doubleday 1966.
Croce, Benedetto. *Æsthetic*. Trans. Douglas Ainslie. London: Peter Owen 1967.
Cunningham, J.V. "Logic and Lyric." *Modern Philology*, 51 (1953–54): 33–41.
Daiches, David. *The Place of Meaning in Poetry*. Edinburgh and London: Oliver and Boyd 1935.
Danby, John F. "Edward Thomas." *Critical Quarterly* 1 (1959): 308–17.
Davie, Donald. *Articulate Energy*. London: Routledge and Kegan Paul 1955.
- *Purity of Diction in English Verse*. London: Chatto and Windus 1952.
Davies, Walford, ed. *Dylan Thomas: New Critical Essays*. London: Dent 1972.
De Man, Paul. *Allegories of Reading*. New Haven and London: Yale University Press 1979.
- *Blindness and Insight*. New York: Oxford University Press 1971.
- *The Rhetoric of Romanticism*. New York: Columbia University Press 1984.
- "Shelley Disfigured." *Deconstruction and Criticism*. New York: Seabury Press 1979.
De Quincey, Thomas. *Thomas De Quincey's Works*. London: A. and C. Black 1897.
Derrida, Jacques. *Of Grammatology*. Trans. Gayatri Chakravorty Spivak. Baltimore and London: Johns Hopkins University Press 1976.
- "White Mythology. " Trans. F.C.T. Moore. *New Literary History* 6 (Autumn 1974): 5–74.
Deutsch, Babette. *Poetry in Our Time*. Garden City, NY: Doubleday 1963.
Dodsworth, Martin. "The Concept of Mind in the Poetry of Dylan Thomas." *Dylan Thomas: New Critical Essays*. Ed. Walford Davies. London: Dent 1972: 107–35.
Doggett, Frank and Robert Buttel, eds. *Wallace Stevens: A Celebration*. Princeton: Princeton University Press 1980.

Doggett, Frank. *Stevens' Poetry of Thought*. Baltimore: Johns Hopkins Press 1966.

– *Wallace Stevens: The Making of the Poem*. Baltimore and London: Johns Hopkins University Press 1980.

Donoghue, Denis. "The Proper Plenitude of Facts." *Marianne Moore: A Collection of Critical Essays*. Ed. Charles Tomlinson. Englewood Cliffs, NJ: Prentice-Hall 1969: 165–71.

Durrell, Lawrence. *Key to Modern Poetry*. London: Peter Nevill 1952.

Dzwonkoski, F. Peter, Jr." 'The Hollow Men' and *Ash-Wednesday*: Two Dark Nights." *The Arizona Quarterly* 30 (1974): 16–42.

Edwards, Michael. "Marianne Moore: 'Transcendence, Conditional.' " In *Modern American Poetry*. Ed. R.W. (Herbie) Butterfield. London and Totowa, NJ: Vision and Barnes Noble 1984.

Eliot, T.S. *Collected Poems 1909–1962*. London: Faber and Faber 1963.

– *Knowledge and Experience in the Philosophy of F.H. Bradley*. London: Faber and Faber 1964.

– *On Poetry and Poets*. New York: Noonday Press 1961.

– "Preface." *Anabasis*. 1931; reprint London: Faber and Faber 1959.

– *The Sacred Wood*. 1920; reprint London: Methuen 1969.

– *Selected Essays*. London: Faber and Faber 1951.

– *Selected Prose of T.S. Eliot*. Ed. Frank Kermode. London: Faber and Faber 1975.

– *The Use of Poetry and the Use of Criticism*. London: Faber Paperbacks 1964.

– *The Waste Land: Facsimile and Transcript*. Ed. Valerie Eliot. London: Faber and Faber 1971.

Farjeon, Eleanor. *Edward Thomas: the Last Four Years*. Oxford: Oxford University Press 1958.

Fenellosa, Ernest and Ezra Pound. "The Chinese Written Character as a Medium for Poetry." In *The Little Review Anthology*. Ed. Margaret Anderson. New York: Horizon Press 1953.

Fitzgibbon, Constantine. *The Life of Dylan Thomas*. London: Sphere Books 1968.

– ed. *Selected Letters of Dylan Thomas*. New York: New Directions 1965.

Foucault, Michel. *The Order of Things*. New York: Vintage 1973.

Fowler, Alistair. "Adder's Tongue on Maiden Hair: Early Stages in Reading 'Fern Hill.' " *Dylan Thomas: New Critical Essays*. Ed. Walford Davies. London: Dent 1972: 228–61.

Freed, Lewis. *T.S. Eliot: The Critic as Poet*. West Lafayette, IN: Purdue University Press 1979.

Frye, Northrop. *Anatomy of Criticism*. New York: Atheneum 1966.

– *A Natural Perspective: The Development of Shakespearean Comedy and Romance*. New York: Harcourt, Brace and World 1965.

– *Fables of Identity*. New York: Harcourt, Brace and World 1963.

– *Spiritus Mundi*. Bloomington and London: Indiana University Press 1976.

Gage, John T. *In the Arresting Eye: The Rhetoric of Imagism*. Baton Rouge and London: Louisiana State University Press 1981.

Gardner, Helen. *The Art of T.S. Eliot*. New York: E.P. Dutton 1959.

Graff, Gerald. *Literature Against Itself: Literary Ideas in Modern Society*. Chicago and London: University of Chicago Press 1979.

– *Poetic Statement and Critical Dogma*. Chicago and London: University of Chicago Press 1970.

Graves, Robert. *The Common Asphodel*. New York: Haskell House 1970.

– *The Crowning Privilege*. London: Cassell 1955.

– *On Poetry: Collected Talks and Essays*. Garden City, NY: Doubleday 1969.

– *Poems Selected by Himself*. Harmondsworth, Penguin 1986.

– *Poetic Unreason and Other Studies*. London: Cecil Palmer 1925.

Graves, Robert and Laura Riding. *A Survey of Modernist Poetry*. Edinburgh: Folcraft Library Editions n.d.

Hadas, Pamela White. *Marianne Moore: Poet of Affection*. Syracuse: Syracuse University Press 1977.

Hall, Donald Hall. *Marianne Moore: The Cage and the Animal*. New York: Pegasus 1970.

Hamburger, Michael. *The Truth of Poetry*. New York: Harcourt, Brace, Jovanovich 1969.

Harding, D.W. "A Note on Nostalgia." *Scrutiny* 1 (1932–33): 8–19.

Hardy, Florence Emily. *The Life of Thomas Hardy 1840–1928*. London: Macmillan; New York: St. Martin's Press 1965.

Harmer, J.B. *Victory in Limbo: Imagism 1908–1917*. London: Secker and Warburg 1975.

Harries, Karsten. "Metaphor and Transcendence." In *On Metaphor*. Ed. Sheldon Sacks. Chicago and London: University of Chicago Press 1979.

Hartman, Geoffrey H. *Criticism in the Wilderness: The Study of Literature Today*. New Haven and London: Yale University Press 1980.

Hassan, Ihab. *The Dismemberment of Orpheus*. New York: Oxford University Press 1971.

– *The Literature of Silence*. New York: Knopf 1967.

Hazlitt, William. *The Complete Works of William Hazlitt*. Ed. P.P. Howe. London and Toronto: J.M. Dent and Sons 1930.

Hofmannsthal, Hugo von. *Selected Prose*. Trans. Mary Hottinger and James Stern. London: Routledge and Kegan Paul 1957.

Holbrook David. *Dylan Thomas and the Code of Night*. London: Athlone Press 1972.

– *Llareggub Revisited: Dylan Thomas and the State of Modern Poetry*. London: Bowes and Bowes 1962.

Holland, Norman N. *The I*. New Haven and London: Yale University Press 1985.

Holroyd, Stuart. "Dylan Thomas and the Religion of the Instinctive Life." *A Casebook on Dylan Thomas*. Ed. J.M. Brinnen. New York: Thomas Crowell 1960: 140–55.

Hosek, Chaviva and Patricia Parker, ed. *Lyric Poetry: Beyond New Criticism*. Ithaca and London: Cornell University Press 1985.

Hough, Graham. *Image and Experience*. Lincoln: University of Nebraska Press 1960.

Housman, A.E. *The Name and Nature of Poetry*. Cambridge: Cambridge University Press 1938.

Hughes, H. Stuart. *Consciousness and Society*. London: MacGibbon and Kee 1967.

Hulme, T.E. *Further Speculations*. Ed. Sam Hynes. Minneapolis: University of Minnesota Press 1955.

– *Speculations*. Ed. Herbert Read. London: Kegan Paul, Trench, Trubner 1924.

Hynes, Samuel. *Edwardian Occasions*. New York: Oxford University Press 1972.

Jameson, Fredric. *The Prison-House of Language*. Princeton: Princeton University Press 1972.

Jarrell, Randall. *Poetry and the Age*. New York: Octagon Books 1972.

Johnson, Barbara. *The Critical Difference*. Baltimore and London: Johns Hopkins Press 1985.

Johnson, Carol. *Reason's Double Agents*. Chapel Hill: University of North Carolina Press 1964.

Jones, Daniel. *My Friend Dylan Thomas*. London: Dent 1977.

Kappel, Andrew J. "Introduction: The Achievement of Marianne Moore." *Twentieth Century Literature* 30 (Summer/Fall 1984): v–xxx.

Kaufmann, Walter. *Nietzsche: Philosopher, Psychologist, Antichrist*. Princeton: Princeton University Press 1974.

Keats, John. *The Letters of John Keats*. Ed. Hyder E. Rollings. Cambridge, MA: Harvard University Press 1958.

Keith, W. J. *The Poetry of Nature*. Toronto: University of Toronto Press 1980.

– *The Rural Tradition*. Hassocks, Sussex: The Harvester Press 1975.

Kenner, Hugh. *A Homemade World: The American Modernist Writers*. New York: Knopf 1975.

– *The Pound Era*. Berkeley and Los Angeles: University of California Press 1971.

Kermode, Frank. *Romantic Image*. London: Routledge and Kegan Paul 1957.

– *Wallace Stevens*. New York: Chips Bookshop 1960.

Kertzer, J.M. "T.S. Eliot and the Problem of Will." *Modern Language Quarterly* 45 (December 1984): 373–94.

Kirkham, Michael. *The Imagination of Edward Thomas*. Cambridge: Cambridge University Press 1986.

Lamb, Charles. *The Collected Works and Letters of Charles Lamb*. New York: Random House 1935.

Langbaum, Robert. *The Poetry of Experience*. New York: Norton 1963.

Langer, Susanne. *Feeling and Form*. New York: Scribner 1953.

Leavis, F.R. *New Bearings in English Poetry*. Harmondsworth: Penguin,1963.

– " 'Thought' and Emotional Quality." *Scrutiny* 13 (1945–46): 53–71.

Lentricchia, Frank. *After the New Criticism*. Chicago: University of Chicago Press 1980.

Litz, A. Walton. "Particles of Order: The Unpublished Adagia." *Wallace Stevens: A Celebration*. Ed. Frank Doggett and Robert Buttel. Princeton: Princeton University Press 1980: 57–77.

Lobb, Edward. *T.S. Eliot and the Romantic Critical Tradition*. London: Routledge and Kegan Paul 1981.

Longley, Edna. *Edward Thomas: Poems and Last Poems*. London and Glasgow: Collins 1973.

MacLeish, Archibald. *New and Collected Poems 1917–1976*. Boston, Houghton Mifflin 1976.

– *Poetry and Experience*. Boston: Houghton Mifflin 1961.

Mallarmé, Stéphane. *Correspondance 1862–1871*. Ed. Henri Mondor. Paris: Gallimard 1959.

– *Oeuvres Complètes*. Paris: Pléiade 1945.

Margolis, John D. *T.S. Eliot's Intellectual Development 1922–1939*. Chicago and London: University of Chicago Press 1972.

Martz, Louis, L. *The Poetry of Meditation: A Study in English Religious Literature*. New Haven and London: Yale University Press 1954.

Melchiori, Giorgio. *The Tightrope Walkers*. London: Routledge and Kegan Paul 1956.

Miller, J. Hillis. *Poets of Reality*. New York: Atheneum 1974.

– "Stevens' Rock and Criticism as Cure." *The Georgia Review* 30 (1976): 5–33, 330–48.

– "The Critic as Host." In *Deconstruction and Criticism*. New York: Seabury Press 1979.

Moore, Geoffrey. "Dylan Thomas." *Dylan Thomas: The Legend and the Poet*. Ed. E.W. Tedlock. London: Heinemann 1960: 248–68.

Moore, Marianne *A Marianne Moore Reader*. New York: Viking Press 1961.

– *Collected Poems*. New York: Macmillan 1951.

– *The Complete Poems of Marianne Moore*. New York: Macmillan/Viking 1967.

– *Predilections*. New York: Viking 1955.

Motion, Andrew. *The Poetry of Edward Thomas*. London: Routledge and Kegan Paul 1980.

Nasssar, Eugene Paul. *Wallace Stevens: An Anatomy of Figuration*. Philadelphia: University of Pennsylvania Press 1965.

Nemerov, Howard. *Figures of Thought*. Boston: David R. Godine 1978.

Newton-de Molina, David, ed. *The Literary Criticism of T.S. Eliot*. London: Athlone Press 1977.

Nietzsche, Friedrich. *The Genealogy of Morals*. Trans. Francis Golffing. New York: Doubleday Anchor 1956.
- *Thus Spoke Zarathustra*. Trans. R.J. Hollingdale. Harmondsworth: Penguin 1969.
- *Twilight of the Idols*. Trans. R.J. Hollingdale. Harmondsworth: Penguin 1968.
- *The Will to Power*. Trans. Anthony M. Ludivici. New York: Frederick Publications 1960.

Olson, Elder. *The Poetry of Dylan Thomas*. Chicago: University of Chicago Press 1954.

Palinurus (Cyril Connolly). *The Unquiet Grave*. 1944; reprint Harmondsworth: Penguin 1967.

Parkenham , Michael, ed. *Les Premières armes du Symbolisme*. Exeter: University of Exeter Press 1973.

Paz, Octavio. *The Bow and the Lyre*. Trans. Ruth Sinns. New York: McGraw Hill 1973.

Pearce, R.H. and J. Hillis Miller, eds. *The Act of the Mind: Essays on the Poetry of Wallace Stevens*. Baltimore: Johns Hopkins University Press 1965.

Perloff, Marjorie. *The Poetics of Indeterminacy: Rimbaud to Cage*. Princeton: Princeton University Press 1981.

Peterkiewicz, Jerzy. *The Other Side of Silence*. London: Oxford University Press 1970.

Phillips, Elizabeth. *Marianne Moore*. New York: Frederick Ungar 1982.

Plato. *The Ion*. *The Dialogues of Plato, vol. 1*. Trans. B. Jowett. New York: Random House 1937.

Poggioli, Renato. *The Theory of the Avant-Garde*. Trans. Gerald Fitzgerald. New York: Harper and Row 1971.

Pound, Ezra. *Gaudier-Brzeska: A Memoir*. 1916; reprint New York: New Directions 1974.
- *Literary Essays of Ezra Pound*. New York: New Directions 1968.
- *Personae: The Collected Shorter Poems of Ezra Pound*. New York: New Directions 1971.

Press, John. *A Map of Modern English Verse*. London: Oxford University Press 1969.

Quintilian. *Quintilian's Institutes of Oratory*. Trans. Rev. John Selby Watson. London: George Bell and Sons 1907.

Rabkin, Norman. *Shakespeare and the Common Understanding*. Chicago and London: University of Chicago Press 1967.

Rajan, Balachandra. *The Overwhelming Question*. Toronto: University of Toronto Press 1976.

Ransom, John Crowe Ransom. "On Being Modern with Distinction." *Marianne Moore: A Collection of Critical Essays*. Englewood Cliffs, NJ: Prentice-Hall 1969: 101–6.

Rees, Ralph. "The Reality of the Imagination in the Poetry of Marianne

Moore." *Twentieth Century Literature* 30 (Summer/Fall 1984): 231-41.
Richards, I.A. *The Philosophy of Rhetoric*. New York: Oxford University Press 1936.
Ricoeur, Paul. "The Metaphorical Process as Cognition, Imagination, and Feeling." In *On Metaphor*, Ed. Sheldon Sacks. Chicago and London: University of Chicago Press 1979.
- *The Rule of Metaphor*. Trans. Robert Czerny. Toronto and Buffalo: University of Toronto Press 1977.
Riddel, Joseph N. *The Clairvoyant Eye*. Baton Rouge: Louisiana State University Press 1965.
- "The Climate of Our Poems." *The Wallace Stevens Journal* 7 (Fall 1983): 59-75.
- "Stevens on Imagination - The Point of Departure." In *The Quest for Imagination*. Ed. O.B. Hardison, Jr. Cleveland and London: Case Western Reserve University Press 1971: 55-85.
Righter, William. "The Philosophical Critic." *The Literary Criticism of T.S. Eliot*. Ed. David Newton-de Molina. London: Athlone Press 1977: 111-38.
Rimbaud, Arthur, *Collected Poems*. Ed. Oliver Bernard. Harmondsworth, Penguin 1962.
Sacks, Sheldon, ed. *On Metaphor*. Chicago and London: University of Chicago Press 1979.
Said, Edward W. *Beginnings: Intention and Method*. New York: Basic Books 1975.
Saussure, Ferdinand de. *Course in General Linguistics*. Trans. Wade Baskin. New York: McGraw-Hill 1966.
Savage, D.S. "The Poetry of Dylan Thomas." *Dylan Thomas: The Legend and the Poet*. Ed. E.W. Tedlock. London: Heinemann 1960: 141-7.
Scarfe, Francis. *Auden and After*. London: Routledge 1942.
Schiller, Friedrich von. *Naive and Sentimental Poetry*. Trans. Julius Elias. New York: Frederic Ungar 1966.
Sewell, Elizabeth. *The Orphic Voice*. New Haven: Yale University Press 1960.
Shattuck, Roger. *The Banquet Years*. New York: Vintage 1955.
Shapiro, Karl. "Dylan Thomas." *Dylan Thomas: The Legend and the Poet*. Ed. E.W. Tedlock. London: Heinemann 1960: 269-83.
Smith, Stan. *Edward Thomas*. London: Faber and Faber 1986.
Sontag, Susan. *Styles of Radical Will*. New York: Farrar, Straus and Giroux 1966.
Stapleton, Laurence. *Marianne Moore: The Poet's Advance*. Princeton: Princeton University Press 1978.
Steegmuller, Francis. "*La Feuille Blanche*: a Valéry rarity." *Times Literary Supplement*. (17 Sept. 1976): 1169.
Steiner, George. *Language and Silence*. London: Faber and Faber 1967.
- *On Difficulty and Other Essays*. Oxford: Oxford University Press 1978.
Steinman, Lisa. "Figures and Figuration in Stevens' Long Poems." *The Wallace Stevens Journal* 1 (Spring 1977): 10-16.

- "Modern America, Modernism, and Marianne Moore." *Twentieth Century Literature* 30 (Summer/Fall 1984): 210–30.

Stephens, Raymond. "Self and World: The Earlier Poems." *Dylan Thomas: New Critical Essays*. Ed. Walford Davies. London: Dent 1972: 21–55.

Stevens, Wallace. *The Collected Poems of Wallace Stevens*. New York: Knopf 1978.

- "Insurance and Social Change." *The Wallace Stevens Journal* 4 (Fall 1980): 37–9.

- *Letters of Wallace Stevens*. Ed. Holly Stevens. New York: Knopf 1966.

- *The Necessary Angel: Essays on Reality and the Imagination*. New York: Vintage Books 1951.

- *Opus Posthumous*. Ed. Samuel French Morse. New York: Knopf 1957.

- *The Palm at the End of the Mind*. Ed. Holly Stevens. New York: Vintage 1972.

- *Souvenirs and Prophecies: The Young Wallace Stevens*. Ed. Holly Stevens. New York: Knopf 1977.

Sutton, Walter, ed. *Ezra Pound: A Collection of Critical Essays*, Englewood Cliffs, NJ: Prentice Hall 1963.

Sypher, Wylie. *The Loss of the Self in Modern Literature and Art*. New York: Random House 1962.

Tedlock, E.W., ed. *Dylan Thomas: The Legend and the Poet*. London: Heinemann 1960.

Thomas, Dylan. *Early Prose Writings*. Ed. Walford Davies. London: Dent 1971.

- *Letters to Vernon Watkins*. Ed. Vernon Watkins. New York: New Directions 1957.

- *The Notebooks of Dylan Thomas*. Ed. Ralph Maud. New York: New Directions 1965.

- *The Poems of Dylan Thomas*,. Ed. Daniel Jones. New York: New Directions 1971.

- *Portrait of the Artist as a Young Dog*. London: Dent 1965.

- *A Prospect of the Sea*. London: Dent 1968.

- *Quite Early One Morning*. London: Dent 1967.

Thomas, Edward. *Algernon Charles Swinburne, A Critical Study*. London: Martin Secker 1912.

- *The Collected Poems of Edward Thomas*. Ed. R. George Thomas. Oxford: Clarendon 1978.

- *Feminine Influence on the Poets*. London: Martin Secker 1910.

- *The Heart of England*. 1906; reprint London and Toronto: Dent 1932.

- *Letters of Edward Thomas to Gordon Bottomley*. Ed. R. George Thomas. London: Oxford University Press 1968.

- *Light and Twilight*. London: Duckworth 1911.

- *A Literary Pilgrim in England*. 1917; reprint Oxford: Oxford University Press 1980.

- *Maurice Maeterlinck*. London: Methuen 1911.

- *Richard Jefferies*. 1909; reprint London and Boston: Faber and Faber 1978.

– *The South Country*. London: Dent 1909.
– *Wales*. 1905; reprint Oxford: Oxford University Press 1983.
– *Walter Pater, A Critical Study*. London: Martin Secker 1913.

Thomas, R. George. "Edward Thomas, Poet and Critic." In *Essays and Studies 1968*. London: John Murry 1968: 118–36.

Thoreau, Henry David. *A Week on the Concord and Merrimack Rivers*. New York: AMS Press 1968.

Tindall, William York. *A Reader's Guide to Dylan Thomas*. New York: Noonday Press 1962.

Tomlinson, Charles, ed. *Marianne Moore: A Collection of Critical Essays*. Englewood Cliffs, NJ: Prentice-Hall 1969.

Treece, Henry. *Dylan Thomas: Dog Among the Fairies*. New York: John de Graff 1956.

Trilling, Lionel. *The Liberal Imagination*. New York: Viking 1951.

Underhill, Hugh. "The 'Poetical Character' of Edward Thomas." *Essays in Criticism* 23 (1973): 236–53.

Unwin, Rayner. *The Rural Muse: Studies in the Peasant Poetry of England*. London: George Allen and Unwin 1954.

Valéry, Paul. *The Art of Poetry*. Trans. Denise Folliot. New York: Vintage 1961.
– *Paul Valéry: An Anthology*. Ed. James R. Lawler. Princeton: Princeton University Press 1956.

Vendler, Helen Hennessy. *On Extended Wings: Wallace Stevens' Longer Poems*. Cambridge: Harvard University Press 1969.
– *Part of Nature, Part of Us: Modern American Poets*. Cambridge and London: Harvard University Press 1980.

Waldrop, Rosmarie. *Against Language?*. The Hague and Paris: Mouton 1971.

Ward, David. *T.S. Eliot: Between Two Worlds*. London: Routledge and Kegan Paul 1973.

Weatherhead, A. Kingsley. *The Edge of the Image: Marianne Moore, William Carlos Williams and Some Other Poets*. Seattle and London: University of Washington Press 1967.

Wellek, René. "The Criticism of T.S. Eliot." *Sewanee Review* 64 (1956): 398–443.
– *Discriminations*. New Haven and London: Yale University Press 1970.

Welsh, Andrew. *Roots of Lyric: Primitive Poetry and Modern Poetics*. Princeton, NJ: Princeton University Press 1978.

Winters, Yvor. *In Defense of Reason*. Denver: Alan Swallow 1947.

Wittgenstein, Ludwig. *Tractatus Logico-Philosophicus*. Trans. D.F. Pears and B.F. McGuinness. London: Routledge and Kegan Paul 1961.

Wordsworth, William. *The Prose Works of William Wordsworth*, Vol. 2. Ed. W.J.B. Owen and J.W. Smyser. Oxford: Clarendon Press 1974.

Yeats, William Butler. *The Celtic Twilight*. New York: Signet 1962.
– *The Letters of W.B. Yeats*. Ed. Allan Wade. London: Hart-Davis 1954.
– *Mythologies*. London: Macmillan 1959.

Index